THE DETROIT TRUE

CHRONICLES

TALES OF MURDER & MAYHEM IN THE MOTOR CITY

SCOTT M. BURNSTEIN

With contributions by Paul Kavieff, Ross Maghliese, Kyle Duda, Dr. James Buccellato, and Alan Bradley

Camino Books, Inc.
Philadelphia

2 3 4   16 15 14 13

Library of Congress Cataloging-in-Publication Data

Burnstein, Scott M.
  The Detroit true crime chronicles: tales of murder and mayhem in the Motor City / Scott M. Burnstein; with contributions by Paul Kavieff [et al.].
      p. cm.
   ISBN 978-1-933822-27-3 (alk. paper)
   1. Murder—Michigan—Detroit—History. 2. Crime—Michigan—Detroit—History. 3. Organized crime—Michigan—Detroit—History. 4. Detroit (Mich.)—Social conditions—History. I. Title.
   HV6534.D6B87 2012
   364.152'30977434—dc23   2012030363

ISBN 978-1-933822-27-3
ISBN 978-1-933822-79-2 (ebook)

Cover and interior design: Jerilyn Bockorick

This book is available at a special discount on bulk purchases for promotional, business, and educational use.

Publisher
Camino Books, Inc.
P.O. Box 59026
Philadelphia, PA 19102
www.caminobooks.com

TO MY BUTTERSCOTCH, RIP

CONTRIBUTORS

Alan Bradley is a lifelong Detroit resident and a noted documentarian. He is the creator of several critically acclaimed productions, including *Murder City, Rollin'*, *The Frank Matthews Story*, and *Detroit Mob Confidential*. Bradley is a graduate of the University of Michigan and Wayne State University.

James Buccellato is a member of the faculty of Wayne State University. He is a recognized authority in the areas of international organized crime and Sicilian-American mob relations.

Kyle M. Duda is an author from the Metro Detroit area. His work has appeared in *The Onion*, and he has worked as a writer and editor at *The Oakland Press*. Duda is a former web editor for the Campbell Ewald advertising agency.

Paul R. Kavieff, born and raised in Detroit, is a noted historian of organized crime. He is considered one of the nation's leading experts on gang violence during the Prohibition era. Kavieff is the author of four books, including important works on Detroit's Purple Gang and the New York gangster Lepke Buchalter.

Ross Maghliese is a journalist at the MLive Media Group in Flint, Michigan. He is a former writer and editor for *The Oakland Press*.

CONTENTS

FOREWORD

The Detroit True Crime Chronicles: Tales of Murder and Mayhem in the Motor City is a unique and special book that balances street culture, organized crime and social ecology. I am indebted to this book and the body of work that Scott M. Burnstein has done over the past decade. As an urban ecologist and sociologist, I rely on information from different sources. Scott is an expert resource, someone who knows the current and latter-day state of affairs of organized crime in the Motor City like very few others I have ever encountered. I have relied on his knowledge extensively in my recent work and will continue to do so. My scholarship and fieldwork are significantly based on observations and participation within a matrix of people, places and professions in different worlds. There are only a few genuine experts like Scott Burnstein, who can connect the history to the present state of organized crime and do it in a way that is fun and exciting as well as informative. Even fewer experts have a full understanding of the complex mix of ethnic groups involved in the diverse cultural network that is Detroit and the Greater Detroit area. Scott clearly does and he imparts his understanding in this book.

A wide array of criminal organizations have played a long-standing role in the social fabric of the Motor City, and *The Detroit True Crime Chronicles* gives a thorough documentation of the relationships between these groups and the overall impact made by gangs and their leaders on the local culture. Organized crime has had a rich history in Detroit. To this day, the city represents an important part of criminal enterprise within the complicated and thorny web of both the national and international underworld.

My study of Detroit over the past four decades has revealed a hidden culture that I call the Third City. It is here that I have learned about and conceptualized an America that is not part of the mainstream. This Third City harbors the marginalized underground of people struggling to enter the middle-class social and economic community. *The Detroit True Crime Chronicles* shows how immigrants from Europe and many homegrown Detroiters refused to accept the social engineering that defined them in terms of poor employment, housing and education throughout the 20th century, and instead used ingenuity and ambition to survive and thrive, climbing through the social strata by any means necessary. This Third City also shows how local organized crime provides a blueprint for Detroit's youth to learn from, emulate and challenge a society that does not see them as equal, capable or desirable.

The criminal organizations created in the early days of Prohibition evolved into the illicit narcotics commerce that came to dominate the local underworld in the second half of the last century. It was an epic awakening, the birthing of a new set of players on the streets, marking a new day where African-American drug lords were no longer dependent on their Italian Mafia counterparts for their supplies or their way of life. This new independence in the city created new rules and in effect a new urban street culture.

Within these pages, Detroit is explored not only historically, but also in terms of the evolution of the postindustrial city. This is critical in understanding what Detroit is like today compared to the hometown of the young Jewish gangsters of the Purple Gang, practically all of them immigrants from Eastern Europe, who ruled the city during Prohibition.

Lastly, this book gives an accounting of tales and dynamics not always mentioned in mainstream gangster lore. We read the story of how those in the Italian Mafia have often crossed paths with African-American street culture, as well as other powerful underworld factions, making for an interesting mix of criminals sharing the same business landscape. We learn about the always-complicated relationships between the city's most infamous gangland leaders and their respective organizations through time—relationships that would ebb and flow and quite often result in bloodshed and brutality.

The vast group of characters and experts that Scott Burnstein has assembled for this project is simply amazing. It is one that presents a thorough dissection of every nook and cranny of Detroit's criminal world. The stories in these chapters jump off the pages. The book is sure to have historical significance, too. Until now, there has been nothing else like this available for researchers and academics hoping to learn or teach about the full history and compelling intricacies of the Detroit underworld. I can promise that those who read *The Detroit True Crime Chronicles* will be well rewarded.

Carl S. Taylor, Ph.D.
Professor of Sociology,
Michigan State University

THE
DETROIT TRUE
CRIME
CHRONICLES

BICENTENNIAL BLOODBATH

The Greek Must Die!

It was Sunday July 11, 1976, exactly one week past the dawning of the nation's much-celebrated Bicentennial. The air in the city of Detroit was thick and muggy, the weather sweltering, carrying on a heat wave that had blanketed the area since the beginning of the month. Nobody felt the heat more than Ernest Kanakis, known in local underworld circles simply as "Ernie the Greek," sitting anxiously alert behind the wheel of his car at the corner of Chalmers and Warren that early evening, frantically going over in his mind what his next move should be. Should he stay and face the music or should he find the nearest highway, get on it and keep driving until he was well beyond the state line? The decision-making process was over in a matter of seconds. The passenger door of Kanakis' car opened abruptly and Detroit Mafia lieutenant Frank "Frankie Razz" Randazzo slipped into the seat beside him. By that point he had no choice. He was in it for the long haul.

Starting to drive eastbound on Warren, Kanakis was on edge from the moment Randazzo got into his car. Frankie Razz was a Sicilian-born mafioso, widely feared and highly respected within the Motor City crime syndicate, and on his bad side is not where you wanted to be. Unfortunately for Kanakis, that's exactly where he was and had been for a while. The closer the pair of wiseguys, former partners in a lucrative illegal gambling operation, got to Randazzo's house, the more uncomfortable Ernie the Greek became.

The two had been on bad terms for a while. A few years earlier, Kanakis broke off their profitable business relationship, and despite Frankie Razz's heated objections, Ernie went on his own. That didn't sit well with Randazzo or his friends in the Mafia who had gotten quite used to the fattened envelopes of cash they were generating from the series of gambling rackets Kanakis was overseeing. Taking that into account, Kanakis was caught off guard when in early July 1976, Randazzo approached him at his restaurant, Ernie's Finer Foods Diner, located in downtown Detroit's Cass Corridor in the Eddystone Hotel, and started to talk him up like there was no bad blood between them. Before Randazzo left, he requested Kanakis' help in moving a defective safe out of his basement, offering Ernie $4,000 if he would help him dispose of it.

While suspicious about the request, Ernie the Greek was broke and needed the money. His beef with the mob had cut into his bottom line and was keeping people away from his restaurant. Knowing full well that the ill will between Randazzo and himself was most likely not forgotten by Frankie Razz or his bosses in the Mafia, Ernie agreed to help. It wouldn't be a wise decision and it wouldn't take him long to figure it out.

◇◇◇◇◇◇◇◇◇◇◇◇

Ernie the Greek's problems with the Detroit Mafia began eight years earlier, at a time long before Kanakis had gone into business with the mob, and concerned a dispute he had nothing to do with and knew nothing about. In 1968, a local mob associate and fruit vendor named Sam Di Maggio found himself in financial debt to the notorious Giacalone brothers, a vicious gangland duo consisting of Motor City crime family street boss Anthony "Tony Jack" Giacalone and his younger sibling, Mafia capo Vito "Billy Jack" Giacalone. The Giacalones, plucked from the streets of Eastern Market and groomed as future leaders of the mob from a very young age, ran a citywide bookmaking and loansharking operation, and Di Maggio, a heavy sports gambler, owed them a couple of thousand dollars.

"Tony Jack and Billy Jack were the Family's junkyard dogs; they enforced the orders of the upper administration and did it with pride," said former U.S. Prosecutor Keith Corbett, who made his living trying to bring down the Detroit Mafia in over two dozen years of service to the government. "I think they relished the roles. They were the kind of guys who liked being gangsters and got off on the fear they instilled in people."

Here is an excerpt resulting from an FBI wiretap that was placed within the Home Juice Company, the headquarters of the Giacalone brothers during the 1960s, in which Tony Jack and Billy Jack were browbeating a colleague for trying to loan out money in their territory:

Billy Jack: I pay the police, I pay the lawyers, I pay the judges, I pay the courts, now I get all of this. So keep your hands off. You're in the bonding business. You handle all the bonding around here. Leave the loans to us. Anybody comes to you looking for a loan, you send 'em to me or my brother.

Tony Jack: You got any other money out right now that we should know about?

Colleague: No, not shylocking at all anymore.

Billy Jack: You sure about that?

Colleague: Positively.

Tony Jack: Now don't let me find out you're lying to us, or I'll bury ya!

Billy Jack: This is it, your one and only warning.

Colleague: I understand, Bill. I'm out of the shy business, I swear.

Tony Jack: That $500 dollars Leo owes you; you lost that one. That one belongs to us now. Don't bother Bob no more either. We're taking that one, too. That's your penalty. Now, get out of here!

Here's another excerpt from the same wiretap of the Giacalone brothers berating another colleague for being a lousy drunk:

Billy Jack: If you don't know how to hold your drinks, I suggest you stop drinking. Next time, I'm gonna…I'm gonna…They're ain't gonna be no fucking next time. I'll chop your fucking head off. I don't go for that shit.

Colleague: I know, Billy. I feel awful about the way I acted. I don't know what I was thinking.

Tony Jack: Just quit this shit about the drinking and the getting out of hand in public. We don't go for that shit around here. We don't take that shit from nobody, I don't care how big or small.

Billy Jack: We don't give a shit about you or any fucking body.

Colleague: I know, I know. I'm sorry.

Tony Jack: I'm gonna tell ya right now, if you get out of line one more time, we ain't giving out any more passes. You respect us, we respect you. Don't be stupid or you'll end up in a ditch.

Sam Di Maggio was well aware of the Giacalones' reputation and knew he had to go to all lengths in order to fix the situation immediately. Not having the money himself to pay the Giacalone brothers, Di Maggio went to area mob loanshark, Bernard "Bernie the Hammer" Marchesani, and borrowed the cash at a substantially inflated interest rate in order to settle his debt. Di Maggio might no longer have been into the Giacalones for money, but then he found himself in debt to Marchesani, a heavy-handed Mafia strong-arm who in perfect underworld synchronization reported to none other than the Giacalone brothers. It was a vicious circle and Ernie Kanakis was stuck in the middle of it with no reprieve.

Bernie the Hammer was Detroit's own Luca Brasi from *The Godfather*, the official go-to guy for the mob on the streets, given all the toughest enforcement assignments from the crime family's top brass. He was gruff and physically imposing, unafraid to break traditional Mafia protocol and sport a thick and bushy beard, sometimes appearing more like a biker than a mobster.

"Marchesani was as tough as they come in that world," said retired FBI agent Mike Carone. "For a lot of years, he did all of the collecting for the Giacalones and they ran the street for the entire Family. So in essence, by doing that, he was doing the enforcing for the Family's official enforcers. They picked him as their representative. That really tells you all you need to know about what kind of guy he was. He put the fear of God in some of the city's most hardened wiseguys."

Things didn't bode well for Sam Di Maggio. A week later and still broke, he failed to fork anything over to Bernie the Hammer when he came to collect the first installment of the loan. Pleading with an angry Marchesani for more time, Di Maggio was sent away with a warning and told he better come up with payment soon or he would be in serious trouble. Two weeks passed and Di Maggio still had no money to give. Infuriated, Marchesani went to Tony Giacalone for guidance in how to handle the problem, and he was advised to assign a crew of strong-arms to rough up Di Maggio as an "incentive" to pay his future loan installments on time. Rounding up three of his foot soldiers—Pete Vassalo, Robert Dunaway and John Palmer—Marchesani sent them to see Di Maggio with specific instructions to beat him up but not to kill him. Tony Jack allegedly told Marchesani that Di Maggio was protected by the fact that he was the cousin of deceased mob soldier Frank "The Iceberg" Di Maggio, a top lieutenant of mobster Pete Licavoli, who was said to have come to Detroit from Chicago in the years after Prohibition.

Eager to impress their superiors in the crime family with their effectiveness as enforcers, Vassalo, Dunaway and Palmer, each wielding blunt instruments, went overboard in their assault of Di Maggio. Approaching their delinquent target outside his home while he tended to his front lawn, they attacked him with several baseball bats and a lead pipe, beating him so badly that he died later the same day at a local hospital. This infraction of direct mob orders infuriated the notoriously hot-tempered Giacalone brothers, and FBI documents allege they ordered Vassalo, Dunaway and Palmer to be executed as soon as possible. Biding its time, a trait of deliberate homicidal plodding that was a trademark of the Detroit Mafia since its inception, Dunaway was murdered in 1971 and Vassalo in 1972. John Palmer disappeared in 1977, shortly after his release from prison on unrelated felony charges.

Although a link between the Giacalones and the four previously described gangland slayings could not be established in a court of law, the brazen Mafia executions caught the collective interest of the federal government and resulted in the opening of a widespread FBI investigation into the brothers' various other criminal activities. Not knowing it at the time and to his great dismay, Ernie Kanakis was about to be unwittingly flung into the center of the whole thing.

Around the same time as Dunaway and Vassalo were murdered, Ernie Kanakis went into business with the local mob and indirectly with the Giacalone brothers. It was a decision he would deeply regret for the rest of his life, but one he had no choice in making at the time. Besides serving up good food and good conversation, Ernie the Greek's diner also served as a backdoor casino, which made him a great deal of money. Since he had opened the establishment in 1967, Kanakis had been closing his diner early three nights a week and running blackjack, dice and roulette games out of the restaurant's basement, independent of the Mafia. By the early 1970s, Kanakis' after-hours gambling extravaganzas became a neighborhood staple, attracting a loyal client base, and unfortunately for Kanakis, the attention of certain organized crime figures who sensed a cash cow to be exploited to their advantage.

"Ernie was loud and obnoxious, but he was a big-time earner and that earned him a certain level of prominence in the city's rackets," Carone noted. "I don't think there was any question either, though, that despite him being a bit of a blowhard, he was quite capable of fending for himself on the street. I mean he wasn't easy to push around. It was known he could handle a gun."

On a stormy October night in 1972, Frank Randazzo and another local mob soldier named Joe Siragusa paid Ernie Kanakis a visit at his diner and made him an offer he couldn't refuse: either go partners with them in their gaming activities and move the location of the game from the diner to an athletic club in Greektown named The Summit, which was owned by Siragusa, or they would shut his casino down themselves and kill him. Kanakis was tough, but he wasn't stupid. Seeing very few options for himself, Ernie the Greek agreed to the mob's demands and moved his gambling operation to The Summit.

Detroit's Greektown, located in a five-square-block radius centered on Monroe Street and long overseen by mob capos and brothers Paul and Pete Vitale, was a hotbed of Mafia activity for a good 50 years, ranging from the 1940s through the early 1990s. For several decades the area has been a popular nightlife district, and local police officers were once explicitly instructed not to socialize in the booming ethnic enclave when off duty.

"It's long been an area with deep ties to organized crime," said Mike Carone of Greektown. "That's not to say that all the shopkeepers and restaurant owners are criminals, just that the atmosphere in that area was always ripe for being taken advantage of by the mob. The Grecian Gardens restaurant on the far west end of Monroe was a big gathering place for organized crime figures and where the Vitale brothers and their crews were centered. There was always a lot of different kind of activity going on at all hours of the day. Guys were earning and socializing down there at the same time."

Just like in the basement of his diner, things were cooking from the start down in Greektown. The "casino nights" held by the club four days a week and overseen by Kanakis immediately became a hot ticket, attracting many of the city's highest rollers and turning a pretty penny, most of which ended up in the pockets of Randazzo, Siragusa and their superiors in the mob. One thing was for sure, Randazzo knew how to keep his bosses happy. He was a longtime moneymaker for the Mafia in Detroit, being charged with looking after its prostitution rackets for a solid 25 years, as well as running a number of other cash-heavy illegal ventures for the mob.

It didn't take long for Kanakis to sour on the new arrangement, and in less than a year he told Randazzo and Siragusa that he was breaking off their business relationship and going back on his own. Disturbed by the chain of events, but not quite ready to make their adversary disappear, the Mafia gave Ernie the Greek a temporary pass. Returning to running his backdoor gaming ventures out of his diner at the Eddystone didn't exactly turn out the way Ernie had envisioned. News of Kanakis' falling out with Randazzo and Siragusa was all over the street, and gamblers that were once his most loyal patrons were now too spooked to frequent his games. This phenomenon carried over to his eating establishment. Former bread-and-butter customers stopped congregating at his diner in fear of upsetting the Mafia. Within months, Kanakis was broke.

After a few weeks of considering his options, Ernie the Greek made yet another decision he would live to regret. Instead of going to a local bank and requesting assistance to save his restaurant, Kanakis decided to go to the mob. He borrowed $1000 from Bernard Marchesani at five percent interest, and went forward in trying to rebuild his diner's reputation and image, but most of all, its profitability. The rebuilding effort quickly went south and Kanakis could not afford to repay his loan to Marchesani, who at that point was demanding double the interest the two parties had agreed upon at the outset. Bernie the Hammer had little sympathy for Ernie the Greek and viewed him as a mark. On several occasions in public, Bernie threatened to kill Ernie and his entire family if he did not make good on the outstanding debt.

Fortunately for Kanakis, not long after his brutal encounter with Marchesani, the Giacalones' loansharking operation was busted by the feds. The Giacalone brothers and Marchesani were each indicted, and the Detroit Mafia soon had much more important concerns on their minds than the money owed to them by one somewhat inconsequential local half-wiseguy. Unfortunately for Kanakis, at the same time the mob was letting him slide on his debt, he was being subpoenaed by the government to appear as a witness at the Giacalones' loansharking trial. This placed Ernie in a very precarious position. He knew that if he didn't appear in court to take the stand against the Giacalones, he would be held in contempt and jailed. At the same time, he also knew that testifying against Tony Jack and Billy Jack in open court could mean a death sentence for himself and anybody he associated with, including his family. Weighing his options delicately, Kanakis decided to take his chances on the street and avoid certain imprisonment by showing up and providing testimony at the highly publicized trial.

Although making no direct statements regarding either of the Giacalone brothers while on the stand, Ernie the Greek did speak on the record at great length about his relationship with their top lieutenant, Bernie the Hammer Marchesani. He told of his monetary transactions with Marchesani, the threats Marchesani hurled his way when things went poorly, and his knowledge that Marchesani took orders from the Mafia. He told of his distaste for the local crime syndicate and how he preferred operating on the streets independent of mob influence and direction. And with that, in essence, Kanakis signed his own death warrant. When you added his falling out with Randazzo and Siragusa to the beef he had with Marchesani, and the fact that he testified against the mob in court, he was substantially more of a headache than he was worth. The Detroit mafia had reached its breaking point, and Ernie the Greek would soon find himself designated to be murdered for his repeated indiscretions.

"I think testifying at the Giacalones' trial was probably the final straw," said Keith Corbett. "He was already on a lot of people's bad sides and that most likely put things over the edge. Plus, I think they [the mob] wanted his gambling business, which might have been down in profits from its peak, but was still a lucrative operation."

Looking for the best way to lure Ernie the Greek to his slaughter without raising suspicion, Tony Giacalone called upon Kanakis' former business partner, Frank Randazzo. Federal documents allege that Tony Jack, the local mob's day-to-day overseer, told him to round up a crew of hit men and carry out the contract on Kanakis as soon as possible. In turn, Randazzo constructed an unusually elderly execution team—everyone chosen was over the age of 70. Besides himself, the team included Joe Siragusa and longtime Motor City gangland assassin Nick "The Executioner" Ditta. Randazzo reputedly met with Giacalone in early June 1976 at Giacalone's headquarters, the Southfield Athletic Club, at Ten Mile and Evergreen, and told him that they planned to hit Kanakis the following month, shortly after the Bicentennial. Giacalone allegedly informed the team to send word through his brother, Billy, if there were any more issues with setting up the contract and then to report back to him after the job was completed. Kanakis had crossed his associates in the mob on one too many occasions and although he didn't know it at the time, he was living his life as a marked man.

◇◇◇◇◇◇◇◇◇◇◇◇

Randazzo was exhibiting strange behavior during the entire car ride to his house. He was displaying outward signs of extreme nervousness and anxiety, constantly watching his rearview mirror and commenting that he was paranoid about government surveillance. Plus, he kept badgering Kanakis about whether he had been followed or had told anybody about where he was going that night. Ernie the Greek was no dummy. He knew something was very wrong.

Pulling up the driveway of Frank Randazzo's house, located on Detroit's Northwest Side, Kanakis parked the car and both he and Randazzo exited the vehicle and entered the residence through the back door. Ernie the Greek was no amateur; he had been dealing with seedy and conniving underworld figures for quite a while and had developed a good idea about how they operated. Accordingly, Kanakis made sure he had covered all his bases before leaving for his encounter with Randazzo on the evening of July 11. That morning, Ernie had telephoned a local gambler friend of his named Thomas "Tommy the Judge" Nicopolous, and told him where he was going that night and who he would be with. As an extra measure of safety, he arranged for Nicopolous to be waiting in a house down the street from where Randazzo lived, just in case he ran into trouble he could not handle himself and had to call for backup. He also took the time to write a note and leave it with his wife, with instructions to deliver it to the FBI if something were to happen to him while allegedly helping Frankie Razz move his safe.

The handwritten note was addressed to an FBI agent that Kanakis had developed a relationship with in his years on the streets. In it, he relayed the events leading up to his meeting with the mob that evening and informed the agent that law enforcement should focus on Randazzo and his cronies if he were to wind up dead or missing. Finally, Kanakis armed himself with a pistol, which he strapped to a holster on his leg, kissed his wife goodbye and left for his rendevous with the Mafia, knowing that by doing so he was leaving life and limb in the hands of fate.

Immediately after the pair of wiseguys entered the house, Randazzo made a quick left turn and opened the door to his basement, inviting Kanakis to lead the way down the stairs. Kanakis agreed and Randazzo closed the basement door behind them, nervously ushering his target to the impending bloodbath. The second the door shut, Ernie the Greek knew something was wrong and began to turn around so he could confront Randazzo about his odd behavior. Before Ernie could turn, Frankie Razz jumped on his back and pushed him down the flight of stairs. Approaching a staggered Kanakis on the basement floor, Randazzo picked him up and attempted to hold both of his arms behind his back while yelling, "Kill him, kill him now!" Suddenly, Joe Siragusa came screaming out of the cellar shadows and began stabbing Kanakis repeatedly in the chest with an ice pick. It was a tornado of terror and Kanakis was ensconced in the eye of the storm, seemingly bound for certain death.

While Randazzo and Siragusa were assaulting Kanakis, a third figure emerged from his hiding spot in the back of the basement. It was Nick Ditta and he was brandishing a pistol with its barrel wrapped in a kitchen towel to act as a makeshift silencer. A devilish grin imprinted on his face, Ditta took two steps toward Kanakis, put the gun to his temple, and pulled the trigger. That should have been the end for Ernie the Greek Kanakis. He should have been killed instantly, but he wasn't. Luckily for Kanakis, Ditta's pistol jammed. The towel he had tied around the gun was too tight and that caused it to malfunction. Surprised he hadn't blown his target's head all the way across the room with his first shot, Ditta fired the gun one more time. Once again, nothing happened.

Meanwhile, Ernie the Greek broke loose from the clutches of his assailants, kicked the gun out of Ditta's hand, and had the presence of mind to make a move for his own weapon. Pulling the gun from underneath his left pant leg, Kanakis took aim at the three men who were trying to take his life just moments before and shot them all at point-blank range. Fleeing up the stairs and out the back door, he got into his car, drove himself to the hospital for treatment, and had nurses call and report the incident to the local police.

Back at the house, Siragusa and Randazzo died instantly, while Nick Ditta held on long enough to make it up the stairwell and call 911. Ditta was a favored hit man of the Detroit Mafia brass for over four decades and had often traveled to other cities on behalf of the crime family to carry out top-secret assignments. He finally succumbed to his bullet wounds on Randazzo's kitchen floor, clutching a telephone in his hands, waiting for the ambulance he wouldn't live to see arrive.

Following his involvement in the carnage-soaked basement massacre, Ernie the Greek went on trial for murder and was eventually acquitted of all charges on the grounds of self-defense. Kanakis had averted death and jail, and with the exception of some scars on his chest from being stabbed with Siragusa's ice pick, he was standing tall and strong, ready to start his life anew. He believed he had escaped the Mafia's murderous wrath and pledge of vengeance against him. However, Ernie the Greek had underestimated the Detroit mob's resolve, and while Kanakis looked to take advantage of his newfound second lease on life, the Motor City crime family stewed in the shadows and plotted their enemy's eventual demise. They would make certain that their target was lulled into a sufficient state of relaxation and security before they struck again.

◇◇◇◇◇◇◇◇◇◇◇◇

Six years went by and it appeared, at least on the surface, that tensions between Ernie Kanakis and the mob had cooled down significantly. It was the 1980s, and Kanakis had left his interests in the underworld behind, deciding to go legitimate and live his life on the straight and narrow. Being interviewed by a local paper on the five-year anniversary of his attempted murder, he rejected the idea that the Giacalones would still want to have him killed: "If the Giacalone brothers wanted me dead, they would have done it already and better than anybody in the world—in complete secrecy." Divorced from his wife, he had a new girlfriend and in his mind, he had successfully outrun all the demons from his past. He couldn't have been more wrong.

"When mob around here holds a grudge, it's for a lifetime," Mike Carone said firmly. "I don't think any single event in the last three, four decades demonstrates that more than the Ernie Kanakis situation."

Despite Ernie the Greek's delusions of safety, the Detroit Mafia had an outstanding long-term memory, especially when it came to unpaid debts. They had not forgotten about him at all. They owed Kanakis another visit, and by the start of the new decade it was only a matter of time before the mob looked to exact their revenge. That time came in December 1982, when crime family lieutenant Frank "Frankie the Bomb" Bommarito, a highly feared local underworld enforcer and trusted member of Vito Giacalone's crew, summoned widely known Motor City hit man Charles Acker to a meeting at a Detroit-area Denny's restaurant. After some initial small talk in a secluded back booth, Bommarito offered Acker $5,000 in cash if he would kill Ernie the Greek Kanakis. In a gruesome added twist, he said he would throw in a $2,000 bonus if, after Acker completed the job, he took photographs of the corpse and crime scene and sent them in a Christmas card to the Giacalone brothers. Acker agreed to the deal and had several more meetings with Bommarito to discuss the logistics of the hit. Eventually, over dozens of cups of coffee spread over a three-month period, the two decided how, where and when they would attempt to kill Kanakis for the second time. This time the mob seemed confidant that they would succeed.

Everything appeared to be going perfectly as planned. The specifics had been worked out and the wheels of the second contract were in heavy motion. But soon a major glitch was discovered—Acker was working for the federal government. Since the very first time he had met with Bommarito at Denny's to discuss the hit on Ernie Kanakis, Acker had been wired for sound, secretly recording every conversation he had with Frankie the Bomb and turning them over to the FBI.

"Charlie Acker came to us and told us that Frankie the Bomb wanted him to hit Ernie Kanakis and all we could think of at the office was how sadistic it was to wait in the shadows for almost 10 years and then come after him like that. It was like an animal stalking its prey, waiting just for the exact right time to pounce and devour it."

Arrested in January 1983, Frank Bommarito was convicted and jailed on the charge of conspiracy to commit murder, and he served close to three years in prison for the offense. On the other hand, Kanakis was in a state of shock, stunned and emotionally shaken by the entire incident, but at the same time refusing to buckle under the pressure being put on him by the local Mafia.

In the years to come, Ernie didn't move from his home in suburban Detroit. He didn't change his name or enter the witness protection program. Instead, he remained in the area and once again stood tall and strong against his adversaries in the mob. He did this by going about his daily life unfazed by the many men in the city's underworld who wanted him dead, never wilting in the face of gangland threats or intimidation. All the money and perks Ernie the Greek once had by living on the wrong side of the law were gone, given up for the mundane job of an ordinary citizen. But he was alive.

Unaware of whether or not the mob had lifted the contract on his life, Kanakis led an uneasy existence, refusing to sit with his back to the door while out in public and turning on the ignition of his car with one foot securely out of the vehicle, so in case there was a bomb inside, he could escape as quickly as possible. It was no easy way to live. And he was bored out of his mind. After some careful thought, Ernie decided he wanted back in.

Always a man who craved action and tired of lurking in the shadows after over a decade removed from streets, in about 1987, Ernie the Greek hooked up with some members of the city's Arab Mafia and went back to running a series of hugely profitable gambling rackets. Partnered with Tahrir "Crazy Tommy" Kalasho, a top lieutenant to his uncle Lou "The Hammerhead" Akrawi, the reputed founder and boss of the local Chaldean (non-Muslim Iraqi) crime syndicate, Kanakis built his gambling business back up to practically the point it had been prior to his falling out with the mob. The only problem was that all the money Kanakis and Kalasho started making and the clientele they were generating began showing up on the Mafia's radar. They hadn't forgotten about their old nemesis, and they wanted to know why the Chaldeans were doing business with him. Furthermore, they wanted Kalasho to serve him up to them so they could finally have him killed like they had been trying to do for 11 years.

In another stroke of good fortune for Kanakis, the Chaldeans refused to deliver their new and high-earning friend to his butchering. Instead, they went to bat for him and ended up saving his life. Reaching out to one of their contacts in the Mafia, Antonio "Tony the Zip" Ciraulo, the Chaldeans requested that Ciraulo, a lieutenant in the Giacalone brothers' regime, arrange for a sit-down to sort out the two parties' differences. Ciraulo, eventually convicted on murder charges in the early 1990s and sent to prison for the rest of his life, had the sit-down arranged for the week leading up to Thanksgiving 1987 at his bar in Warren.

Delivering a sizable chunk of cash to the Giacalones at the meeting and offering them a percentage of their gambling interests, the Chaldeans asked permission to have the contract lifted on Kanakis' life. Tommy Kalasho said he would personally vouch for Ernie the Greek and take responsibility for all issues related to his work on the street. The Italians had always respected the Chaldeans for their iron-fisted approach to leadership and gutsy takeover of territory almost as soon as they arrived in Michigan from Iraq in the early 1970s. This finally led the Giacalones to remove the contract on Kanakis and let him off the hook. From that point forward, Ernie the Greek was one of the rarest commodities in the world—someone who unflinchingly challenged the Mafia head on and lived.

"Lady Luck was definitely on his side because there aren't many people who stare down the Mafia in Detroit and can say they lived to talk about it," Keith Corbett observed. "Ernie was a colorful character and his story is without question one of the most intriguing I came across in my time working for the government. It really tells you everything you need to know about the way the mob operates in this city."

After a few solid years making money with the Italians, Kanakis retired and moved to Las Vegas where he died of a heart attack in 2005. Bernie Marchesani served time for his role in the Giacalone-backed loansharking operation and then was nailed shortly after his release on an extortion case. The charges were highlighted by his leaving a dead bird on the porch of an associate he believed owed him money and sending that associate letters and cards implying that he would be hurt if he didn't pay up.

Marchesani was eventually jailed in 1985 after close to five years on the run from the law; he died behind bars of stomach cancer in 1998. Tony Giacalone died of cancer at 82, a free man under indictment awaiting trial on racketeering charges, Billy Giacalone died in 2012, and Frankie Bommarito remains. Giacalone is alleged to have been named the syndicate's underboss, or official second in command, in 2004. He was later forced to relinquish the post due to increasing bad health. Ascending above his longtime status as a mere enforcer, Bommarito is reputed to have been named captain of his own crew in 2003.

By way of the public street war with Ernie Kanakis, the Detroit mob further solidified its well-deserved reputation as a syndicate that will seek revenge on its enemies at all costs, no matter how long it takes to finish the job. This reputation sticks with the Family to this day; it is an underworld legend that members will go out of their way to protect and perpetuate.

"Even though they [the Mafia] were ultimately unsuccessful in killing Ernie Kanakis, I think they like the lore and mystique that has been associated with the entire situation all these years," Corbett noted. "They might have failed in what they were trying to do, but the whole thing went a long way to even further enhance their reputation. Those guys reaped a lot of benefits from that endeavor [and] gained a lot of street capital that they were probably able to leverage to their great advantage."

A DOZEN YEARS OF DESTRUCTION

Power, Powder and Prestige

The years 1978 to 1990 on the streets of Detroit represent one of the most violent eras of crime in American history. Practically all of the bloodshed in that period could be attributed to the local drug trade. Experts and local criminologists place the death toll at well over 1,000 gangland-related homicides. Throughout those dozen years, both the product and the consumer changed drastically, but the landscape itself stayed pretty much the same—as treacherous as humanly possible.

"The streets were decaying, people were fleeing the city in masses and the dope peddlers took over what was left," said Robert De Fauw, former head of the Drug Enforcement Administration in Detroit. "First it was heroin and then it was cocaine. Things got pretty chaotic. Murder was rampant and life was cheap."

One retired DEA agent likened the climate to military combat:

"I served in Vietnam in the 1960s and that experience was the only thing I can equate to my experience working the narcotics trade in Detroit in the 1980s. In terms of how much you're observing death in its most raw and visceral sense, they were almost identical. Whatever side you were on, whether you were a cop or a dealer, you were constantly surrounded by death. Violence and murder was so commonplace that after a while everybody became immune to it. Not that I didn't feel for the victims, especially the innocent ones, but that it just became routine, kind of ho hum. Every second you turned around another bottom dropped. By the time I left Detroit, I was numb."

Besides the carnage of the era, it was a time known for its decadence. And accordingly, the men who made their names in the era lived their lives lavishly with flamboyant showmanship and media-friendly panache and charisma. Eye-popping excesses were displayed all around town by these urban "crime czars," flashed for everyone to see at all the city's trendiest nightclubs, finest restaurants and front row at any number of local professional sporting events and music concerts.

"Some of those guys were walking around with chains around their neck that were worth as much as my entire year's salary," said one former Detroit police officer. "You'd see kids that you had once known as these little tykes on 10-speed bicycles bouncing around the neighborhood and all of sudden…they're driving a $50,000 Mercedes and flashing a cash roll that would choke a horse. That's how fast you could get rich."

The start of the 1970s saw the death of Detroit's first genuine African American Godfather, Henry Marzette, and the emergence of more traditional black street gangs like the "Black Killers" and the "Errol Flynns." The "BKs" and "Flynns," or "Flynn Nastys" as they became known, were into minor drug dealing and did engage in murder, but these things weren't the gangs' primary motivation and never came close to the level achieved by their successors.

While early gang life in Detroit's black community was more of an outlet for juvenile angst, male bonding and random petty crime than a means of making truckloads of money, this new era on the streets brought outright bloodlust in the quest for dominance of the drug market and created demigods of aspiring kingpins. The gangs that formed in the latter 1970s and in the first half of the 1980s were considerably larger and more organized than their predecessors like the BKs or Flynns, and they would far exceed in money earned, body count and overall exposure any urban criminal faction or gang leader of the past.

"There was a significant shift that took place on the streets around here in the late '70s and early '80s," recalls former drug lord-turned-author Rob Boyd. "Things moved from strictly gangbanging to pushing weight in the drug trade. All of a sudden everyone is scrambling for the same dollar and a spot to sling and it ain't about gangbanging anymore. That's when it became about business. Nobody could get rich from gangbanging. With powder, everybody could get fat and the market never went dry, so there was always more money that could be made. It was not about being brothers or being homeboys like it was before. It was about stacking as much paper as you can and showing it off."

The renowned sociologist Dr. Carl Taylor, a Detroit native who wrote his dissertation on urban crime and gang activity in the Motor City, concurred with Boyd's assessment:

"The entire paradigm changed. When things got organized and young black men realized they could reach for the American Dream on the street, which wasn't just to get paid, but to get paid in full and they would be applauded for it by a lot of people, the game was immediately altered from that point forward. What spawned from that renaissance were highly efficient war tribes. These weren't just thugs or hooligans anymore. These were true sophisticated criminals with a mind for free enterprise."

Following the 1977 imprisonment of Eddie Jackson, Marzette's replacement atop the city's self-proclaimed Black Mafia, a void was created that was eventually filled by a pair of drug gangs going in opposite directions and representing opposite ends of the spectrum in the city's narcotics industry at that time. The aptly named and slightly archaic Murder Row gang represented the old school and the flashy and innovative Young Boys, Inc., or simply "YBI," represented the new wave in the black drug game. While Murder Row was always subservient to a well-entrenched and immensely powerful middle man in order to get its product, YBI sought and eventually achieved almost complete independence in the supply department.

Formed around 1975, the Murder Row gang was led by Francis "Big Frank Nitti" Usher and Harold Morton. Until about 1979, it could stake claim to being the largest and most feared drug conglomerate in Detroit. Usher and Morton oversaw a lethal crew of lieutenants and street workers that grew to nearly 50 people and slung the finest of European heroin all across the state. Like many black drug lords of the past, the Murder Row boys were supplied with their product by the city's Italian mob contingent.

The relationship between the mob and Murder Row was a natural one. Big Frank Nitti was allegedly introduced to Detroit kingpins Giovanni "Papa John" Priziola and Raffeale "Jimmy Q" Quasarano, a pair of men with deep ties in the international narcotics market, by mob street boss Anthony "Tony Jack" Giacalone, Usher's early mentor in the underworld. Most Italian mobsters traditionally look down on aspiring black criminals and racketeers, but Tony Jack took a quick liking to the young Usher in the 1960s. He kept a close eye on him and put him to work as a gofer. For years, Usher could be found flanking Giacalone at his usual haunts around town, eagerly absorbing everything he could from the city's toughest mobster and taking pride in being allowed to be part of his inner circle. In the ultimate sign of acceptance, Tony Jack tagged Usher with his nickname, "Frank Nitti," a reference to Frank "The Enforcer" Nitti of the infamous Al Capone mob in Chicago during the Prohibition era.

"Frank Nitti Usher was most likely the final black drug kingpin in the area to be doing a majority of his business with the Italian mob," said retired FBI agent Mike Carone. "The relationship between the Mafia and the black drug gangs was really starting to change right around the time Usher went to jail. There wasn't as much of a reliance on the Italians anymore for their product, so the landscape evolved away from the mob dominating the local drug market."

Opposite in mindset to the Murder Row crew, YBI's leadership did everything in its power to separate itself as quickly as possible from becoming dependent on the Mafia for their drugs. They were inspired by Henry Marzette, who had successfully cut the mob out of his operations, acquiring a non-Italian source for his drugs in Southeast Asia before his death. Starting in 1978, YBI founders Milton

"Butch" Jones, Raymond "Baby Ray" Peoples, Dwayne "Wonderful Wayne" Davis, and Mark "Block" Marshall constructed a steady supply line of "China White," the purest of Asian heroin, directly from the Golden Triangle straight into downtown Detroit. The organization, which at its peak had close to 400 employees, completely changed the landscape of how drugs were bought and sold in the state of Michigan from that point forward.

"They were the new breed," Robert De Fauw recalled. "When YBI became the predominant drug faction in the city, the rules changed."

◇◇◇◇◇◇◇◇◇◇◇◇

Much of what separated gangs like Murder Row and YBI from such predecessors as Eddie Jackson or the BKs and Flynns was pure ruthlessness. Chester Wheeler Campbell, possibly the Motor City's most feared assassin ever, was Murder Row's top enforcer and his exploits were legendary. Frank Usher and several Murder Row lieutenants were involved in a headline-grabbing triple beheading in 1979 that decimated the organization in its aftermath and set the stage for the ascension of YBI.

Campbell, known on the streets by such ominous nicknames as "The Angel of Death," "Dr. Death," and "The Undertaker," got an early start on his life of crime by first being incarcerated for burglary in 1946 at age 15. From that point forward, he would rack up a laundry list of felonies that would make even the most hardened and incorrigible of criminals envious. Between 1946 and 1986, Campbell, who scored close to genius level on an IQ test administered by a court-appointed psychiatrist, would spend 30 years behind bars. Crafting a legacy of terror second to none in the city's gangland history, Campbell is thought by federal authorities to have killed personally over 50 people in his time as a free man. Well aware of his villainous character traits, Campbell was known to call himself "one of God's unfortunate creatures," this with a slight grin as he downed shots of whisky with his friends at his favorite area watering holes.

"There aren't many criminals I locked up that I still have nightmares about, but Chester Campbell is one of them," said one former federal agent. "He was pure evil."

In 1955, Campbell was convicted of second-degree murder charges and served a 13-year prison sentence. Upon his release in 1968, he began working as a freelance hit man for a variety of local organized crime groups, including the Mafia and a number of top-tier drug gangs. He was known to dress only in black in an attempt to accentuate his morbid aura and was soon being recruited by out-of-state criminal groups to carry out executions across the nation for fees that topped the $15,000 mark, at the time an astronomical amount for that type of work. A surprisingly cultured man after years of reading and acquiring a wide variety of worldly knowledge while locked up, he was known to fill his time by attending plays, browsing in museums and studying foreign languages.

For a short period in the early 1970s, Campbell hit a run of good luck and successfully dodged two top-priority government investigations against him. In 1971, he was charged with intent to murder a star witness scheduled to testify at a drug-ring trial in which he was a defendant, but had the charges dropped. While he was awaiting trial on another murder charge a few years later, the government's star witness, James "Watusi Slim" Newton, a onetime Campbell confidant and business partner, wound up being executed in the protection wing of a maximum security federal prison in Ohio. Once again, Campbell skated and had the charges against him dropped before the case could ever reach a jury.

Around this time, Campbell started associating and doing business with Frank Usher and Harold Morton, two up-and-coming young heroin dealers from the East Side. Introduced by mutual acquaintances in the Mafia in late 1973, Campbell became the newly created "in-house enforcer" for the Murder Row gang. Usher and Morton cut him in for a piece of their drug business, and with his muscle and reputation, the pair of burgeoning kingpins took their organization to the top of the Motor City underworld. For a solid three to four years, Usher and Morton's Murder Row crew was the biggest drug operation in the entire state of Michigan.

Interestingly, just when the gang was reaching its pinnacle, Chester Campbell was brought down by his own reckless behavior. On February 6, 1975, Campbell turned a routine traffic stop on Orchard Lake Road in Keego Harbor into a high-speed chase that ended with his running a police car off the side of the road before finally being apprehended several miles later. When the arresting officers searched Campbell's vehicle, they found two semi-automatic pistols, a rifle, a sawed-off shotgun and several ounces of heroin. They also found a trunk load of notebooks with the names and addresses of over 300 law enforcement and government officials, as well as the names and daily habits of several recent murder victims and heaps of photocopied classified police documents. During a subsequent trial at which Campbell was convicted on drug and weapons charges, federal prosecutors alleged that the notebooks and their contents constituted a "hit list" of past and potential targets.

With Chester Campbell imprisoned, enforcement duties for the Murder Row gang passed to Adolph "Doc Holiday" Powell, a grizzled and well-traveled felon who had migrated to Detroit from New Orleans in the 1950s. The selection of Powell as a top lieutenant in the gang by Usher and Morton proved a mistake, as the power of his new position quickly went to his head. Tensions started to swell between Powell and Usher and as the decade came to a close, they were ready to boil over. The standoff tilted decidedly in Powell's favor due to the fact that Frank Usher's main backers, Harold Morton and Tony Giacalone, were both in the midst of serving jail sentences when tempers were reaching their highest pitch in mid-1979.

This lack of support left Usher vulnerable, and Powell pounced. Recruiting a pair of notorious hit men—James "Red" Freeman from Detroit and Robert "Lefty" Partee from California—to help eliminate Usher and his inner circle, Powell prepared to seize control of the whole Murder Row organization for himself. Luring Usher, a female companion named Joanne Clark and Usher's two closest associates at the time, William "Dirty Dirt" McJoy and William "Straw Hat Perry" Jackson, to the Michigan Federated Democratic Social Club, located on Garfield not far from Woodward, on July 18, 1979, Powell is alleged to have ordered Freeman and Partee to murder all four of them.

Big Frank Nitti somehow convinced Freeman and Partee to spare his life. Some claim he bribed them with drugs and money. Other say he simply used his quick wit and politician-like savvy to talk his way out of being killed. McJoy, Jackson, and Clark weren't so lucky. It is alleged that Freeman and Partee shot all three of them execution style in the back of the head and then chopped off their heads and hands and left their mutilated corpses in a van parked on the East Side.

Usher, Powell, Partee, Freeman, and a social club employee named Benjamin "Shorty" Fountain would all be charged with the murders and go on trial in 1980. Despite testimony and evidence pointing to Usher as an intended victim of the slaughter, he was convicted of the killings along with Partee, while Fountain had his charges dropped and Freeman and Powell were each acquitted.

After serving close to a decade of his life sentence, Usher had his conviction overturned by a Recorders Court judge and was granted a new trial in 1989. He pled guilty to being an accessory after the fact and was soon released after being credited with time served. Adolph Powell's fate wasn't so fortunate. He was murdered while having an afternoon drink at La Player's Lounge on Joy Road on January 22, 1983, amid rumors that he had become a government informant. Powell was blown away by a shotgun blast as he was about to take a shot of cognac and tip the bartender with a $50 bill, which was found by police in his clenched hand.

For all intents and purposes, the killings that took place at the Michigan Federated Democratic Social Club marked the end of Murder Row as a megawatt drug organization, splintering the gang into factions that either backed Usher or stood behind Powell in the dispute between the two. When Usher was jailed, his men were dispatched from the gang, allowing Powell to sweep up the pieces of what was left and set out under his own banner until he was killed three and a half years later.

Chester Campbell emerged from prison in 1984, but by that time the Murder Row crew was no longer active and he went back to work as a hired gun until his imprisonment in 1987 on charges stemming from an arrest practically identical to his 1975 roadside encounter with the cops. Just like the first incident, when police searched his car, they found several firearms, a suitcase full of drugs and another address-filled notebook that contained what authorities dubbed a hit list.

"A lot of people breathed a lot easier the day Chester Campbell was locked up for good," Mike Carone commented.

◇◇◇◇◇◇◇◇◇◇◇◇

Sprouting up in the late 1970s on the city's West Side around the areas surrounding Dexter, Monterey, and Linwood Avenues, Young Boys, Inc. started out as a small group of loosely connected drug dealers sharing a common supply source and soon was on its way to becoming a mega narcotics empire that operated with assembly-line efficiency and expert criminal acumen. YBI, as the group became known, completely changed the drug game in Detroit. The organization was a pioneer in underworld marketing and sales strategy, and in just five years it would erupt as a notorious part of the city's historical fabric while becoming its most financially successful narcotics gang ever. Authorities estimated that the gang cleared close to half a billion dollars cash in the 1982 calendar year alone.

"YBI was the first real iconic criminal organization to emerge out of the city since the old Purple Gang of the Prohibition era," Carl Taylor has pointed out. "They crafted the mold for all who came after them in the game. They were the model of how a well-run, large-scale narcotics gang operated. The emergence of YBI changed everything and really opened up a Pandora's Box of activity that hasn't stopped to this day."

The first traces of the gang emerged around 1976 when aspiring kingpins Raymond "Baby Ray" Peoples, Dwayne "Wonderful Wayne" Davis, and Mark "Block" Marshall brought their individual crews together and started selling heroin out of a bar on the corner of Prairie and Puritan. When Milton "Butch" Jones, a close friend of both Block and Baby Ray, was released from prison in February 1978, after serving a four-year sentence for manslaughter stemming from a robbery in late 1973, and joined up with the fast-growing operation, YBI was officially off and running. The four YBI founders were a good mix. They complemented each other well. While Peoples and Davis were more of the hustler type, master movers and shakers, Jones and Marshall were straight thugs, heartless street soldiers with itchy trigger fingers. In his autobiography, which he self-published in 1996, Butch Jones admitted carrying out his first of many murders when he was only 15 years old.

It's alleged that seed money for the gang's first large-scale narcotics purchase came from an $80,000 insurance settlement that Mark Marshall received when his father was killed. Collecting the money was no easy task, since Marshall himself was conspicuously charged with a heinous crime: the mass murder of three people and a dog whose corpses were all ejaculated on. Although he wound up being tried twice for the triple homicide, Block was never convicted and subsequently was able to collect the insurance payout. Although he was the last man on the scene, Butch Jones quickly ascended to the top of the gang's leadership and immediately imposed his will on the direction the syndicate would take. He was a natural bully and not a person who liked to share power.

"Butch Jones was a pretty menacing guy," Robert De Fauw remembers. "He bullied his way to the top of the gang and once he was there he ruled with over-whelming force. He and his crew were just coldhearted, ruthless people. I know one of his favorite enforcement tactics was to beat his enemies with a baseball bat. He did a lot of damage and hurt a lot of people."

Intent on building YBI in the mold of a Fortune 500 corporation, Jones culti-vated an infrastructure that was highly organized from top to bottom. Trying to diversify the gang's activities as much as possible, he split the operation into several distinct street factions, each responsible for a different aspect of the syndicate's overall bottom line. At the top of the food chain were Butch and Block, who ran their own individual army called "The Wrecking Crew" and oversaw the day-to-day affairs of the entire organization. Baby Ray and Wonderful Wayne, who went by the alias "WW," were each given responsibility over individual crews and oper-ated with general autonomy, deferring to Jones only for basic policy decisions and mediation of intra-gang disputes. Beneath the founders was an enforcement crew known as "The A Team" and led by teenage hit man Curtis "Kurt McGurk" Napier as well as a finance and supply crew led by Sylvester "Seal" Murray. Within Wonderful Wayne's faction were separate subfactions, jointly overseen by Davis and Jones, that dealt specifically with the cutting and marketing of the drugs. These master mixers cooked up enticingly potent brands of heroin and slapped on their packaging slick and catchy names like "Atomic Dog," "Purple Haze," "Hocus Pocus," "Starlight," "Whippersnapper," "Rolls Royce," "Hoochie Con," and Jones' own personal concoction dubbed "Check Mate" in honor of his love of the game of chess.

Butch was never one to abide by the status quo, so he also made sure that YBI was the first gang of its era not to have to rely on the Mafia for its drugs. Said to have been enamored with the city's original "Black Godfather," Henry Marzette, the area's first dealer to oppose the mob's control of the marketplace, Jones pat-terned his legacy after him. So it was only natural when he got out of jail and hooked up with Baby Ray, Block, and WW—who were all being supplied by Italian-backed sources—that he steered them away from relying on the Mafia for their product and encouraged complete independence. Jones and the fledgling Young Boys found that independence when they secured former Marzette lieuten-ant John "Milwaukee Jack" Mayes as their first primary heroin supplier. Mayes would soon introduce Jones to his protégé Seal Murray, who would go on to become Butch's top advisor and main conduit to the wholesale drug community outside of Michigan. Even further down the ranks, making up perhaps the most integral cogs in the entire organization, were the teams of street dealers, all boys and girls between the ages of 8 and 12, that sold the product on their elementary school playgrounds and delivered it on 10-speed bicycles and in taxi cabs paid for by their superiors. These juveniles were the same ones who did most of the gang's marketing footwork, plastering the city's various housing projects with handwritten coupons and notices of sales and new product development.

When the gang reached its peak of power in 1981, it controlled a staggering 90 percent of the drug trafficking taking place within the city limits. The epidemic of young children dealing on behalf of YBI became so ingrained in neighborhood culture in the late 1970s and early 1980s that little girls jumping rope would sing out rhythmic cadences like "Starlight, Hoochie Con, Rolls Royce round and round" among other rhymes that referenced the narcotics their peers were selling at the time.

"They were history makers all right," said De Fauw. "By the end of YBI's run, they had reshaped the way the drug game was played on both sides of the law. We had to adjust our methods as law enforcement, up our game if you will, to get an accurate beat on these guys. They were the first gang to start really exploiting preadolescent kids to their advantage and using them as shields. It made things a much more delicate process on our end in terms of investigating them."

YBI gang members tended to travel in bulk. When members showed up at a nightclub or concert, they were often 50 deep. Usually dressing in unison, they sported the trendiest clothes and styles of the era. One day they would all be wearing red Adidas tracksuits and white Adidas Top 10 running shoes, the next, brown and green military fatigues and steel-toed boots. During winter the gang favored fur-lined Max Julian hooded jackets, and they were known to wear "John Dillinger derbys" — Styrofoam political campaign hats adorned with red, white and blue stripes around the brim. Modes of transportation were of the utmost importance as well. And as with their clothes, members of YBI were notorious for purchasing in lockstep. Two dozen or more Mercedes and Corvettes were bought at the same time and then promptly shown off during massive caravans to places like Cedar Point or Kings Island amusement parks in Ohio or sporting events and concerts in locations within a day's driving distance.

Dissatisfied with living in the city where they grew up and plied their trade to great riches, Butch and Baby Ray hightailed it to the plushy suburbs as soon as they could. Both relocated in ritzy Oakland County, with Butch moving to Oak Park to a house he built with an indoor pool and Baby Ray moving further north to Troy where he purchased a three-story residence in a leafy and secluded, newly developed subdivision.

"I knew the second I laid eyes on these guys we were dealing with a different breed," said Carl Taylor, who spent time working in the private security business. "It was an eerie feeling that came over me because I immediately realized how much destruction a group like this could do. These cats were young, but so sophisticated and organized. They had an aura unlike any group like them I had encountered before. The neighborhood kids all gravitated to them. There was a prestige on the streets when you were affiliated with the Young Boys. It was like saying you played with the L.A. Lakers or New York Yankees."

The good times lasted a half-decade, from roughly 1977 to 1982. And then the common perils of the industry started to set in and the gang self-destructed. The core of YBI, which consisted of about 50 people, was torn apart at the seams by greed, jealousy and resentment. Like a circling shark that smelled blood in the water, the government came in and delivered the deathblow, levying back-to-back-to-back federal indictments that spelled complete decimation for the gang by 1987. It was an ugly dismantling process.

◇◇◇◇◇◇◇◇◇◇◇◇

The first cracks in the armor appeared in late 1980 when Baby Ray Peoples and Block Marshall had a falling out over a woman they were both seeing at the same time. Marshall might have had the reputation of a killer and Peoples that of a suave, laid-back smooth-talker, but make no mistake about it, Baby Ray could more than hold his own in a fight. When he was 19 years old, Peoples was charged with, but eventually acquitted of, a racially motivated murder of a man who was dragged from his car on Livernois Avenue and beaten to death with a piece of broken-off concrete. Things boiled over between Peoples and Marshall in early 1981. In the last of several heated verbal altercations the pair had engaged in that spring, Baby Ray shot Block, who survived the attempt on his life, but picked up and left Detroit for California as a result.

Around this same time, Wonderful Wayne began to chafe under the thumb of Butch's heavy-handed leadership methods. Jones was power drunk and didn't like to share credit or profits. Davis felt stifled and split town. First he went to Seattle and set up a small distribution operation in Washington State. Then he trekked cross-country to Massachusetts and in a matter of months had seized control of a majority of the heroin market in Boston. Returning triumphant to the Motor City in early 1982, Davis started an offshoot gang of his own called the "H2O Crew," and although he was still officially considered YBI, he refused to kiss Butch's ring. It started when Wonderful Wayne's crew took over much of the drug dealing in Pontiac, a traditionally independent town in northern Oakland County, a good 45 minutes out of the city, and didn't offer any tribute or commission to Butch or Baby Ray. WW did the same thing a few months later when he branched off further up I-75 to working-class Flint and began selling powdered cocaine, a product that had just become cheap enough to sell in the inner cities.

This perceived lack of respect didn't sit well with Jones and the rest of the YBI administration. Tensions came to a head between Davis and Jones over a territory squabble involving selling space on Lawton Avenue in Northwest Detroit. In

Butch's mind, all of Lawton belonged to YBI. When the H2O lieutenants, many of whom were recent Boston transplants, started pushing a new mix of heroin called "Freak of the Week" in the area throughout the first part of 1982, Jones was personally offended. Things escalated when Kurt McGurk reported back to Butch that Davis was talking subversively and reportedly had said "Fuck that guy," in reference to Jones.

On Mother's Day, Baby Ray Peoples took a shot at an associate of WW's while he was leaving a Hallmark store after purchasing a card to take to his mom on the way to dinner at her house. The summer came and went, and Davis was still tooling around the city in his triple-black Mercedes, outwardly disavowing anything and everything YBI. While standing outside a residence on Philadelphia Street on the city's West Side in early August, Peoples was shot as he assaulted a woman he had been dating named Cherrisse Jones. Some informants told authorities that the shooting was related to the infighting going on between Davis and his former cohorts in YBI, since the woman in question was said to have also been seeing a member of Davis' H2O Crew. Baby Ray survived the shooting, but months later, Cherrisse Jones was found shot in the head, her body dumped by some railroad tracks near the city's New Center area.

WW's brash and careless behavior finally caught up with him on September 28, 1982 when he was shot in the head in broad daylight by two assailants, one of which he had engaged in conversation, on the corner of Columbus and Lawton. Butch, Kurt McGurk, and another pair of YBI lieutenants named Keith "Kethon the Terrible" Green and Maurice "Mo Heart" Gibbs were charged with the crime six years later, but each soon had the charges dropped.

Following Wonderful Wayne's high-profile homicide—an audacious killing that was preceded by the brazen murder of a Detroit narcotics officer by YBI member Carey Goins a few months before—the government turned the heat up on the gang and pushed its investigation into overdrive. The first nail in the coffin was a multi-count, 41-person federal racketeering indictment levied on December 8, 1982 that ensnared the entire hierarchy of YBI, including Butch Jones, Raymond Peoples, Seal Murray and Kurt McGurk. At the press conference announcing the bust, the DEA said the gang was making close to eight million dollars a week pushing heroin. A raid of Murray's luxury penthouse apartment atop the Jeffersonian downtown discovered nearly a million dollars in cash. One of the young men arrested was wearing $100,000 worth of diamond-encrusted jewelry. It was soon revealed that a DEA undercover agent had infiltrated the operations of Murray and his right-hand man, Daryl "Dynamite D" Young, as early as 1981, and the information gleaned from that part of the investigation put things over the top in the government's favor.

Jones, who by that time was 28 years old, didn't take the indictment lying down. With word of the upcoming bust reaching him by Thanksgiving, Butch scooped up his wife, Portia, who would also end up being charged in the case, and his two kids and relocated to a mansion he had recently bought in Arizona. Encouraging his attorney, Richard Lustig, to make a deal with prosecutors, Jones turned himself in to federal custody on March 22, 1983, agreeing to plead guilty of being head of a continuing criminal enterprise in exchange for a sentence of 12 years in prison. Most of Jones' underlings followed suit and pled guilty to the charges. Two of his Wrecking Crew enforcers, Karl "Fat Pratt" Gatlin and Kevin "Lughead" Wilson, couldn't take the heat of the bust and became government witnesses.

The crushing legal assault on YBI, unfortunately, did little to temper the violence the gang exhibited, and although it shook the organization to the core, there were still enough remnants to keep things active within the ranks for another five years. Immediately following the indictment and subsequent guilty pleas, further friction developed between Butch and Baby Ray. With Butch locked up and Peoples out on bail awaiting sentencing, the pair are alleged to have bumped heads over how the gang would be governed and the previous earnings distributed with the entire original administration either currently or soon to be behind bars. This feverish dispute was complicated by the fact that Baby Ray's brothers, Timothy "Timmy Slim" Peoples and Nathaniel "Nate the Great" Peoples, were both key members of Butch's crew. Timmy Slim was viewed as Butch's top emissary, often acting as Jones' eyes and ears on the streets.

According to federal documents, Butch wanted to tidy some things up within the gang before everyone turned themselves in to start serving their prison time. Most of the tidying, the documents say, related to Jones' desire to eliminate certain members of Baby Ray's inner circle who were unscathed by the recent bust. On May 12, 1983, Moe Heart Gibbs, one of Butch's closest confidants, and Kurt McGurk, whose nickname derived from an obscure comic strip character from the early 1970s, ambushed Joseph "Wamp" Brown and Gregory "Special K" Kendricks, two of Peoples' top henchmen, on separate street corners in the same afternoon. Brown was killed when McGurk shot him on the corner of Concord and Benson, but Kendricks survived his attack on the corner of Beaubian and Erskine. Right before he died, Wamp told police that "Kurt McGurk and Mohawk [another alleged nickname of Gibbs] shot me," leading the judge in his drug case to revoke both of their bonds and issue arrest warrants.

Gibbs turned himself in and was eventually acquitted of the charges. Not surprisingly, McGurk, described by street informants as a "bloodthirsty psychopath" who had been doing hits for the gang since he was 15 years old, went underground. While at large, he made front-page headlines twice—first, in September, for taking aim at a pair of uniformed police officers with a sawed-off shotgun in the midst of fleeing on foot from an alley on Richton and Cortland on Detroit's near Northwest Side, and then shortly thereafter by allegedly sending a letter containing a death threat to Gil Hill, the Detroit Police Department's Chief of Homicide. A citywide manhunt for Kurt McGurk ensued, with the 19-year-old hit man being declared Public Enemy No. 1 by the Wayne County Sheriff's Office. He was finally apprehended in November and pled guilty to the Brown murder following a high-speed chase that took police from Pontiac onto I-75 before finally ending on the lawn of the D'Arcy-McManus & Masius advertising agency on Woodward in Bloomfield Township.

The coming years didn't bring peace or stability to the already iconic criminal empire. Further housecleaning was deemed necessary, and through the first half of 1984 there were six gangland homicides attributed to backbiting between the gang's quickly emerging two factions. Before the end of the year there were three more. Looking to drive a stake right through the heart of Baby Ray's power base, Butch's crew killed Norman "Snead" Johnson, a key Peoples associate, on February 17th, and then Carl Garrett, his onetime bodyguard and driver, on July 17th, gunned down as he rode a moped at the intersection of Six Mile Road and Schaeffer.

Just two months earlier, in May, Ricky Gracey and two other assailants—all said to be Peoples loyalists—robbed Butch Jones' suburban Troy residence, where his wife and children were staying when he was imprisoned, and then tried to rob it again two days later. The second robbery attempt was thwarted, according to court testimony, when Butch's wife Portia—on probation for her role in the 1982 bust—shotgunned Gracey as he ran from the house. Butch's son "Mo Mo," 10 years old at the time, is alleged to have taken part in the shooting as well, and according to court testimony begged his mother to let him finish off the wounded Gracey with his own weapon. Instead, Portia Jones called for help from "The A Team" to dispose of Gracey. Arriving on the scene to aid Jones' family were Charles "The Big O" Obey, Spencer Holloway and Andre Williams. Led by Obey, The A Team tortured Gracey to find out the names of his co-conspirators and, according to Williams, who testified against the gang in court, killed him by unloading an Uzi clip into his body and leaving his mangled corpse in an East Side alley at Cardoni and Russell Streets.

Carl Garrett's death was linked to the planning of the heist. Prior to Garrett's murder in June, his stepfather, Dennis Bankston, who authorities also connected to the failed robbery, was found slumped over the steering wheel of his car, shot to death in a parking lot in northeast Detroit. The week following Garrett's murder, Reggie Stringer, another suspected accomplice in Gracey's break-in, was found dead in his car on Winder Street from multiple gunshot wounds to his head and body.

Baby Ray Peoples came out of jail on parole at the age of 29 in late April 1985 and, at least according to his family, tried to go straight. He got married in June and was looking to get involved in the real estate business. It never happened. The past, specifically his beef with Butch Jones, caught up with him on August 10th when he was killed, shot to death sitting in his beige-colored Chevy Citation, waiting to meet an associate in an alley on Sturdevant Avenue, between La Salle and 14th Street.

Even following the Davis and Peoples homicides and the jailing of Jones and McGurk, the government remained aggressive in its pursuit of bringing down whatever was left of the organization. In 1985 and 1987, investigations dubbed "YBI II" and "YBI III" were capped with sweeping federal racketeering indictments, the latter of which spelled the official demise of the legendary drug organization. For a while, things on the YBI front were dead. And then Butch Jones got released from prison.

◇◇◇◇◇◇◇◇◇◇◇◇

Back on the scene in the city of Detroit in the early 1990s, after eight years behind bars for his role as the ringleader of the remarkably notorious YBI gang, Butch Jones had no intention of going clean. Despite spewing rhetoric of his supposed rehabilitation to the press and telling tales of wanting to do everything in his power to dissuade young kids from a life on the streets, Jones went back into the drug and murder business. Combining forces with John "The Bread Man" Bass, a much-feared crime lord who had emerged on the scene while Jones was serving his time in prison, Butch joined and eventually seized control of Bass' "Dawg Pound" gang. The Dawg Pound was smaller yet eerily similar to YBI, and ran its operations out of a series of residences on Monterey Avenue, right back in the epicenter of his old stomping grounds. Just like in the '80s, drug dealing, fierce intimidation tactics and cold-blooded murder were center stage. Although Jones has never been convicted on any specific counts of homicide, police files estimate that this latter-day urban Godfather, referred to in some newspaper accounts as the "Henry Ford of heroin," can be linked to the planning, ordering or carrying out of some 35 gangland executions.

Similar to what happened back in 1978 when Butch came out of prison to muscle his way to the top of an already-functioning crime conglomerate, Jones basically showed up on Bass' doorstep and declared himself in for half of the Dawg Pound organization. Too intimidated to refuse his declaration, Bass welcomed Butch on board with a smiling face and an extended hand, knowing at the very least that being associated with the former YBI boss could only increase his street cred. However, unlike in his YBI days when he was alleged to have killed his way to complete leadership supremacy, Jones assumed command of the Dawg Pound due to simple good luck. Working relatively well in cahoots with each other, Jones and Bass coexisted peacefully for about five years before the Bread Man was brought down by a crippling federal bust in February 1997, allowing Butch to be on top of the gang's power structure all alone. Included in the indictment were charges that Bass ordered the June 1996 murder of his partner and half-brother Patrick "Pat the Ram" Webb, carried out by Dawg Pound lieutenant Armenty "Fat Moe" Shelton, who was killed four days later by Bass himself in order to cover his tracks.

From 1994 to 2001, Butch Jones oversaw a large-scale marijuana and cocaine distribution network that committed at least two murders of rival dealers. Based on his name and reputation alone, Jones was also allegedly able to strong-arm his way into the extortion racket, simply taxing other drug organizations for doing business in his neighborhood. By way of his association with Bass, Butch was also reputed to have gotten into the world of dog fighting, one of the derivatives of the gang's moniker. Indicted in the summer of 2001, the U.S. Prosecutor's Office declared its intention to seek the death penalty against him, but just as in 1983, thanks to some nifty lawyering, Jones walked away with a lesser-than-expected penalty of 30 years incarceration. With time off for good behavior, Butch could be home by the mid-2020s, getting the chance to live out his final days among his friends and family at home.

◇◇◇◇◇◇◇◇◇◇◇◇

If Young Boys, Inc. was the McDonald's of the Motor City drug trade in the 1980s, then "The Pony Down Gang," "The Davis Family Gang," and "The Curry Brothers Gang" were the Burger King, Wendy's, and KFC. These narcotics franchises might have lived in the shadow of Butch Jones and YBI, but they were just as dangerous, successful and violence-prone, though with fewer headlines.

"Those gangs were all copying the blueprint of YBI," Robert De Fauw explained. "That said, they were wreaking equal amounts of havoc within the city limits. While at one time, you might have had only a small handful of big-time organizations, by the 1980s, these types of groups were sprouting up all over the place, simply following the path set by the Young Boys."

The only one of these gangs that actually tried to take on the Young Boys head-to-head was the Pony Down Gang. While the Davis and Curry crews carved out obvious non-YBI territory for themselves to make a living, the Pony Down Gang had the gall to plant its flag in the middle of the Young Boys' well-established West Side turf, to start poaching their roster of employees and to enter into direct competition with them by trying to undercut their prices. From the very start, it was war.

Pony Down was started by Leroy "Gun" Buttrum and got its name from the gang's trademark Pony-brand shoes and athletic gear, worn in direct and purposeful contrast to YBI's signature Adidas ensembles. Unlike Butch Jones, Baby Ray Peoples and Block Marshall, who were all teenagers when they started YBI,

Buttrum was just short of his 30th birthday when he founded Pony Down in 1980. A junior high school dropout, Buttrum had his first arrest in 1964 at the age of 14 for burglary. He wasn't yet 16 when he had already stacked up a rap sheet that included charges of auto theft and assault with intent to commit murder. In 1970, he was busted for assault with intent to commit armed robbery and sentenced to five years in prison, of which he served three. Paroled in 1973, Buttrum went temporarily legit, coming back to Detroit and starting a home improvement business, helping rehab houses. It didn't stick.

Building his own drug empire in the exact same mold and using an identical business model as his adversaries in YBI, Gun Buttrum recruited his best friend, Robert "Bobby the Pimp" Lantine; his brothers, Walter "WB" Buttrum, Larry "LB" Buttrum, and Tony "The Snake" Buttrum, and several onetime Young Boys soldiers. By mid-1980, the Pony Down Gang was up and running in full swing. Buttrum immediately had dozens of adolescent street dealers posted across Seven Mile Road on the far Northwest Side of the city, slinging his own brands of slickly marketed heroin sporting flashy names like "GQ," "Shotgun Special," "Papa Smurf," "Nod City," and "Devil's Dust." Gang members raided and destroyed YBI drug houses, telling YBI dealers that they could either "Pony down or pack up and leave town." This meant they could either join the new crew of drug bandits and turn their backs on YBI or get out of the business altogether.

The phrase "I Pony Down" was spray-painted everywhere possible, especially on YBI property. Handwritten YBI fliers advertising its new brands of drugs and certain buy-one, get-one-free deals were ripped down from the housing project hallways and street posts and replaced with similar offers sponsored by the Pony Down boys. These aggressive leadership tactics were more than fruitful as authorities placed the gang's profit margin at $100 million annually.

Moving out of the city and into a quaint, residential manor in suburban Farmington Hills, Gun Buttrum went around calling himself the "new and improved Butch Jones," outwardly showing his disdain for the YBI kingpin, while at the same time mimicking practically every one of his ruling methods. It was a contradiction that didn't escape Jones and his compatriots, and only fueled the bitter rivalry. Tensions simmered under the surface for a while, then in late 1982, when YBI was under siege from the government, a series of violent altercations broke out between the battling drug syndicates—mostly drive-by shootings—with Buttrum and his Pony Down crew making a move to seize territory when their rivals were at their weakest. After New Year's, the hostility increased and bodies started to drop.

In response to Pony Down's takeover of a pair of YBI drug houses in the months after Butch Jones' jailing, YBI lieutenants George "Scandalous Butch" Young, Vincent "Sharkie" Reed, Kevin "Bibbie" Terrell, and John "Potsie" Piner staged an assault on three teenage Pony Down dealers on an East Side street corner in April 1983. Driving up to the trio in the mid-afternoon, the YBI contingent exited their vehicle and opened fire with automatic weapons. One of the boys was killed and the two other victims of the attack were wounded. The next month, members of Pony Down responded by beating a YBI associate named Douglas Pace with baseball bats and then leaving him to die in an abandoned house on Pickford Street.

The bloodshed wasn't exclusive to YBI either. Anybody who infringed on Pony Down's rule was gambling with his life. An independent drug peddler named William "Chilly Willie" Hunter was killed outside a West Side apartment on June 17th, and several other dealers were gunned down over the course of that summer in murders the police attributed to Pony Down's further consolidation efforts. That fall, rivals of Gun Buttrum and his brothers struck a very personal blow to the Pony Down Gang and the Buttrum family itself. In an act of supreme contempt and disrespect, Leroy Buttrum's two-year-old nephew was kidnapped in September and held for a $100,000 ransom. The Buttrum brothers were incensed. Despite being warned numerous times by authorities to stay out of the investigation, that just wasn't realistic. Striking a blow at the organization was one thing. Attacking the Buttrum family personally took things to a whole new level. At a police-monitored delivery of the ransom, Walter Buttrum and one of his henchmen disrupted the arrest of the assailants by opening fire on the man who came to make the pickup. When word of an alleged $250,000 bounty on the heads of the kidnappers reached the streets in the hours after the botched ransom drop, the Buttrums' nephew was returned unharmed before the end of the day, dropped off at a local McDonald's.

The reign of Gun Buttrum and the Pony Down Gang came crashing down on November 20, 1985 when the federal government hit them with a 35-person, 50-count indictment featuring numerous drug, firearm and tax evasion violations. Gun Buttrum didn't stick around to see his fellow gang and family members arrested and hauled off to jail. Once again copying the actions of his biggest adversary, Butch Jones, Buttrum went on the lamb and became a fugitive of the law. In January 1986, he was arrested after a traffic stop in Berrien Township in western Michigan, apparently heading for Chicago, where the gang was said to have affiliations. Like all of his brothers, Leroy Buttrum pled guilty to the charges against him and was sentenced to six and a half years in prison. LB, the gang's reputed third-in-command, was back in the news after his release from jail when he pled guilty to further drug conspiracy charges stemming from a 2006 arrest in Missouri for intent to distribute marijuana and Ecstasy.

The Davis Family Gang, soon to be known just as "DFG," was started in the early 1970s and was headed by Reggie Davis and his brothers and sisters. Reggie, only 18 when he began his organization, thought in bigger terms than just Detroit. Bigger even than the state of Michigan or the whole Midwest. He thought intercontinental. Finding a California-based heroin connection, Davis relocated to a mansion in Beverly Hills in 1977 and set up several of his siblings at a base of operations in Miami. With more siblings and cousins looking after things back in Michigan and further supply connections developed from sources in Jamaica, Ghana, Nigeria, Holland, Haiti, Thailand, and Britain, the gang began flooding multiple cities throughout the country, including a good percentage of Detroit's non-YBI territory, with high-grade heroin, cocaine and marijuana.

The weak link in the DFG chain proved to be Reggie's younger brother, Ricky, who had a well-known big mouth. After Ricky talked his way into a transaction with an undercover DEA agent in October 1979 and soon after introduced him to his brothers Duane and Reggie, DFG was infiltrated at the very top of the heap. Due to this security leak, authorities were able use extensive audio and video surveillance to learn of a June 1982 meeting in a luxury suite at a downtown Detroit hotel. Reggie and several other kingpins met to discuss the negative effect that YBI's outlandish behavior was having on their business.

Davis, whose son Reggie Jr. would go on to become a popular local hip-hop radio disc jockey, had good reason to be worried about what was going on with YBI. During the raid of Seal Murray's penthouse apartment at the Jeffersonian in December 1982, the DEA seized documents and phone records that chronicled a business relationship between the pair. Earlier in the decade, Duane Davis was often seen driving around town in an audacious yellow Cadillac Fleetwood registered in the name of Seal Murray, a fact that reached the local press and caused a flare-up between Murray and Butch Jones over where his allegiances lay.

The levy had actually broken three months earlier in August when a female DFG courier working on behalf of Duane and his wife, Alicia, was busted coming into Chicago's O'Hare International Airport from Amsterdam with 1.5 kilos of pure heroin hidden in coffee cans. The courier agreed to be debriefed by federal agents and to divulge her intimate knowledge of the DFG smuggling process. Among other things, she told of the practice of getting drugs through customs in hand-carved religious statues carried by men and women posing as traveling Christian missionaries. The courier's cooperation was the first domino to fall. There would be more.

DFG's fate was sealed on August 4, 1983, when the federal government unveiled a 57-count drug and income tax evasion indictment that essentially closed the lid on any further dealings with the group as an entity. While most of the gang's members either were convicted on the charges or pled guilty, Reggie fled and eluded the law for the next three years. He was finally apprehended in September 1986 inside an Ann Arbor hotel room with over two pounds of uncut cocaine. In press releases relating to Davis' status as a fugitive, he was called one of the "Top 10 heroin dealers in North America" and the leader of a drug ring "that stretched to four continents."

Unlike the Buttrum brothers and their Pony Down crew, who looked to challenge top-dog YBI at every opportunity, or DFG, which did an end run and went out of state to move the bulk of its drugs, the Curry brothers were content to play second fiddle to Butch Jones and his Young Boys empire. Minus the flashy handle and juvenile preening, the Currys didn't interest the press. Their story didn't have enough glitz and glamour, but that was fine by them. Lurking in the shadows, the Curry Brothers Gang sat back and watched as YBI and Pony Down went to war with each other, racking up headlines and flouting the law with bloodshed and overly boastful behavior. The fallout eventually spurred their downfall and allowed the Curry gang to swoop in and coyly pick up the scraps left behind. Run by twin brothers Johnny and Leonard Curry, the gang was centered on the East Side, conveniently stashed away from primary YBI and Pony Down sales districts further west. Federal files allege that the Curry brothers' dad, Sam "Sammy Mack" Curry, acted as the gang's top advisor and reputedly chipped in with startup cash back in 1978 when the gang was formed. Also along for the ride was the family's baby brother, Rudell "Boo" Curry, an eager lieutenant almost always at his older siblings' sides, being groomed for a future leadership role.

The most recognizable figure from the Curry gang proved to be Johnny's ace protégé, Richard "White Boy Rick" Wershe, a teenage street prodigy with a fierce and flamboyant reputation that he had earned by the time he was 15. Wershe's rise to fame shocked many people and created frenzied news coverage. He had no business holding as much power as he did, but somehow he climbed to heights in the urban underworld that few of his age or skin color have ever achieved. Being white and not even old enough to have a driver's license, Rick stuck out like a sore thumb, yet it made no difference. The lanky, mop-topped, fresh-faced 15-year-old was Johnny Curry's right-hand man and that said it all. If Johnny trusted him and treated him like a son, the rest of the street had no choice but to respect him.

"They were an odd coupling," said one former federal law enforcement official of Johnny Curry's association with the drug-dealing wunderkind Wershe. "Seeing those two tooling around town together in Johnny's Benz was like watching Superfly tote around the kid from *Leave It to Beaver*. At first glance, everybody was shocked. Then it was just accepted by everybody. It's like on the streets and in law enforcement after everyone got over the novelty of the two of them running together, all of a sudden he changed skin color. Within a few months, everybody just viewed him as black. There was no differentiation. That was the way he acted and those were the type of girls he dated and people he hung around with. It appeared very effortless for him. He lived the culture, so people didn't view him as an outsider playing gangster. Surprisingly, the assimilation process was very fast; he was accepted very quickly by all the major players outside the Curry boys as one of their own. To his credit, he was very business savvy for a kid his age. He had a deep understanding of street politics and he knew how to exploit certain very complex and dangerous angles and use them to his advantage."

Johnny and Leonard Curry might not have been as well known to the general public as many of the other kingpins of the day, but on the street, they were as big as it got. Anybody who made a living in the drug trade at that time would tell you that Johnny (known as "Little Man") and Leonard (known as "Big Man") were as respected and feared in the Motor City underworld as Butch Jones, Gun Buttrum, Reggie Davis and Frank Usher. By 1986, they were the only ones left standing.

"The funny thing about that time is that a lot of guys who made major paper, guys like Little Man and Big Man, were considerably less well known to the public than the guys who had these big personalities and were in all the headlines but didn't hold a candle to cats like the Curry boys when it came to hustling," Rob Boyd commented. "Nobody outside of the game back then would have been able to tell you who Little Man and Big Man were. They liked it that way. In the 'hood on the other hand, where it mattered the most, everybody knew the Currys weren't anybody to mess with."

As a result of their ability to avoid the spotlight, the Currys wound up being the longest-lasting of all the Detroit drug syndicates of their era. YBI and Pony Down lasted five years apiece. So did Murder Row. The Davis Family Gang did them one better and lasted six. However, the Curry brothers ruled for almost a full decade, acquiring equal riches with far less fanfare and acquiring the type of highly placed connections in both local politics and law enforcement that their contemporaries like Jones or Buttrum could only dream of.

"Little Man was real slick, a behind-the-scenes guy who got things done," Boyd recalled. "Big Man was out front, a little more outgoing and willing to engage with people outside their inner circle. They weren't on your TV screen at night on the nightly news, but they were the guys coming down the street or riding around Belle Isle with the freshest new cars and hottest threads."

The Currys were in business for so long that their gang's activities spanned two distinct narcotic booms. They were a true anomaly. When the gang started up in the late 1970s, like everyone else, the Currys sold heroin. When the curtain finally came down on the gang's tenure in the late 1980s, cocaine was the product being pushed, and specifically crack. Around mid-1984, the more than two dozen Curry-owned heroin dens scattered throughout the city nearly all became crack houses. Being supplied by local wholesale moguls Arthur "AD" Derrick and Sam "Doc" Curry (no relation), the Currys had an endless supply of powdery goodness that they cut and sold for an estimated $200 million over the next three years.

Operations within the Curry organization were significantly aided by Johnny's influential contacts outside the drug industry. Little Man had allies in almost every nook and cranny of the city's political structure, inroads that reached all the way to the mayor's office. Most of these connections were consummated the day Johnny married Cathy Volsan, a favored niece of longtime mayor Coleman A. Young whom he treated as a daughter.

"Cathy was a ghetto princess," said one former FBI agent. "She was beautiful, educated, and carried herself in a very high-powered manner. But for some reason, she was attracted to drug dealers. I don't know if it was a rebellion thing, growing up around the mayor's mansion or whatnot, but she strictly dated dopers. And big-time guys, with lots of juice already without her in the picture. Landing Cathy Curry was like bagging the kingfish. It was a prize. Being with Cathy meant you were tied into the mainframe of the mother ship. She provided the kind of access criminals killed to have. When Little Man married Cathy, he went from just another big-time dealer to being practically untouchable. I say practically because he wound up getting busted, but only after he stayed around probably a good five years longer than he should have."

Coleman A. Young was Detroit's first black mayor and served five terms in office. In the first half of Young's two decades in the mayor's office, the diminutive yet extremely charismatic grassroots politician was celebrated. In contrast, the second half of his time on top was plagued by increasing violence on the city's streets and constant speculation of wrongdoing. Heavily investigated by the FBI, IRS, and DEA for a variety of alleged illegal activity, Young was never charged with a single crime. Leaving office in 1993, he had a complex legacy and was plagued with speculation about his ties to the local underworld. Rumors abounded for years about Young's connection to the area's drug industry. It started in the 1970s with investigations by multiple government agencies regarding narcotics activity possibly being conducted out of his family's restaurant, Young's BBQ. The investigations concluded as Young left office with rampant accusations of corruption and convictions of several members of his inner circle for running a police-sponsored protection racket for drug dealers both in state and out.

Many of Young's problems later in his mayoral tenure could be traced directly back to the soft spot he had for his niece Cathy, a drug-addicted diva with a penchant for associating with some of the city's most dangerous and high-profile felons. The daughter of Young's sister Juanita and his close friend Willie Volsan, an alleged associate of a number of area drug kingpins, Cathy was the apple of her uncle's eye and he spoiled her. He also watched her back intently. During court proceedings in the 1990s, it would come out that Young personally authorized around-the-clock private security for Cathy provided by a special service unit of the Detroit Police Department. Orders to the unit were expressly not to disrupt the activities of Cathy's criminal associates, but merely to make certain if any violence erupted in her presence that it be thwarted and that she be shuttled to safety immediately. The top-secret security detail was on duty from 1985, when the mayor's niece married Johnny Curry, through 1988, when she was having an affair and sharing living quarters with her husband's right-hand man, White Boy Rick Wershe.

Through the years, Cathy was a fixture at the mayor's residence, the Manoogian Mansion, and through her uncle she was introduced to some very powerful people. One of these was Police Commander Gil Hill, with whom she became very close. Some federal investigators claim too close. Besides holding several top positions within the Detroit Police Department, Hill gained minor Hollywood celebrity in 1984 when he appeared in the film *Beverly Hills Cop* as Eddie Murphy's superior officer on the Detroit police force. In 1989, Hill would be elected Detroit's City Council president, and he would eventually stage an unsuccessful mayoral campaign in 1996. Between his brush with movie fame and his foray into local politics, however, Hill was investigated by the FBI for reputed connections to none other than Cathy's husband, Johnny Curry. Cathy testified under oath in 1992 that Hill tipped her off in 1986 about the Currys' home telephone being bugged by federal surveillance experts. Later that year, a *Detroit News* article reported an ongoing investigation into Hill's possible role in leaking information and taking a payoff from Johnny Curry to impede progress in the case of a gangland homicide that was allegedly pointing in the direction of Curry and his crew.

The homicide was that of 13-year-old Damion Lucas, an innocent bystander struck by a bullet in a drive-by shooting aimed at his uncle, a rival Curry drug dealer, on April 29 1985. Lucas' uncle had allegedly screwed the Curry brothers on hotel reservations in Las Vegas for the Marvin Hagler–Tommy Hearns fight, which the gang had attended weeks earlier. According to Curry, Cathy and he met with Hill in his office the day after the Lucas murder and were informed that a member of Curry's crew was the top suspect in the crime. Hill then allegedly told them, "You have nothing to worry about," and according to Curry, accepted a bribe of $10,000 in cash to keep him and his inner circle out of the investigation. Although he admits to speaking with Cathy on the phone the day after the Lucas homicide, Hill denies disrupting the investigation of the murder and taking any money to help shield Curry from harm.

The run for Johnny and Leonard Curry atop the city's drug world came to an end in the spring of 1987, when the government indicted the Curry brothers and 18 of their foot soldiers in a racketeering case, with charges of mass narcotics trafficking and tax evasion dating back close to a decade. Cathy wasn't arrested, but was named as an unindicted co-conspirator in the case, which mapped out her husband's airtight control of numerous East Side drug houses and his increase in power and territory acquisition after the incarceration of Butch Jones and Leroy Buttrum. The following winter, the Currys and all of their underlings pled guilty, with Johnny and Leonard each getting hit with 20-year sentences, of which they served a little more than half.

Taking over Johnny Curry's organization and stealing his wife to boot, 17-year-old Rick Wershe's time as king of the hill was short-lived. He was convicted for possession with intent to distribute eight kilos of cocaine in January

1988, stemming from an arrest shrouded in mystery since police found the drugs, following a routine traffic stop, buried in someone's yard over a block away. In the years that followed, it would come out that Wershe had been recruited at age 14 by a federal task force to infiltrate the city's drug world and report back with intelligence on a variety of local underworld figures. At some point in 1987, the task force cut ties with Wershe, laying the groundwork for his ascension to the top of the Curry organization.

Wershe went back to work for the government in exchange for a promise of future parole while he was in prison serving a life sentence. He subsequently aided federal investigators in setting up a sting to nail Willie Volsan, Cathy's father and Coleman Young's brother-in-law, and Jimmy Harris, a Young confidant and the onetime head of his personal security staff, for running a protection racket for wholesale narcotics suppliers doing business in Detroit. For a hefty price, Harris and Volsan would arrange to have out-of-town dealers picked up at the airport in a standard-issue black-and-white police cruiser and driven to the site of their "sales meeting." If you were a dealer who already lived in the city, it was alleged that you could pay Harris and Volsan for information related to specific investigations and heads-up alerts on pending busts, search warrants and surveillance activity.

Offering their services to an undercover FBI agent in the early part of 1991, the protection ring was busted up by a federal indictment in May. For Harris, a 30-year veteran of the police force, it was a long fall from grace. Although well-respected and well-decorated as an officer of the law, he was never far from controversy. In the 1970s, Jimmy Harris was a member of the highly publicized STRESS unit, an undercover brigade that came under heavy scrutiny for its aggressive tactics. He was involved in the 1972 shooting of a Wayne County sheriff's deputy, but was later cleared of any wrongdoing when he proved to investigators that he had reason to believe the deputy was a criminal trying to attack him.

When the STRESS unit was disbanded as a result of too many on-the-job killings, Harris was reassigned to the DPD's Homicide and Major Crimes Division and cracked a series of high-profile murder cases that gained him a number of headlines and department accolades. Due to his close relationship with the mayor as his niece began getting into increasingly hot water with the men in her life, Coleman Young had Harris transferred into the Special Service Squad and put him personally in charge of looking after Cathy. The judge in the case didn't go lightly on Harris and slapped him with a 30-year prison sentence in 1993. Before leaving the Oval Office, President George W. Bush pardoned Harris in the fall of 2008, setting him free from custody more than 10 years ahead of schedule. Rick Wershe remains in prison and has not been given a maximum release date on his sentence.

◇◇◇◇◇◇◇◇◇◇◇◇

If Butch Jones was the quintessential Motor City drug kingpin of the early 1980s, Demetrius Holloway held that title for the latter half of the decade. Holloway was a businessman's gangster with a lethal reputation on the streets. He dressed like a corporate CEO, yet wasn't afraid to get his hands dirty when the situation called for it. Smart, magnetic, feared and respected, Holloway embodied every quality of the consummate crime lord. It was a powerful mix that took him to astronomic heights.

"It sounds clichéd, but in this case it couldn't be more true; if Demetrius had been brought up under different socioeconomic conditions, he could have been a business mogul or a CEO of a major corporation," said Steve Fishman, his attorney at the time of his death. "That obviously didn't happen and he became the Demetrius Holloway we all know today, but I know he had a lot of natural qualities that would have translated to the legitimate world. He was razor sharp and an entrepreneur in the most basic sense. People gravitated to him."

Starting out as a disciple of Frank Usher and his Murder Row gang back in the 1970s, Holloway took a bust for transporting stolen goods across state lines in 1980 and did five years in federal prison. Released in 1985, he hit the streets and began to cobble together his legacy. Using an inheritance from his grandfather and some money he had stashed away before being incarcerated, he purchased his first major cocaine shipment from Art Derrick and Doc Curry. Parlaying the money he made from his early drug sales, Holloway put together a successful legitimate business portfolio. Within two years, he was supplying over three quarters of the city's crack houses.

Quickly emerging as the city's top wholesaler, Holloway sold most of his drugs to the Chambers Brothers Gang, a drug empire headed by four siblings from Arkansas who operated over 100 crack houses throughout southeast Michigan. He became close with the gang's two leaders, B.J. and Larry, and they became his workhorses. B.J. ran all the street activities and Larry bought the Broadmore apartment complex on West Grand Boulevard and turned it into a vice emporium, a one-stop shop offering drugs, sex and gambling 24 hours a day, seven days a week. By maintaining ownership of a popular chain of athletic shoe stores called The Sports Jam and hulking quantities of real estate both locally and across the country, Holloway was able to wash his money just as fast as he was making it. Known as a heavy gambler, he frequently jaunted to Las Vegas and Atlantic City for card and dice binges that could either win or lose him hundreds of thousands of dollars at a time.

Born on the East Side of the city, Demetrius Holloway grew up in the same neighborhood and the same social circles as future world-champion prizefighter Tommy Hearns. Before he got into a life of crime, he tried to live on the straight and narrow, taking a job as a postman. But it was a half-hearted venture. Holloway was drawn to the streets like a moth to a flame. And he was a natural. Headquartering his operations in the Chalk and Cue, a pool hall he ran on West Seven Mile, Holloway recruited his childhood friend, Richard "Maserati Rick" Carter to be his right-hand man and immediately started a rapid ascension up the gangland ranks. Before long, he went from buying a dozen kilos at a time from Art Derrick and Doc Curry to consummating a wholesale deal with Colombians in the Bahamas, cutting out the middle men and smuggling the bricks through U.S. Customs himself.

"Demetrius was a true Don," Rob Boyd recalled. "Him and Maserati Rick were holding it down for real. Rick was more flamboyant, but Demetrius was calling all the major shots. They both used to hit the clubs all iced up and sporting full-length mink coats. We all knew from the day Demetrius got out of prison from doing his five-piece in '85, it was only a matter of time before he became The Man. That's just how he was. A couple of old G's hooked him up to start and he got his feet wet, learned the new game on the street, which was crack, and blew up quick."

While Holloway was dangerous but deliberate, those he surrounded himself with were simply dangerous. They were brash and ruthless with absolutely no method to their madness, and they would turn out to be his downfall. Quick to remove himself from the day-to-day street operations of his organization, Holloway outsourced much of his strong-arm work. Maserati Rick, although an able-bodied enforcer—he was a Golden Gloves boxing champ as a teenager—and Holloway's eyes and ears on the street, was only one man. He needed help and a crew of heavily strapped foot soldiers watching his back. That help would come in the form of the Brown brothers, four siblings, each a year a part in age, raised on the East Side, who headed a crew of like-minded goons called "The Best Friends." Terrance "Boogaloo" Brown, Reginald "Rocking Reggie" Brown, Gregory "Ghost" Brown, and Ezra "Wizard" Brown were hungry for a piece of the pie in the local underworld and made sure everyone knew it with their quick-trigger antics.

Scowling and brutish, they each cut imposing figures, all standing six-feet-two and weighing over 234 pounds. Ghost and Wizard, the two eldest brothers, had T-shirts, jackets, and hats made up with the words "Best Friends" embroidered across the front in big, bold letters. They were all known to drive the same cars—different-color BMWs or custom-made Suzuki Samurais—and kill anyone who dared get in the way on their climb to the top. Not to mention countless others. While its predecessors like YBI and Pony Down murdered in the name of profit and greed, the Best Friends did it for pure fun. Upon meeting the Browns and their crew at a downtown nightclub, Holloway tabbed them his official enforcement unit and began dispatching them to mete out justice on the street as he saw fit. They were burly and intimidating and took pleasure in hurting people.

"There was a no-tolerance policy with Demetrius," said Boyd. "If you crossed him once, you were done. Maserati, on the other hand, who was Demetrius' guy on the street, was more laid back and some people probably thought they could take advantage of it. That was why they brought in the Best Friends to use as muscle. They were straight thugs, coldhearted killers that hired themselves out for different enforcement jobs. Eventually things got out of hand with them, and Demetrius and Rick couldn't control their activities anymore."

The arrangement worked beautifully for a good year and a half. Holloway rode the Best Friends brawn all the way to the top. The Brown brothers made a name for themselves by simply being associated with the dapper-dressed crime lord. Not to mention the pure glee and heinous satisfaction they took in their job. Then things went south. And fast. Realizing they could only make so much money doing strong-arm work for Holloway, the Browns sought to branch off on their own. They wanted to move up the underworld ladder and expand their activities beyond the murder-for-hire gigs that originally made their name and into the drug-trafficking business. Specifically, they wanted Holloway to concede some of his territory to them as a good-faith gesture and allow them to earn on their own in addition to doing muscle work for him.

This idea didn't sit well with Holloway, and he told them he didn't approve. The Browns, whose position was enhanced by the fact that Maserati Rick had recently introduced them to one of Holloway's foreign suppliers, didn't care and left Holloway's organization anyway, seizing prime street-corner dealing territory by force within days of the split. Holloway restocked his enforcement wing and named Clifford Jones, an alleged assassin with a reputation for bloody chaos equal to that of the Best Friends, as his new sergeant-at-arms. He then hunkered down for what he knew would be a corpse-riddled conflict with his onetime lieutenants. It was war and it would get ugly.

"He didn't know it at the time, but the second Demetrius started doing business with the Best Friends, which in itself acknowledged their importance and validated them in a lot people's eyes, he created a monster," a former DEA agent commented. "They were sociopaths. For the Best Friends, killing was like eating, breathing and sleeping for the rest of us. It was just something they did every day and didn't even think about it twice. Demetrius really should have known better than to have gone into business with them. I'm sure he realized right off the bat that those guys would be impossible to reel in and he would have to cut bait. But once they got that little bit of rope, they ran with it, and then eventually tried to strangle Demetrius with it."

The Holloway faction struck first and delivered multiple blows directly to the fabric of the Brown family itself. Wizard Brown, 24, was shot and killed on December 20, 1986 as he and his younger brother Boogaloo sat in a car down the street from the city's 7th police precinct on Mack Avenue. The holiday season assault didn't stop there. Exactly one week later, Ghost Brown, 25, was killed after attending his brother's funeral in a drive-by shooting on Gratiot. Leaving an East

Side bar where he and his crew were toasting Wizard's memory, Ghost, the family's eldest sibling, was wearing the same white tuxedo he had worn to the lavish burial ceremony at the cemetery just hours earlier.

Staying out of harm's way for the time being, Holloway stood back and watched as the Best Friends went on a killing spree and expanded its business operations to out-of-state locations such as Indiana, Ohio, Illinois, and Kentucky. DEA records indicate that the gang was responsible for close to 100 murders over the next five years. An estimated dozen of the gangland homicides perpetrated by the Best Friends over this time period were tied to the feud festering between themselves and their former boss.

Things became increasingly complicated for Demetrius Holloway when further rifts in his camp started to develop in 1987. First, an offshoot faction of Holloway's organization, led by Edward "Big Ed" Hanserd, a former close friend, sprouted up right in the middle of Holloway's East Side stronghold and began cutting into his bottom line. Cultivating a new supply source from the West Coast, Hanserd started selling drugs to customers of Holloway and Rick Carter at a cheaper price. In addition, he's alleged to have accrued a debt of $100,000 from money owed to Carter that was related to two shipments of drugs given to him on consignment months earlier. When Carter approached Hanserd about the issue at one of Hanserd's East Side beauty parlors that summer, a monumental verbal altercation ensued and led to threats being hurled back and forth before Maserati Rick spat on the floor and stormed out. The bad blood increased when Hanserd, all of five-feet-six, began telling local press outlets that he was dubbed Big Ed by Maserati Rick's mother because of his well-endowed penis.

Over the next half-year, Hanserd, whose new drug connection was Los Angeles crime lord Richard "Freeway Ricky" Ross, would engage in a string of public shootouts with Carter, each marked with more vitriol than the last. Whenever the pair crossed paths, shots rang out no matter where they were. In one instance, Hanserd was shot by Maserati Rick outside a nightclub, survived the hit attempt and then, abiding by the code of the street, refused to identify Carter to the police as his attacker.

"Ed didn't want to pay Maserati Rick what he owed him, he didn't think he had to," said Rob Boyd, who was present at one of the shootouts. "Rick went to Ed and just wanted what was rightfully his. The next thing you know, they were both trying to kill each other. We all used to be friends growing up, but that's the kind of stuff that happened when the drugs and money came into play and started to change everyone's motivation."

The Hanserd situation coincided with a falling out involving White Boy Rick and his right-hand man, Stephen "Freaky Steve" Roussell, with the Brown brothers over Roussell's love affair with one of Rocking Reggie's girlfriends. Boogaloo and Rocking Reggie reached out to Holloway and Carter through an intermediary and requested help with taking out Roussell in exchange for an ending of their own beef. Considering White Boy Rick and Roussell important allies, Holloway steadfastly refused the request, and tensions between the two sides grew even deeper. Several violent incidents broke out between Freaky Steve and Rocking Reggie throughout the late spring and summer of 1987. Whenever the pair crossed paths, whether late at night in a club or in the middle of the street in broad daylight, heated words were exchanged, fists were thrown and guns were drawn. More often than not, shots would be fired. After police responded to one scuffle in early September, Brown was placed on probation. According to FBI documents and court testimony, Rocking Reggie got word on where Roussell was staying one day—a house in the 13600 block of Glenwood—and came storming through the front door with an automatic submachine gun in hand. Encountering Roussell and his cousin, Patrick "Little Pat" McCloud, asleep on the couch, he opened fire, killing Freaky Steve and severely wounding McCloud.

Rocking Reggie, a suspect in close to a dozen other homicides at the time, was eventually convicted of Roussell's murder, leaving Boogaloo, soon to be facing a murder indictment himself, the only Brown brother left on the street. In March 1989, former Best Friends associate James "Mr. Big" Lamont, a 30-year-old crime czar who was looking to carve out a piece of territory on Best Friends turf, was shot in the head and neck as he sat in the driver's seat of his purple Suzuki Sidekick, waiting at a light in front of the St. Regis Hotel on West Grand Boulevard. The killing was perpetrated drive-by style using automatic weapons, and Boogaloo Brown was charged with the crime, though eventually he skated and was acquitted at trial.

Maserati Rick Carter's vendetta with Big Ed Hanserd ended in the most dramatic of fashions in the fall of 1988. On Saturday, September 10th, Carter and Hanserd's top enforcer, Lodrick "Ricky the Hitman" Parker, got into a gunfight in front of a car wash owned by Carter on the corner of Mansfield and Seven Mile Road. Parker was shot in the shoulder, treated at Sinai Hospital and released that same day. Carter was wounded in the stomach and forced to undergo several hours of surgery at Mt. Carmel Hospital before stabilizing.

On Monday, September 12th, in a scene out of a Martin Scorsese film and a crime that goes down as possibly the single most brazen in Detroit history, Maserati Rick was killed as he slept in his hospital bed in Mt. Carmel's intensive care unit, shot in the head by a man wearing a doctor's lab coat. Lodrick Parker was charged with the headline-grabbing homicide, but gained an acquittal at trial in December, despite the fact that the prosecution presented an eyewitness to the murder who identified Parker as the shooter.

Going out in death in the same manner in which he lived, Maserati Rick Carter was sent off with flair and panache in a funeral ceremony and procession fit for a king. With thousands of mourners on hand, Carter was buried in a $25,000 custom-made Mercedes Benz coffin, equipped with silver-plated rims and gold exterior. Making most of the arrangements for the lavish burial was his brother Clyde, who himself would be killed in a gang-related drive-by shooting the following year in the midst of a turf war raging over control of the Holloway and Carter organization.

Almost the second Lodrick Parker was acquitted of Rick Carter's murder, he was back on the front pages and in trouble with the law again. Less than a month following his release from custody, Parker, who was a childhood friend of Hanserd's dating back to their days growing up in Mississippi, was arrested after the shooting of a drug-dealing rival near Gary, Indiana. Federal documents allege that throughout the 1980s, a number of Detroit-area narcotics syndicates had made inroads out of state, including Hanserd, who was said to have sent Parker down to Indiana to handle another Detroit-based dealer who was encroaching on his territory.

No less than three weeks later back in Michigan, Parker survived an assassination attempt at a house on Greenbriar, near the intersection of Coolidge and Eight Mile Road in Oak Park. Sometime around 3:00 a.m., assailants threw a tear gas canister through the front widow to draw Parker outside, at which point two gunmen fired several rounds at him from automatic weapons, wounding him in the hip and leg. Parker's trouble with the law continued through 1989 and into 1990. In January 1990, he was charged with the firebombing of Blessed Candles, a candle store on West Seven Mile Road, owned by a rival of the Hanserd organization named Thomas Tye. A few months earlier, three significant things happened: Parker was indicted on drug charges, Tye's sister was killed outside her apartment, and he and his wife were injured in a shooting at the store. Informants told police that the events were all related and stemmed from a dispute involving Tye, Parker and a former mentor of Ed Hanserd's named Waymon "World Benji" Kinkaid, who was behind bars on a murder conviction, but still wielding power.

On August 10, 1990, Tye's uncle, Charles Byrd, a co-owner of Blessed Candles, was killed in the same apartment complex where Tye's sister had been slain 11 months earlier. An eyewitness to the firebombing, Byrd was slated to testify against Parker, who awaited trial for the firebombing incident as well as the murder of Tye's sister and the shooting of Tye and his wife. Even without Byrd's testimony, Parker was convicted of the firebombing assault and the shooting attack on Tye and his wife in September 1989. The fact that he was acquitted of the murder of Tye's sister, Charmaine, meant little. He was going away for life.

The nightmare for Tye, unfortunately, didn't end with Lodrick Parker's imprisonment. Thomas Tye and his wife, Alice, were murdered in the parking lot of their Sutton Place apartment complex, an upscale residential community in Southfield on Nine Mile Road. Pulling out of their reserved parking spot on the morning of June 6, 1991, the couple was hit with a barrage of automatic weapon fire, their bodies found by apartment security personnel in their Chevy Corsica with the engine running and the lights on. Even behind bars, Parker was considered a suspect.

While his top enforcer was under siege by a team of elite law enforcement figures assigned to take him down, so was Big Ed Hanserd. Jailed on a pair of gun charges in 1988, Hanserd, who had to forfeit close to a million dollars because of various arrests that year, was released and given probation in early 1989. His time back on the street would be limited. Big Ed violated his parole in June and was taken into custody as he exited Northland Mall in Southfield and headed to his red BMW in the parking lot. Hit with additional weapons charges, Hanserd was sentenced to three to five years in prison, but a year into his sentence he was indicted as the mastermind of a $55 million-a-year drug conspiracy. Pleading guilty in order to prevent the mother of his son from going to jail, Big Ed received a sentence of 40 years. In the end, the government was able to do to Hanserd, a man who survived a total of nine gunshot wounds in his days as a drug baron, what his enemies could not—bring Big Ed down to size.

The conclusion to Demetrius Holloway's career on the street was not as neat and clean as Hanserd's, and considerably more painful. In the wake of the murder of his top lieutenant, Maserati Rick Carter, in September 1988, Holloway and his organization were under fire. Besides the constant police surveillance that he and his inner circle encountered on a daily basis, his gangland adversaries were starting to close in. A month after Carter's murder, Steve Washington, another of Holloway's lieutenants and a former close associate of Cliff Jones, was killed while sitting in his Mercedes Benz on an East Side street corner. Holloway himself was the victim of several unsuccessful drive-by shootings, and between Labor Day and Halloween 1988, more than a half-dozen of his drug houses were firebombed. Feeling the heat, he staged his own disappearance. On the evening of November 12th, witnesses saw gunfire erupt between Holloway and four men in ski masks at an East Side Top Hat hamburger stand on the corner of Gratiot and the Ford Freeway. After exchanging shots, the four men grabbed Holloway, threw him in the trunk of their car and sped away. It turned out to be a big ruse and he resurfaced before New Year's.

Eerily similar to his boyhood pal Rick Carter's demise, Demetrius Holloway was taken out in a brash and very public execution. Almost a year after his staged kidnapping, Holloway was killed while shopping at a popular downtown men's clothier, The Broadway, on October 8, 1990. At approximately 4:00 p.m., as Holloway was at the store's checkout counter, two men entered through the front door. With one man standing lookout, the other approached Holloway from behind, pulled out a gun and shot him in the back of the head. Satisfied with his work, the man snapped his fingers, uttered "Got 'em" and exited the door with his accomplice literally whistling a happy tune. Getting into a 1990 black BMW, which had been left idling at a nearby car park, they fled.

Nearly a decade later, Lester "Little Les" Milton and his younger brother Thomas "Toe-Tag Tommy" Milton, a pair of long-known criminals, were charged and convicted as the two assailants. Little Les was fingered as the triggerman, and Tommy the lookout man. Where the order actually came from has long been debated. Government records point to three main possibilities; the most commonly held belief is that the hit came from Holloway's longstanding rivals, the Best Friends. One former Best Friends member, in an interview with *F.E.D.S.* magazine, claims responsibility, alleging Boogaloo Brown ordered the hit in retaliation for the murders of his two older siblings, Ghost and Wizard. Others believe that the hit was orchestrated in tandem by Brown and Holloway's then second-in-charge, Cliff Jones. The theory is that they conspired to kill Holloway so they could split up his lucrative drug operations between themselves. Jones and his crew, an enforcement unit that authorities believe had carried out close to 75 contract hits, would only last another couple of years on the street themselves; they were brought down and jailed in February 1993. Another school of thought is that the contract was put out from behind bars by Benji Kincaid due to a personal beef with Holloway and had nothing to do with the Best Friends or any intra-gang turmoil between Holloway and Cliff Jones, who had taken Carter's place as his right-hand man in the final years of his life. No matter what the motive behind the Broadway hit, the fact was that Demetrius Holloway was dead and the Brown Brothers were on their way out.

The ultimate downfall of Boogaloo and Rocking Reggie Brown was worthy of being penned by a top Hollywood screenwriter. It was dramatic and bloody and didn't end well for either of the remaining founders of the Best Friends gang, arguably the most violent crime syndicate ever to walk the streets of Detroit. Things started to go bad with Reggie Brown's 1988 murder conviction. The defection of the gang's chief assassin, Nathaniel "Boone" Craft, a six-foot-five, 300-pound gangbanger with elite military training who would kill on command for the Brown brothers, came next and would prove crushing. Upset by the execution of his little brother when he was doing a short bit in prison in the late 1980s, the man they called "Boone" as in Daniel Boone, due to his crafty work with a knife, went to work for the feds. A spitting image of Academy Award nominee Michael Clarke Duncan, Craft admitted to murdering 30 people on contract from the Best Friends, while also sometimes working as a bodyguard for Maserati Rick Carter. In 2010, Craft was named Most Notorious Gangster in America by the History Channel's hit show, *Gangland*. His decision to turn his back on the Brown brothers, who had recruited him to join their ranks after watching him demolish opponents in a strongman contest held at Cobo Hall in 1985, sent the Best Friends reeling. When Boogaloo and Rocking Reggie found out about Craft's cooperation with the authorities, they scrambled. Boogaloo split town. Rocking Reggie had his murder conviction in the Steve Roussell case overturned and in 1992, he was released on bond pending his retrial. Paranoid because of Craft's defection and rumors of other informers within his organization, Reggie joined his baby brother on the run. But not before he took care of a little business.

On May 12, 1992, Reggie Brown approached a lieutenant of his named Alfred Austin on his porch at a residence located on the corner of Buckingham and Mack. He was surrounded by a group of onlookers—innocent bystanders who had no idea of the danger they were in. A bloodthirsty Rocking Reggie opened fire on the group with an Uzi. Four people, including Austin and a three-year-old girl, were killed in the attack. Austin, who had recently been arrested in Kentucky and was facing federal gun charges, had been offered an immunity deal by the FBI, information the government alleged came through a tip-off by one of the gang's attorneys. Meeting up with Boogaloo in New York City, Rocking Reggie and his brother hid out on the East Coast for the next year. Being protected by some of their powerful underworld associates in Harlem, Brooklyn, and the Bronx, the Browns avoided detection until June 1993 when Boogaloo, Rocking Reggie, and the rest of the Best Friends organization were hit with a 56-count federal drug and racketeering indictment. The feds traced the Brown brothers' location to Manhattan and on the afternoon of June 17th, they pounced, surrounding the pair outside a BMW dealership where they had gone to pick up a car they had purchased the previous day.

Rocking Reggie was taken into custody, but Boogaloo got away, jumping on a nearby motorcycle and outrunning police in a high-speed chase that made its way through three different boroughs. Heading south, Boogaloo Brown went to Georgia and stayed low for a couple of months until his lifestyle finally caught up with him. In a grisly scene, Brown's body was found in the back of a stolen pickup truck parked at a Ramada Inn in an Atlanta suburb on August 9th. It was wrapped in a Ralph Lauren Polo bedsheet, faceted by silver masking tape and shot in the back of the head. The most commonly held theory is that Brown was killed by a member of his inner circle in a power struggle that developed in the aftermath of the bust.

Despite the best efforts of Boogaloo and Rocking Reggie, when the dust settled and the case eventually got to trial in 1995, there were a lot more gang members than just Boone Craft that ultimately jumped ship. Besides Boone, the government gained the cooperation of other top Best Friends hit men—Stacey "The Machine" Culbert and Charles "Chuckie Do" Wilkes, little brother of co-defendant William "Bumpy" Wilkes—and with their testimony brought the syndicate to its knees. All 29 gang members indicted either pled guilty or were convicted of the charges, effectively bringing an end to the Best Friends and their sinister reign as well as the entire crack era in the Motor City which they so well embodied.

"That whole time will be remembered as a very dark period in the city's history," Robert De Fauw commented. "We as law enforcement did the best we could do considering the circumstances, and we stopped a lot of drugs from being sold and a lot of people from dying and being killed. But catastrophic damage was still done. Lives were ruined and families were torn apart. And I would suspect that much of the ripple effect is still being felt by people till this very day."

This viewpoint on the era isn't reserved just for former feds like De Fauw. Some onetime drug bosses like Rob Boyd feel the same way: "The stuff that happened back then is nothing to glamorize. There were some real bad decisions made by a lot of people, myself obviously included. At the end of the day it just isn't worth it. It's hard to get that perspective when you're young and ambitious and think you want to become a street king. You don't know any better. You just see the money and the power. But what's the point of making $20 million if you ain't gonna be able to spend it, or getting a bunch of juice and respect on the streets if you ain't gonna be on the streets for more than a second or two. The reality is no matter how much money you make or power you achieve, you're always gonna wind up in one of two ways: you're gonna end up in a cell or a box. That's the bottom line and it won't ever change no matter what year in history we're in."

NOT-SO-EASY RIDING IN THE MOTOR CITY

Five on the Floor

John Wolfenbarger got paroled from prison in mid-2002 after serving eight years on an armed robbery conviction. Far from rehabilitated, he had no intention of going straight. In fact, it wasn't long before Wolfenbarger, at the time 31 and an associate of some of Detroit's most ruthless biker gangs, was calling up Dennis Lincoln, his old cellmate from Boyer Correctional Facility in Carson City, Michigan, and telling him about some jobs he was planning on pulling off around the holiday season. Lincoln, then 27 and residing in Flint, was known as a safe-cracking specialist and Wolfenbarger requested his services down in metro Detroit.

In the weeks leading up to Christmas 2002, Lincoln and Wolfenbarger, some-times referred to by the nickname "Solo," scouted numerous locations, mostly jewelry stores in Wayne County, before deciding to focus on spots in the city of Livonia. They made their way to the Livonia Mall at the corner of Middlebelt and Seven Mile Road and followed one jewelry store owner out of the mall parking lot with the intent of robbing him at his home, but lost their intended victim in the late-afternoon rush-hour traffic. Later that same week, Wolfenbarger and Lincoln returned to the intersection and found a nearby strip mall to stake out. Within minutes, they locked their eyes on Marco Pesce, a successful 38-year-old business-man who just happened to be in the wrong place at the wrong time. Pesce owned Italia Jewelers, located in a strip mall down the street from the mall where the two sat parked, casing potential victims. Waiting for him to close up shop for the day, Wolfenbarger and Lincoln followed Pesce to the 37500 block of St. Martins Street—still in the city of Livonia—to see where he lived. Wolfenbarger phoned Lincoln the next morning, December 21st, and told him that he wanted to "do the Italia Jewelry thing." At that point there was no turning back, and fate would wind up being extremely unkind to some very innocent people.

The plan was for the pair to force their way into the Pesce home posing as deliverymen and then make one of the residents call Marco home, where he could give them access to his personal safe. They borrowed a truck and on their way to the Pesce residence, Wolfenbarger and Lincoln stopped at a local Hallmark store to purchase a teddy bear, which they planned to use as a purported Christmas gift, and at Kmart to buy clipboards, fake uniforms and ski masks. When they arrived at the home, Pesce's mother, Maria Vergati, visiting her son and his family from Italy, was cleaning up around the garage, which had an open door facing the street. Approaching Vergati in disguise, Wolfenbarger and Lincoln fooled the elderly woman, who spoke and understood little English. They coaxed her into the house through the door in the garage. The moment they set foot inside the residence, Wolfenbarger pulled a gun and Vergati became confused and disoriented. Taking her into the living room, Wolfenbarger ordered Lincoln to the strip mall where Marco's jewelry store was located to monitor activities there.

With Wolfenbarger holding Vergati hostage in the living room, Marco dropped off his three children—Carlo, 12; Sabrina, 9; and Melissa, 6—in his driveway, following an afternoon with their mother in Ann Arbor, and then drove back to his store. Once the children were inside the house, Wolfenbarger contacted Lincoln and told him, "Dad just dropped off the kids." When Marco returned to the jewelry store, Wolfenbarger had his son Carlo phone the store and tell his dad that he was needed back at the house because his sister Melissa had fallen and chipped her tooth. Just like when they conned their way into the house by fooling Vergati, the story about Melissa was a ruse. And just like with Vergati, Marco was hoodwinked and returned to his residence, having no clue of the coldhearted treachery in store for him and his entire family in the coming minutes. After trailing Marco back to the house, Lincoln sat in his car on the side of the street, waiting for Wolfenbarger to come out with further instructions. Those instructions never came. Instead, Wolfenbarger exited the house, jumped in the car with stolen cash and jewelry in tow, and remarked bluntly, "Five dead."

The pair split up in the hours after the homicides. Before he left for Flint, Lincoln was given $3,200 in cash by Wolfenbarger—half of the money taken from the Pesce home. The next day, authorities doing a check of the St. Martins residence at the request of Diane Pesce, Marco's ex-wife, found Marco, his mother and his three children all dead, dispatched execution-style. Vergati was killed in the living room, while Marco, Sabrina, Melissa, and Carlo were found in a circle in the basement, each shot to death. It was a brutal scene. A local law enforcement official called it "one of the most heinous and vicious crimes in the history of the Metro Detroit area." Fortunately for the victims' families, it wouldn't be long until the murderers were brought to justice and made to account for their horrific crimes. Help in solving the quintuple homicide would come from the most unlikely of sources—Wolfenbarger's uncle, a hardened criminal and local biker boss with a fearsome reputation.

◇◇◇◇◇◇◇◇◇◇◇◇

In the early morning hours of December 22nd, William "Billy Wadd" Smith, was awakened by a loud knock at the front door of his Dearborn residence. One of the city's top outlaw biker leaders, Smith was accustomed to dealing with sudden catastrophe at all hours of the day, yet he was still taken aback at what he saw when he came downstairs in his bathrobe to greet his nephew. Standing there in a blood-spattered shirt, toting a duffle bag full of cash and jewelry, and asking to borrow a change of clothing was John Wolfenbarger. He had a mischievous grin on his face and was beaming with pride. Before Smith could get a word out, Wolfenbager admitted that he had just killed five people. Trying to convince his uncle that he wasn't joking, he remarked, "When they find out what I did, it's going to be on CNN."

The next afternoon at Smith's bar, the Copa Lounge, a popular biker hangout located near the corner of Schoolcraft and Outer Drive, Wolfenbarger asked Smith to help him fence some of the stolen jewelry he had taken from the Pesce home. "I wanna get rid of it real cheap," he allegedly told his uncle. Around this same time, Wolfenbarger asked a number of people in the bar and elsewhere to help him melt down a portion of the gold he had stolen. He definitely wasn't shy about bragging to anyone who would listen about his recent big score. Over a period of four days, Wolfenbarger allegedly told close to a dozen people either all or portions of the story surrounding the Pesce family robbery-homicide. It was only a matter of time before somebody went to the cops. Surprisingly, that person was the one man Wolfenbarger trusted and looked up to the most.

Following his nephew's disturbing revelation, "Billy Wadd," nicknamed for his ability to generate large amounts of cash for his gang, experienced an epiphany, a spiritual breakthrough of sorts. He called a friend of his who was a cop in the Dearborn Police Department and told him he had information on the Pesce murders. Eventually, Smith would not only agree to testify against his nephew in court, but would aid the government in launching multiple investigations into several of the area's most notorious biker gangs. Like relatives of the Pesce family, Billy Smith's life would never be the same after the grisly events that took place on December 22, 2002. Unlike the Pesce relatives, Smith's monumental life alteration was by choice.

◇◇◇◇◇◇◇◇◇◇◇◇

William Smith was born and raised in Detroit, in the area around Seven Mile Road and Brightmoore. As a teenager, his family moved out of the city and into the Downriver suburb of Taylor. Even though he enrolled in Taylor Center High School and eventually became a football star, Smith continued to spend time in his childhood neighborhood, running with a primarily black street gang known as "The Seven Mile Dawgs" and selling drugs. It was at that time he was tagged with the street handle of Billy Wadd, since the black gangbangers he was running with had never seen a white kid able to make so much money by selling drugs. During his senior year at Taylor Center, around the same time college recruiters were thinking about extending him a scholarship offer, he blew out his knee in an early-season home game. Suddenly his dreams of playing football at the next level were destroyed and without much forethought, he turned to the streets to start making his living as an adult.

A few months out of high school, Smith got into riding motorcycles and joined the Detroit Drifters, a local "family-style" club that went on weekend trips throughout the Midwest. After spending some time with the Drifters, making a name for himself as someone who knew how to make a lot of money in a variety of endeavors, not all of them legal, Smith left and declared himself a free agent. Because of his reputation, he quickly started getting offers to join some of the most fearsome motorcycle gangs in the city. It was like he was a college athletic recruit again with each club trying to entice him to join their ranks. While attending a party at the Mt. Elliott headquarters of the "Devil's Diciples," a nationwide outlaw biker gang, the club's president, Jeff "Fat Dog" Smith, was so impressed with Billy Wadd, and the potential leadership and earning potential he could bring to the gang, that he offered him full membership without having to go through any probationary or initiation period.

"We were all partying at the clubhouse and Fat Dog took me back into a separate room away from everyone else, removed the "DD" patch off his own jacket and gave it to me," Billy recalled. "I was respected enough that I automatically became a full-patch member."

The Diciples, who intentionally misspell their name, started in California in 1967, but by the 1980s, the gang had relocated its national headquarters to the Detroit area. Their most famous alumnus is popular television reality star Duane "Dog" Chapman, who left his life as a biker to become a bounty hunter. Significantly smaller in size than some of the area's better-known and higher-profile gangs, it's alleged that the Diciples make up for their lack of roster length by sheer fearlessness and smart business practices. Within less than a year of joining the Diciples, Billy was named boss of the club's entire West Side operations. It wasn't long, however, until the glamour of running with an outlaw biker gang lost its luster. Billy was quick to realize that the much-preached allure of biker life—brotherhood—was really nothing but a myth.

"People who are enamored with the life and want to join a gang have no clue what the whole thing is really about which is putting money in certain people's pockets, nothing else," he said. "If you think brotherhood has anything to do with the life, you couldn't be more wrong. Any and all brotherhood in that life comes with a price tag. There's no loyalty and you're only valuable for what you can do for the person in front of you."

◇◇◇◇◇◇◇◇◇◇◇◇

The city of Detroit has a rich and storied tradition of renegade biker gangs. Nationally feared clubs like "The Outlaws," "The Highwaymen," "The Devil's Diciples," and "The Avengers" have each called the Motor City home, thus making the area in and around southeast Michigan a simmering hub of Midwest biker culture.

"They're certainly a different breed of criminal," said former FBI agent Bill Randall. "These are the type of people that live on the fringes of society and hold grave contempt for anyone but themselves. Even within the criminal sect, they're viewed as kind of out there doing their own thing, renegades in the truest sense I suppose you could say."

Newspaper accounts as far back as 1913 document recreational motorcycle activity in Metro Detroit. The criminal element in the local and national landscape didn't really start to appear on a large scale until the late 1960s and '70s. According to some sociologists, this may have been affected by the return of tens of thousands of disillusioned Vietnam War veterans. It was a time when biker gangs around the country were morphing into fully functional crime conglomerates. The Illinois-based Outlaws hosted the nation's first post-World War II road rally, an event that would go on to become the cornerstone of any U.S. biker club's social calendar, at Soldier's Field in 1946.

The Detroit area became home to a number of gangs with ruthless reputations spearheaded by men who were one-of-a-kind leaders prone to streaks of unparalleled criminal innovation. Ward "The Anvil" Wright, president of the Michigan chapter of the Avengers, based in Pontiac, was arrested for stealing a half-dozen U.S. Forestry Service planes and using them to ferry drugs between Detroit and Medillen, Colombia. Wright fled town after committing a murder in Ohio, but was eventually caught and shipped off to prison in 1997. Thomas "Big Foot Tommy" Khalil then became not just boss of the gang in Detroit, but the club's national president. During his reign, he oversaw a brutal street war between the Avengers (made up of chapters in Michigan, Ohio, Indiana, Illinois, and West Virginia) and two rival gangs, the Iron Coffins and the Forbidden Wheels.

According to court documents, Khalil instructed the Avengers to go out and kill as many members of the Iron Coffins as possible and then take the patch off their "cuts"—sleeveless denim or leather jackets on which a gang's colors and emblems are displayed. In a November 1998 tongue lashing that he gave his lieutenants, which the government happened to get on tape due to a hidden recording device, Big Foot Tommy was heard saying, "I'm surprised that somebody hasn't gotten their first fucking Coffins patch. I guess I'll have to go out there and get one myself."

Paul "Rocky" Dye, president of the Detroit chapter of the Forbidden Wheels, was convicted in 1983 of the murder of Glenda Collins and Donna Bartels, two associates of the gang, and sentenced to life in prison. As recently as 2007, tensions between the Forbidden Wheels and the Avengers reached a fevered pitch and boiled over into a violent public fracas in the parking lot of the Red Dog Saloon in downtown Milford.

While Khalil and Wright's Avengers, Dye's Forbidden Wheels and Billy Wadd's Devil's Diciples could more than hold their own in the Motor City biker world, the Outlaws and the Highwaymen are without a doubt the two most prominent gangs in metropolitan Detroit and they share a bitter rivalry. The Highwaymen, founded in Detroit in 1954 by the city's original biker Godfather, Elburn "Big Max" Barnes, is to this day is the state's biggest motorcycle club. They view the Outlaws as interlopers, encroaching on their rightful home territory. Formed in Chicago in 1935, the Outlaws made their major inroads into the Motor City in the 1970s and '80s as a result of the rise to power of Harry "Taco" Bowman, a menacing, Michigan-raised hellion who developed a cult-like following and a legacy that grew larger than any American biker boss of the last 30 years.

These two clubs rule the biker world in Detroit with brute force and find themselves at constant odds over turf, respect and a cornucopia of rackets. Both clubs are deadly and engage in every seedy and illegal business venture imaginable. The Outlaws also have long been at war with the West Coast-based Hells Angels, a situation that has led both the Highwaymen and the Devils Diciples to make alliances with the Angels in local affairs—relationships bound by their mutual hatred for the Outlaws and a desire to undermine the club's every move. According to club lore, the animosity between the Outlaws and the Hells Angels, the country's two most high-profile outlaw biker clubs, started in the late 1940s when the Hells Angels rejected a request from the Outlaws for permission to set up a charter in California.

The first time the Outlaws club really made a name for itself in the Detroit press was in 1967 when John Wadles and Don Graves, two Detroit-area Outlaws, were arrested in Florida for nailing a young woman to a tree for stealing money from an Outlaw clubhouse in Palm Beach. It wasn't more than a decade later that the Highwaymen burst onto the local media scene in the same violent manner when the homegrown club had several of its members arrested and convicted for bombing, robbing, and ransacking a number of homes and businesses owned by Outlaws. Jason Gray, president of the Detroit chapter of the Highwaymen in the 1980s, actually attacked the agent in charge of the DEA investigation into the club's activities with gunfire as he drove to work. Although the attack did not result in serious injury to the agent, the brazen assault on authority did wonders for the gang's reputation.

Biker power officially shifted in the Outlaws' direction in 1984 when the club's international president, Harold "Stairway Harry" Henderson, a beloved and dynamic head of state who was the first club president to expand chartership outside of U.S. boundaries, was forced to step down due to legal issues and his vice president and protégé, Harry "Taco" Bowman, was named his successor. Bowman, who got his nickname because of his dark complexion and Latino looks, followed in Stairway Harry's footsteps and built up a strong and loyal support network made up of juiced-in advocates and menacing enforcers and assassins. An underworld rarity, he was both loved and feared. Behind his hypnotic leadership ability, the Outlaws swelled to record numbers with a national roster of more than 1500 full-patch members and over 200 total chapters worldwide.

The chameleon-like Bowman has been called by the authorities the first "businessman biker boss," a trendsetter in guiding the Outlaws into more diverse rackets and more sophisticated business ventures than just owning bars, strip clubs, and tattoo parlors. He expanded his power base by forging sturdy ties with other crime syndicates, including the Mafia, and with upstanding members of legitimate society, including wealthy philanthropists, politicians, and policemen. His zen-like leadership style would sometimes send his underlings into states of mass hysteria, chanting, and reacting emotionally to his every gesture and command. Fascinated by Adolf Hitler, he would wear a full-length black cape embroidered with a swastika when he presided at chapter meetings or held court in his well-stocked clubhouse library.

Known to dress and act according to the company he was trying to impress, Bowman was just as likely to be seen in his club colors, carousing with the boys in a seedy bar as he was to be clean-shaven, neatly coiffed and decked out in a $5,000 suit, looking like he was ready to attend a board of directors meeting. Upon becoming president, he bought a house in the upscale suburban neighborhood of Grosse Pointe Farms and enrolled his children in a leafy private school nearby. He could be often seen around town, being driven to appointments in a custom-made, bullet-proof Cadillac, always accompanied by one or two bodyguards. Unlike most of his breed, Bowman did not have long hair, a beard, or a body covered with tattoos. Your typical biker he wasn't.

"Taco was interesting because he kind of went against the grain and kept one foot in the straight world and the other in the biker world, while most of those guys want to stay as far away from the two-car garage and picket fence thing as possible," ex-FBI agent Bill Randall commented. "I mean Taco used to drive his kids to school and was active in neighborhood type stuff. He might have wanted to blend in more than usual, but he was a pretty ruthless individual who definitely raised a lot of hell in his time."

Immediately stamping his personal imprint on the organization, Bowman moved the club's international headquarters from Chicago to his own hometown of Detroit. Then he is alleged to have ordered the execution of a Chicago-based Outlaw member in the days following the move as a means of sending a message that his regime would be a hellish and bloody one. And it was.

Using a fortified clubhouse on Warren Avenue, a mile east of the Southfield Freeway, as his command center, Bowman made a big splash right off the bat, conquering the hearts and minds of his minions with his garish and gung-ho leadership style. In his next major decision, he tapped Wayne "Joe Black" Hicks, a Toledo-based Outlaw and a man with a vicious reputation as a psychopathic killer, to be president of the club's integral Ft. Lauderdale chapter. Having a stronghold in Florida is imperative for any biker club's success on a nationwide level, since the state acts as a hub for biker culture in the South and for much of the East Coast as well. Hicks, a gruffer, more physically imposing version of Bowman, became his most trusted lieutenant and quickly gained a reputation as the overlord of biker activity in Florida. With the aid of the state's regional president, William "Wild Bill" Pilgrim, and his own personal bodyguard and top lieutenant, Stephen "DK" Lemunyon, Hicks ruled the Sunshine State with a heavy hand. The rest of the decade was relatively tame compared to what was on the horizon for the future. Taco Bowman's diabolical reign hit its stride in the 1990s, when the strapping and handsome biker boss upped the ante in his battle with enemies both foreign and domestic. Taco was on the warpath and his bloodlust had few limits.

During the early part of 1991, Bowman ordered the murder of Raymond "Bear" Chaffin, a former Outlaw member in Florida who had left the gang and affiliated with The Warlocks, a rival biker club backed by the Hells Angels. He gave the contract to Hicks, who in turn had club enforcers Houston "Tex" Murphy and Alex "Dirt" Ankerich shoot Chafin to death on February 21. A little over a year later in March 1992, Bowman oversaw and directed the beating of an Outlaw probational member, Irwin "Hitler" Nissen, at Biker Week in Daytona Beach—an event that serves as one giant annual weeklong extravaganza for the entire American biker nation. Nissen was being punished for getting into a physical altercation with Atlanta Outlaw chapter president James "Moose" McClean the previous afternoon at a wet T-shirt contest held at an Outlaw-owned bar. Brought to Bowman's hotel room, Nissen was beaten, threatened with a knife, and then thrown over the balcony by Bowman and fellow Outlaw members Tex Murphy, Dennis "Dog" Hall, and Christopher "Slasher" Maiele.

Around this time, Bowman's relationship with the local Mafia began to go sour. The longstanding bond that Bowman himself had constructed between the Outlaws and the mob was coming apart at the seams due to his own greed. Not satisfied with the percentage of the gambling operations he shared with the Italians, Bowman ordered his men to muscle in on several traditionally Mafia-backed floating dice games. The games belonged to Jack "Jackie the Kid" Giacalone, a fast-rising soldier in the local mob and someone who had been viewed from an early age as a future leader of the crime family. Deeply disturbed by the biker boss' move on its territory, Anthony "Tony Jack" Giacalone, the Detroit Mafia's longtime street boss and Jackie's uncle, sent Frank "Frankie the Bomb" Bommarito, the veteran liaison between the two crime factions, to tell Taco to back off. Bommarito's message didn't properly resonate with Bowman, and the Outlaws continued to infringe on the Italians' gambling interests. At that point, Tony Giacalone allegedly issued a murder contract on Taco Bowman and gave it to Nove Tocco and Paul "Big Paulie" Corrado, a pair of thuggish street soldiers who were in the process of making a name for themselves by shaking down every two-bit criminal in sight. Tocco and Corrado, who were discussing sensitive mob business while driving around in a bugged car, spent several months trying to carry out the contract to no avail. Informed by the FBI of the Mafia's intention of killing him, the sly-mannered Bowman was too elusive for Tocco and Corrado to take down.

In the midst of trying to plan another attack on their target, Tocco and Corrado started to question the merit of their assigned duty. They felt it was possible that Jackie Giacalone was using them as pawns to settle his own personal vendetta against Bowman. It was all caught on tape by the FBI.

Nove Tocco: "Something's going on here that's not right. I don't know exactly what it is right now, but things ain't sitting right with me. Uncle Tony warned me yesterday about Taco."

Big Paulie Corrado: "What did he say?"

Tocco: "He says something's not right. He says this story's not right. Something is wrong with the whole thing."

Corrado: "In what way?"

Tocco: "He says he don't know whether it's Jackie for sure, but something's not right about this fucking story. He thinks Jackie might be playing us into Taco for his own reasons."

Joe Tocco (Nove's brother): "'Cause Jackie feels Taco is a threat to Jackie."

Corrado: "Right. Fucking exactly."

Nove Tocco: "Yesterday when I went to pick up some vinegar from my father [Mafia soldier Paul Tocco], he says, 'I'm glad you're here; I want to talk to you alone.' Now he starts telling me that this whole thing feels wrong to him, too. He wants to corner Tony Giacalone and make him get to the bottom of it. From what he can tell, they backed off because they wanna know how much

Jackie knows about all this. He says Jackie gave up a craps game and Taco and his boys took it. I said I thought it was two separate games. He says, 'How the fuck does Jackie let Taco take his game?' And then he says, 'From what I hear, Tony Jack is pissed about it. He tells me he thinks fucking Jackie is pushing you and me at Taco. This came out of his mouth, okay?"

Corrado: "Yeah."

Joe Tocco: "I told you I believed that from the start."

The contract on Taco Bowman's life was eventually lifted when a sit-down was brokered and the two parties settled their differences. According to law enforcement reports, Bowman agreed to stop squeezing the mob's dice games and the Italians gave up a slightly bigger piece of some joint narcotic and juice-loan rackets being run out of a series of biker bars in the Detroit area.

Continuing his ruthless ways, in the late spring of 1993, Bowman ordered the kidnapping, beating and torturing of Florida Outlaw member Kevin "Turbo" Talley, who had signed a document with Canadian officials in Ontario, admitting that the Outlaws were a criminal enterprise. The betrayal led Bowman to make an example out of him for everybody in the club, and Talley was ordered to report to Detroit immediately upon his release from custody in Toronto. He was picked up at Metro Airport by two Bowman lieutenants and taken to an isolated room in the Outlaw's Detroit clubhouse, where he was detained for five days as well as beaten, humiliated, and sodomized. After being set free, Bowman and Hicks personally took Talley to the airport and told him bluntly that he was lucky they hadn't killed him for his gross indiscretion, and that he was being stripped of his colors and banished forever from Outlaw property.

A decade into his reign of terror, Taco Bowman was as secure as ever in his post. He inspired a devout loyalty with his charm and aggressive antics and had a genuine affection for his troops. As a result, law enforcement had an incredibly difficult time finding a way to crack the shell of his operations and obtain informants from anywhere near his inner circle. Being at the peak of his power after a decade in control, Bowman had the ability to take the club in any direction he desired. Perfectly in sync with his brash persona, he chose to raise the stakes. On New Years' Eve, 1993, Bowman held a meeting of top Outlaw brass in a Florida hotel suite and declared his intent to escalate the club's war against the ever-hated Hells Angels. The decision was overwhelmingly well received and became an immediate priority.

On a visit to Chicago in early 1994, Bowman ordered Chicago Outlaws president Peter "Greased Lighting Pete" Rogers to begin plotting an attack on the Hells Henchmen, a Hells Angels-backed biker gang based in Illinois. Rogers was upset with the untimely nature of this request, so in September, Bowman met with Indiana Outlaw member Randall "Mad Dog Randy" Yager and Chicago Outlaw member Carl "Jamming Jay" Warneke at his suburban Detroit residence, instructing them to bomb the Hells Henchmen's clubhouse as soon as possible. By the conclusion of November, following two attacks on the clubhouse, the property was burned to the ground and condemned by the city. Before the year was out, Bowman ordered fire-bombing attacks against two Hells Angels clubhouses in Ohio and two clubhouses belonging to the Warlocks in Florida.

Not a man of even temper, the smallest slight or sign of disrespect sent Bowman into a fury. During October 1994, he became enraged when he saw a newspaper photograph taken at the funeral of Hells Angels member Michael "Mad Mike" Quale, killed in a gun battle with Outlaw member Walter "Buffalo Wally" Posjinak, who was also slain in the altercation. In the photo, Bowman saw a member of the Fifth Chapter motorcycle gang, an affiliate of the Outlaws, hugging a mourning Hells Angels member. An extremely close friend of Posjinak, Bowman was incensed at the act of compassion that he interpreted as outright treason. In the days following the funeral, Bowman ordered the entire Fifth Chapter club, a group of bikers based in Southeast Florida, to the Outlaws clubhouse in Tampa, at which time he led a mass beating of the gang's members with chains and bats. Literally throwing the nearly two dozen Fifth Chapter members out on the street outside the clubhouse, Bowman informed them that he was disbanding their club and they could never associate with any Outlaws again.

Before the end of the year, Bowman ordered the murder of a Chicago-based Outlaw named Donald Fogg, a suspected informant that Wayne Hicks wound up killing on behalf of his boss and the gang. Bowman held another New Year's Eve meeting, this one in Detroit, where he declared his intention to "take the war to them out west" and start attacking the Hells Angels on their own turf in California. Early in 1995, he sent a group of lieutenants, headed by Hicks, out to Los Angeles to begin making arrangements for the assassination of Hells Angels leader and founder Ralph "Sonny" Barger.

While in the midst of scheming to kill Barger, Bowmen's men blew up a number of Hells Angels-backed businesses in Southern California and began planning more attacks to take place in the coming year, including the murder of George Christy, one of Barger's closest underlings. But before the attempt on Barger's or Christy's life could be carried out, Taco Bowman's empire began to crack at its very foundation. His self-anointed "sergeant-at-arms," Wayne Hicks, turned government informant and with his aid, in early 1997, the government levied a voluminous, multi-tiered racketeering indictment against Bowman and several of his lackeys. Knowing full well that he wouldn't be granted bail and having no desire to wait behind bars for his trial to start, Taco split town and disappeared off the authorities' radar. Said to have been hidden by his fellow Outlaws across the country and aided by his contacts in the mob on the home front in Michigan, the charismatic crime boss avoided the government's effort to track him down and arrest him for 28 months, reaching number two on the FBI's most-wanted list.

Time finally ran out for Bowman in the summer of 1999, when he got caught trying to sneak back into town to visit his family. Acting on an informant's tip, on June 7th, the FBI converged on a house in Sterling Heights, on Griggs Drive near the intersection of Fifteen Mile Road and Ryan, and apprehended the high-profile fugitive without incident. Sporting a long beard and a tan, Bowman was found socializing with numerous fellow members of the Detroit Outlaw hierarchy.

Convicted in 2001 of all charges, Bowman was sentenced to life imprisonment and replaced as the club's international president by James "Big Frank" Wheeler, an Indianapolis Outlaw who moved the gang's headquarters to Tampa, Florida. Wheeler, a more traditional biker type with long hair and beard and covered with tattoos, was a considerably less successful leader than Bowman, a former confidant of his, and was jailed and convicted of similar charges in 2006. The Outlaw nation is now rumored to be headed by Wisconsin-based biker boss John "Milwaukee Jack" Roziga. Locally, the power vacuum left within the Outlaws leadership by Taco Bowman's incarceration was allegedly filled by Leroy "Black Region Roy" Frasier, a former chapter president from Bay City.

◇◇◇◇◇◇◇◇◇◇◇◇

The feds might not have known it at first, but Billy Wadd's defection to Team America would serve as a jumping-off point for three major investigations, indictments and convictions. While building criminal cases, especially high-profile cases involving organized crime, access is everything. Billy Wadd might not have been the biggest biker boss in town. He might not even have made the Top 10. Not to mention that his gang's local power base paled in comparison to that of the Outlaws or Highwaymen. However, he had the ultimate access to both.

Opening the Copa Lounge in the mid-1990s, Billy Wadd's new business venture quickly became a trendy spot for many of the area's biker elite to socialize. Members of all of the city's major motorcycle clubs were known to party and hang out there, and it became known across the city as a sort of de facto "no man's land" or violence-free zone, a location where rival factions could appear at the same time and not have mayhem break loose. As a result, the Copa also gained a reputation as one of the best locations for "sit-downs," a type of formal underworld meeting held to resolve gangland disputes.

Just because the area bikers viewed the bar as a temporary reprieve from the heated chaos of the streets didn't mean they wouldn't use their time there to plan, brag or discuss any and every criminal scheme under the sun. And there to hear and see it all transpire was the Copa's owner, Billy Wadd Smith. It was a perfect situation for the government to exploit to its advantage in its war on organized crime and the criminal biker element in Detroit. The feds would never have had a chance to get Billy even to think of cooperating with them if it wasn't for his nephew, John Wolfenbarger, and his cold-blooded behavior. Wolfenbarger's senseless mass execution of the Pesche family set in motion a series of events that spurred Billy to turn his back on his brothers in the local outlaw biker hierarchy. Always a troublemaker, even before being locked up for close to a decade when he was just 18, Wolfenbarger got out of prison in early 2002 and had nowhere else to turn for a job but to his uncle. Using his friendship with a fellow powerful biker, Billy got Wolfenbarger employment at a Downriver collection agency. It didn't take long for the habitual felon to lose interest in living his life on the straight and narrow.

"He came out of prison talking that 'I want to clean up my life' business, but come on, who are you kidding, game recognize game," Smith reflects back almost a decade later. "The kid had been stealing since the time he was five, 10 years old. He's been locked up since before he was 21 and become totally institutionalized. Life on the outside is hard for a convict. He didn't want to put in a day's work, he couldn't cope, so he went back to doing what he knew how to do, breaking into people's houses and stealing. It never surprised me that he went back and turned crooked again. But I never saw him going off and starting to murder old ladies and kids."

After returning to his house and heading to bed with his wife after his club's annual Christmas party, there came a frantic knock at Billy's door. His son opened the front door to find a crazed and manic John Wolfenbarger, carrying multiple bags of jewelry and cash and screaming that he wanted to see his uncle immediately.

"I walked down the stairs and saw jewelry and bags spread all over my living room floor," he recalled. "My nephew just says 'five dead' and smiles. I thought he was bullshitting me. Then, a few hours later, I see it on the news."

Though he never hesitated about turning in his nephew for what he did, Billy Wadd's decision to help the government build cases against his fellow bikers was not an easy one, nor was it one he thought he would ever make. That was until he found out that his own gang and some people in other gangs were plotting to kill him for his helping the cops break the Pesche case. After barely averting death in a daring freeway drive-by that almost killed him and some of his family, Billy finally saw the life he was leading for what it really was.

"Those guys smelled blood and saw the whole situation as an excuse to move on me," said Smith. "They wanted to knock me off my pedestal because they were jealous. I had money and businesses on the street they wanted for themselves. It was that simple. Brotherhood meant nothing to them. I wasn't telling on them, I was helping solve the murders of three little kids and a man and an elderly woman who never had any reason to have their lives taken from them whatsoever. But when you start shooting at me and my family, then it's on and I don't care what I have to do to set things straight."

Thanks to Billy Wadd's cooperation, the FBI, DEA, and ATF launched a trio of top-priority investigations of the Outlaws, the Highwaymen and Smith's own gang, the Devil's Diciples. With Smith's permission, the Copa Lounge was outfitted with state-of-the-art surveillance equipment. The tables and bathrooms were bugged, as was the bar, and hidden video cameras were everywhere. Being a primary hangout for virtually the entire Motor City biker world, it was like shooting fish in a barrel. The evidence that was collected was copious and lethal. It was a federal agent's wet dream. Starting in 2006, after four years of building what would turn out to be an impressive collection of airtight cases, the arrests began to pile up. In November 2006, the DEA nailed a major methamphetamine operation being run by seven members and associates of the Detroit-area Devil's Diciples chapter. It would be the first in a series of high-profile busts.

In February 2007, close to 40 Detroit-area Highwaymen were indicted on drug and gun charges. Then, on August 15, 2007, over a dozen members of the Outlaws' Detroit chapter were charged in a wide-range racketeering case filed in federal court. The 18-count indictment included charges of assault with a deadly weapon and large-scale narcotics trafficking. A number of the charges stemmed from an April 2006 attack on a group of rival Hells Angels in Indiana, employing hammers and steel motorcycle parts.

The takedown of Outlaw dignitaries included "Black Region Roy" Frasier, the club's Midwest regional president; Kenny "Moe" Galaviz, Frasier's former vice president while still operating out of Bay City; Ramon "The Razor" Rios, the Detroit West Side chapter president; and William "Slick Billy" Guinn, the club's Downriver chapter president; as well as Norm "Storm'n Norman" Box and William "Tom the Bomb" McCowan, two of the club's regional heads of enforcement. It put a serious dent in the biker syndicate's local activities, forcing the gang to reorganize. Currently, Joseph "Joey Donuts" Holloway sits as president of the Detroit-area Outlaws and is alleged to have recently been elected regional boss of the club.

The Devil's Diciples, whose Detroit-area chapter serves as the club's national headquarters, are currently under a widespread government siege seeking to shake the club to its very core. Close to two dozen local gang members were federally indicted on racketeering and drug charges, most notably the Diciples' national president, Jeff "Fat Dog" Smith (no relation to Billy Wadd); Paul "Paulie D" Darrah, Smith's vice president; and Glen "Gun Control" Vandiver, the gang's reputed "warlord." Diciples' clubhouses in both Clinton Township and Port Huron were raided in April 2009.

Although the charges were eventually dropped in anticipation by the government of a larger and more fruitful bust in summer 2012, the DEA wound up seizing $50,000 in cash, 85 automatic firearms, 4,000 vicodin and oxycontin pills,

110 pounds of high-grade marijuana, and two and a half pounds of meth in the raids. Fat Dog Smith's ties in the legitimate world are alleged by the government to go deep. Paul Cassidy, a boyhood pal of Smith's and a former district court judge in New Baltimore, retired from the bench following an investigation into his affairs and possible preferential treatment given to Diciples members on behalf of his childhood friend.

Interviewed by *The Detroit Free Press* in the days following his arrest, Smith denied that the Diciples were criminals: "We're just a bunch of guys who like to barbecue and ride Harley-Davidson motorcycles," he said. "We've got the largest diabetes fundraiser in the state. It's a club, not a gang."

The mother-lode bust took place almost exactly six weeks after the futile Devil's Diciples raid when in May 2007, the FBI hit the Detroit Highwaymen chapter with the biggest assault on biker gang organized crime in history, an eventual 83-person, 35-count racketeering indictment alleging attempted murder, assault, extortion, interstate theft, and drug dealing, among other things. Of the close to 100 people brought up on charges, 20 of them were identified as "high-ranking" members of the Highwaymen, including Leonard "Big Daddy" Moore, the club's overall "Godfather"; Joseph "Little Joe" Whiting, the club's national president; Aref "Scarface Steve" Nagi, Whiting's former vice president and top enforcer; and Dave Tomlan and Randy Hutchinson, two former Metro Detroit cops. Moore, Whiting, and Nagi were pegged by prosecutors as the "lead defendants" in the high-profile case.

Assigned to the government task force assembled to bring down the Highwaymen, Hutchinson was alleged to have passed sensitive information to the gang regarding the federal investigation into their affairs and the existence and whereabouts of audio surveillance equipment in their clubhouse. Tomlan, known in the gang as "Stifler," was reputed to moonlight as a member of the Highwaymen while serving with the Garden City Police Department.

Scarface Steve Nagi, 43 at the time of his arrest, was a new millennium version of Taco Bowman, someone equally comfortable navigating between the business world and the biker world. Like Bowman had done during his reign of power, Nagi invested his money wisely in legitimate endeavors, making himself a wealthy man by legal means like ownership in a series of local bars and restaurants as well as a janitorial services company. He also held a bachelor's degree from Wayne State University. Like Bowman before him, Nagi favored a cleaner, more conservative image on the streets, preferring business suits, a shorter haircut, and expensive jewelry to denim cuts, a long beard, and tattoos. The Highwaymen's onetime warlord and sergeant-at-arms was a dangerous figure.

When a federal task force raided Nagi's Sterling Heights home, they found 30 firearms, including several that were stolen. In the over 300 hours of telephone conversations intercepted by the federal government, Nagi can be heard bragging about stabbing and beating up one of his employees at a Mexican restaurant he owned in Dearborn and then throwing him in a dumpster. Because of flight risk and concern for the safety of future witnesses, Nagi and his former boss, Little Joe Whiting, were both jailed without bail pending trial. Unlike Nagi and Whiting, a majority of the defendants were granted bail and given their freedom in the time leading up to the courtroom battles of their lives. "Big Daddy" Moore and "Mad Anthony" Clark had faced similar charges two decades before, where both were taken down in a major federal bust of the gang in 1987, in which Moore had to do prison time.

When word leaked out in late 2009 that Gerald "Bird Dog" Peters, a former club national president and one of the defendants in the massive indictment, had started cooperating with federal authorities, he was visited by three of his co-defendants: Erik "Poke-a-dot" Manners, Michael "Coco" Cicchetti, and Robert "Bizzy" Whitehouse. Manners and Cicchetti, who had just recently been elected as the Highwaymen's Detroit chapter president, told him in no uncertain terms to "hide his family" if he had been considering turning his back on the gang.

It was soon discovered that both Peters and fellow defendant-turned-informant Robert "Bad News Bobby" Burton had their names on a list of FBI snitches that somehow got into the hands of the club's leadership. In addition, Peters' estranged wife had been tipping them off as to her husband's discussions with the feds. Manners, Cicchetti, and Whitehouse all had their bond revoked and were jailed alongside Whiting and Nagi, who had both been in custody for over two years awaiting the start of their trial. Peters and Burton were each immediately placed into witness protection as a result of the club's reputedly putting bounties on their heads, and they waited patiently for their time to testify.

Federal U.S. Judge Nancy Edmunds also ordered Moore and his son and co-defendant, Leonard "Bo" Moore Jr., to be placed in home confinement for the younger Moore's attempt to coerce a fellow defendant and for "Big Daddy" Moore's continued involvement in gang leadership. In early 2010, just a few months before the gargantuan case made it into the courtroom, Edmunds ordered Whiting released on bond, despite evidence presented by the prosecution that he had been involved in planning the murder of a potential witness. Just as she did weeks earlier with Nagi, the judge ruled that both had been locked up too long pending trial.

Although it would prove unrelated to the case, less than two weeks before opening arguments were slated to start, one of the defendants, Dennis "Denny Gone" Vanhulle, was shot on the porch of his house in Northwest Detroit. Vanhulle, who was 43 years old and sometimes went by the nickname "Knothead," was shot in the throat on March 26, 2010, as he answered the front door of his residence at Danbury and Eight Mile Road, by rival biker Ronald "The Tank" Thompson, of the Liberty Riders. The pair had been feuding for over a year. After 19 days in intensive care, Vanhulle died on April 13th, but not before he identified his killer for authorities by scribbling the word "Tank" on a piece of paper.

Starting in early April and lasting for over two months, the well-publicized Highwaymen trial was filled with excitement and intrigue, as would be expected with a group of defendants having criminal rap sheets the size of phone books. Things started off with an impassioned opening argument from Assistant U.S. Attorney Christopher Graveline, highlighted by his telling the jury that the gang was "just what they say they are—the meanest motherfuckers on the open road."

It only got seedier and more lurid. Halfway through the proceedings, Coco Cicchetti suffered a massive heart attack that required emergency open-heart surgery, taking him away from the trial altogether. Besides Peters and Burton, two other former Highwaymen—Daniel "Danny Rocket" Sanchez, a onetime vice president, and Phillip "Jocko" McDonald, a former president of the club's Downriver chapter—testified at the trial, transfixing the jury with tales of life inside a renegade biker gang.

Sanchez's testimony provided real-life drama worthy of a sudsy Lifetime channel TV movie when a woman stood up in the middle of his time on the stand, pointed her finger directly at him and screamed, "He murdered my son," referring to an unsolved 1999 homicide that she was told had involved Sanchez. Explaining a conversation he once had with Big Daddy Moore about why Moore didn't want the club's national presidency, Sanchez recounted that the imposing biker don told him, "The title wasn't important because I have all the control" and "I don't need the feds coming at me; I don't need no RICO."

After deliberating for 25 hours, on June 3, 2010, the jury came back with guilty verdicts for many of the gang's kingfish. Big Daddy Moore, Whiting, Nagi, Cicchetti, former national president "Mad Anthony" Clark, and Gary "Junior" Ball, the club's reputed contact with the local Mafia, were all convicted.

◇◇◇◇◇◇◇◇◇◇◇◇

Billy Wadd Smith took his family and went underground as soon as he heard there was a contract on his life for cluing in the police on his nephew's role in the Pesce murders. He briefly popped his head back out in Detroit in May 2003 to testify at John Wolfenbarger's trial, at which his nephew was convicted and sent back to prison for life. Today, Smith is out of the underworld and living in an undisclosed location.

"I'm not hiding from anyone and I'm not afraid; I'm just trying to live my new life in peace and quiet and keep making changes for the better," Billy Smith stated. "I can't change the past and I don't live with regrets. I did things on my own terms, and when I made the decision to leave the life, I left it for good and have never looked back."

BLOOD AND BEER

The Prohibition Era in Detroit

By Paul Kavieff

In 1927, Detroit was the fourth largest city in the United States, with a population of more than 1.5 million. The rapidly expanding automobile industry and the major manufacturing plants were attracting job seekers from all over the world. This prosperity, coupled with National Prohibition, also made the Detroit area a hotbed for underworld gangs. During this period, both the Chicago and New York underworlds often grabbed the headlines of major newspapers with their beer wars and gangster escapades, yet the Detroit underworld in many ways was worse.

When statewide Prohibition became law on May 1, 1918, Detroit became the first city in the nation with a population of over 250,000 to go dry. Detroit went from approximately 1,800 licensed saloons in 1918 to a conservatively estimated 25,000 illegal establishments, or "blind pigs," by 1925. Detroit's proximity to Ontario made it an opportune place for rumrunners and smugglers. By the mid-1920s, an estimated 500,000 cases of Canadian whisky were coming across the Detroit River every month. Despite this staggering figure, more whisky and beer than that was being made in Detroit by an extensive backstreet brewing industry. Opium dens operated openly throughout Detroit. The illegal Detroit gambling industry, which included everything from alley crap games to fancy roadhouses, was actually making the Detroit underworld more money than the $250 million-a-year alcohol rackets. Detroit was a wide-open city. Literally anything legal or illegal could be easily purchased there.

With the advent of National Prohibition at midnight on January 16, 1920, the soon-to-be-infamous Purple Gang and the men who would create the traditional Detroit Mafia began to claw their way to the top of the city's underworld. While the future Purples were still in short pants, shaking down hucksters and rolling drunks, local Mafia gangs were already well established on Detroit's lower East

Side. During the great wave of immigration between 1880 and 1920, many mainland Italians and Sicilians left their homes for U.S. shores. After arriving at eastern ports, they were attracted to Detroit and its industrial prosperity. Along with many hardworking and law-abiding new Americans came Old World criminals. These gangsters were either looking for greener pastures or were forced to leave their homeland because they were wanted by the authorities.

This new breed of criminal first came to the attention of local police as the result of the Black Hand extortion racket. Although organized underworld groups such as the Sicilian Mafia and the Neapolitan Camorra engaged in this racket, it was an extremely popular form of theft often carried out by small-time criminals with no affiliation to any organized group. All that was required was to write an anonymous letter to a prosperous individual in the community, threatening to murder him or his wife, kidnap their children or destroy their place of business if certain demands were not met. Crude drawings of daggers dripping with blood, skulls and crossbones, or black handprints would complete the letter. The victims of Black Hand letters often attributed them to the traditional Mafia or Camorra. Being superstitious and not trusting local authorities, they paid. There were always examples in the Italian community of what happened to people who ignored these letters. This extortion racket became so widespread that most large U.S. cities had special Black Hand squads in their police departments to investigate and deal with these crimes in the Italian community.

The Black Hand racket was sometimes employed by Salvatore and Vito Adamo, immigrant brothers from Alcamo, Sicily, who arrived in Detroit at the turn of the 20th century. Starting about 1905, the Adamo brothers were leaders of a Mafia gang on Detroit's lower East Side that preyed on the Italian community and that most likely constituted the first semblance of modern-day organized crime in the Motor City. The Adamo mob was involved in the typical ethnic underworld rackets of the time, which included making beer and wine, extorting protection money from local citizens, and running the Italian lottery. Vito resided in Wyandotte, while Salvatore, known as "Sam," ran his operations out of Eastern Market.

The first serious threat to the Adamo brothers' rackets came in about 1910 from the arrival of three Sicilian immigrant brothers: Antonino, Salvatore, and Gaetano Gianolla. Soon after coming to Detroit from Tersini, Sicily, the Gianollas began plying their old country trade in the Italian community. For a short time there was a shaky peace agreement between these two Mafia factions. But the Gianolla brothers, who became known in local underworld circles as the Triumvirate of Terror and who controlled all rackets downriver from their produce business, the Wyandotte Fruit Company, were quick to start chafing under the Adamos' rule. By 1911, the Gianollas were expanding their burgeoning empire into the Eastern Market district and other East Side neighborhoods that the Adamos had been controlling for over half a decade.

It was not long before open warfare broke out between the Adamo and Gianolla factions. The gang war lasted for approximately two and a half years, from 1911 to 1913, and left dozens of bodies from both sides in its wake. The Gianollas eventually claimed victory by murdering both Adamo brothers as they walked together near the corner of Mullett and Russell Streets in Eastern Market in November 1913. One of the Gianollas' top lieutenants was Giovanni "Bloody John" Vitale, an integral enforcer for the gang in its war with the Adamos. Vitale was allowed to run a crew that was independent from the Gianollas, and in a lot of ways he was perceived as an equal with the official leaders. This arrangement lasted without a hitch until 1917 when a falling out between Bloody John and his bosses led to another all-out street war for supremacy in the Detroit underworld. The war was jump-started when Antonino "Tony" Gianolla ordered the murder of Sam Bosco, a close friend and trusted associate of Vitale's, over a dispute regarding a joint business venture from which Gianolla believed Bosco was stealing. When the Vitale faction attempted to hijack a load of liquor belonging to the Giannola brothers, the Giannola-Vitale gang war officially began.

Over the next three years, more than 100 men were killed in the gang war. Tony Gianolla was killed in January 1919 by his bodyguard and surrogate son Tony Alucci as he was about to attend a wake. Striking back with intense ferocity, on February 28, 1919, Salvatore "Sam" Giannola and several of his henchmen staged a daring attack, ambushing three Vitale thugs in the corridors of Detroit's Wayne County Jail. The Vitale gangsters, including the boss' son Joe, had gone to visit John Vitale, who was in the Wayne County Jail, locked up on a murder charge. When Sam Giannola got this information, he and several of his men went to the jail and waited quietly for John Vitale's visitors. When the Vitale thugs appeared, the Giannola gunmen opened fire, fatally wounding Vitale lieutenant Vito Renda and seriously wounding John Vitale's son Joe and Salvatore "Big Sam" Evola, another Gianolla strong-arm, both of whom survived the attack. They had originally planned to shoot down John Vitale as he lay trapped in his cell, but they could not gain access to the cellblock. Vitale retaliated by having Sam Gianolla murdered in October 1919, after lulling him into a sense of security by agreeing to a peace accord two months earlier that Vitale never intended to honor. Shooting from a moving car, Vitale assassins hit Gianolla 28 times, killing him on the spot as he exited a downtown bank after cashing a $200 check.

On August 17, 1920, the gang war that had been raging for the better part of four years finally started to catch up with John Vitale when he and his son Joe were ambushed by Giannola gunmen armed with shotguns outside their Russell Street home on Detroit's East Side. Joe Vitale was killed instantly in the barrage of buckshot. Somehow John ducked behind a car and survived. But it would only be a short reprieve, and on October 2, 1920, Vitale was set up by his own men, shot to death as he returned to his residence in the early hours of the morning from a night on the town. The Giannola-Vitale war was finally over. All of the major leaders of both gangs had been killed.

A peace conference was called right after Thanksgiving in 1920 with the city's remaining Mafia factions in attendance. Salvatore "Singing Sam" Catalanotte, a respected Giannola advisor, presided over a meeting of the minds and helped forge a peace agreement. Territory was divided between the East Side and West Side gangs, with former Gianolla lieutenants Joe Zerilli and William "Black Bill" Tocco leading the Eastsiders and Chester "Big Chet" La Mare, a longtime counsel to Catalanotte, heading the Westsiders. The remaining Gianolla brother, Gaetano, the eldest sibling and the least involved in the violence sparked by the preceding conflict, was allowed to retire, his life spared by Singing Sam, who felt loyal to him from their previous association.

By 1925, the all-Jewish Purple Gang, led by the four Burnstein brothers, as well as the Eastside-aligned "River Gang," led by St. Louis transplant Pete Licavoli, had become major factors in the city's bootlegging industry. As the Eastsiders and Westsiders had done years before, the Purples and the River Gang agreed to Salvatore Catalanotte's territorial restrictions and were welcomed into the city's underworld. Along with Zerilli and Tocco's Eastside Gang, the Purples and Licavoli's river rats controlled most of the large-scale rum running on the Detroit River north and south of the city. La Mare, whose headquarters were in his opulent Hamtramck restaurant, the Venice Café, and the Westsiders controlled the rest of the bootlegging through a pair of offshoot Downriver gangs that worked as La Mare's proxies in the liquor smuggling rackets.

Hamtramck is a city that lies within the boundaries of Detroit. At that time it was dominated by the Dodge's huge main auto plant. Hamtramck was notoriously corrupt—so corrupt in fact that in 1923, Governor Alex Groesbeck sent the Michigan State Police into the city to impose martial law and take over the city government. The mayor and a number of city officials were arrested, later convicted of Prohibition violations and sent to prison. Police duties in Hamtramck were temporarily taken over by the Wayne County Sheriff's Department. More than 400 soft drink parlors—which sold everything but soft drinks—were closed, 150 brothels shuttered, and many gallons of "alley brew" destroyed. For a ruthless gangster like La Mare, Hamtramck was heaven on earth.

Throughout the '20s, Detroit's underworld factions enjoyed a period of relative peace. Many bodies still piled up in the city's morgues, but as a result of Singing Sam's peace agreement, the majority of the homicides were rooted in intra-gang disputes, rather than battles over turf between warring sides. Catalanotte, a man who gained his nickname from his love of Italian opera and his willingness to show off his vocal skills for his friends and family at small, intimate gatherings, was a highly respected and much-loved don and Detroit's first modern-day Godfather. The delicate peace treaty that Catalanotte helped craft started to fall apart at the seams when, on February 17, 1930, he died suddenly of complications from pneumonia. Relations between the Eastsiders and Westsiders quickly deteriorated and resulted in what the local press dubbed the "Crosstown Mob War."

It was during this period that murders in Detroit reached their zenith. By July 1930, a month referred to by the press for years after as "Bloody July," there was a gangland murder literally every day. Things came to a head on July 23rd with the murder of WMBC Radio commentator Gerald Buckley in the lobby of the LaSalle Hotel. Buckley was an immensely popular radio personality who was reported to be on the payroll of the Detroit underworld. He had supposedly been bankrolling Mafia still operations in certain parts of the city. In July 1930, a recall election movement was under way for Mayor Charles Bowles. Bowles was reported to be doing business with the underworld. The escalating gang wars and murders were directly blamed on the mayor. It was reported that Buckley, who was originally against the recall campaign, made an about-face and came out in support of it. Some journalists suggested that his change of heart was to put pressure on his underworld partners to get a bigger piece of the take. Whatever the underlying facts, Mayor Bowles was recalled on July 22, 1930, the only mayor in Detroit history to be voted out of office. Gerald Buckley was promptly shot to death in the lobby of the LaSalle Hotel early that morning by local Mafia gunmen. Three Detroit mob thugs were later tried and acquitted of the murder. Historically, journalists and police officers are off limits to underworld gunmen unless they are dirty. Although none of the charges against Buckley was ever proven, the circumstances surrounding his murder are shrouded in mystery.

After the murder of Gerald Buckley, the Crosstown Mob War took on a much lower profile. In the spring of 1930, Chester La Mare feigned interest in attempting to broker a cease-fire with his rivals and set up what he said would be a peace meeting between the top leaders of the two factions at the Vernor Avenue Fish Market on May 31st. It was all an elaborate ruse. Never intending to compromise from the outset, La Mare planned to have two gunmen waiting at the market. They would rush into the meeting and murder the Eastsider hierarchy on a given signal. Angelo Meli, a former La Mare lieutenant who had recently switched sides in the war, suspected a double-cross and advised Joe Zerilli and Bill Tocco to send emissaries to the meeting instead of attending themselves. The savvy gangsters took Meli's advice and assigned Gasper "The Peacemaker" Milazzo, a New York-bred wiseguy sent to Detroit in the 1920s to aid Zerilli and Tocco's Eastside Gang, and his bodyguard, Sam "Sasha" Parino, to attend in their stead. It was the smart move. La Mare's two gunmen executed both Milazzo and Parino as soon as they entered the front door of the fish market.

Big Chet La Mare's downfall turned out to come from within his own inner circle. He was murdered in his home on the evening of February 6, 1931 by two of his own men. The gunmen, both bodyguards to La Mare, had been ordered to murder their boss by the Eastside leadership, who had supposedly found out that they had been the triggermen in the fish market slayings six months earlier. The choice was simple: Either kill La Mare or die in his place. With La Mare eliminated, the Eastsiders came out of the war victorious and sat firmly atop the Motor City underworld, unquestioned holders of the throne. When a similar-themed mob war concluded in New York about this same time, Sicilian-born East Coast gang leader Charles "Lucky" Luciano called a major conference of all mob leaders across the country and created a nationwide organization called La Cosa Nostra, or "This thing of ours," that would have 26 regional "Families" and an overall board of directors known as "The Commission" to make policy and mediate disputes.

Black Bill Tocco was named the first official boss of the Detroit Mafia family in late 1931, and the criminal conglomerate that was subsequently formed would be known as "The Partnership" or "The Combination," a nod to all of the city's mob factions coming under one banner. Tocco and Zerilli—first cousins, best friends, and brothers-in-law—would be the founding fathers of the present-day Detroit Mafia. Other former bootlegging powers, such as Pete Licavoli, Angelo Meli, Giovanni "Papa John" Priziola, and Pietro "Machine Gun Pete" Corrado, would all join Tocco and Zerilli as future leaders of the syndicate, which would eventually grow to have more than 100 members and 500 associates at its peak in the 1960s.

◇◇◇◇◇◇◇◇◇◇◇◇

In about 1917, a predominantly Jewish mob began to form in the old Hastings Street section of Detroit's lower East Side. The original 18 to 20 boys met at the old Bishop School and quickly became a neighborhood nuisance. They rolled drunks, beat up other youngsters, and extorted money from local merchants. This teenage street gang would eventually evolve into one of the most notorious underworld groups of the Prohibition era. No one knows for sure the origins of their colorful name, the Purple Gang. One story was that two Hastings Street shopkeepers were complaining to each other about the depredations of these juvenile gangsters. One said, "These boys are not like other youngsters, they're tainted. They're like the color of bad meat, purple." "Yes," said the other shopkeeper, "They're a purple gang." Another rumor had it that they were named after two delinquents who ran with the gang when they were kids, Sam and Ben Purple. The name most likely evolved during a period of labor strife known as the Cleaners and Dyers War. One of the Purple Gang's terror tactics was to throw purple dye on clothing to force tailor shops to join the union. With the advent of statewide Prohibition on May 1, 1918, and national Prohibition on January 16, 1920, the Purple Gang was on the way to becoming the rulers of the Detroit underworld by 1927.

The young Purples went to work for two local mobsters who were secret owners of a legitimate corn sugar warehouse, which sold supplies to people who wanted to make beer and wine for family consumption only. A certain amount for personal use was allowed under the 18th Amendment. In reality, Charles Leiter and Henry Shorr became the mentors of the juvenile Purples, who quickly graduated from childhood nuisance crime to hijacking and the extortion rackets. The Purples made their early reputation in the Detroit underworld as vicious hijackers who would take whisky from other mobs and kill everybody who was hauling the load. They also cut themselves in on the profits that other gangsters made from gambling, prostitution and drug dealing.

Charlie Leiter and Henry Shorr were experts at setting up brewing plants in old barns and warehouses around the city. These "alley" breweries could produce thousands of gallons of product a week. Using the young Purples as muscle, Shorr and Leiter began to push into the territory of other mobs. The young Purples divided their time between working with Shorr and Leiter, extorting money from local businesses—legal and illegal, and sometimes working as guards in the local gambling houses. At this early point in the mob's evolution, they were known as the Oakland Sugar House Gang. Under the tutelage of Leiter and Shorr, the Purples set up and ran their own alcohol cutting plants. By cutting hijacked whisky with water and other ingredients, one bottle could be made into five. This whisky was then sold by the case as the original product. Original manufacturers' labels were removed from the bottles and bootleg labels, or "tickets," affixed. One of the Purple Gang's bootleg labels became widely known as Old Log Cabin Whisky.

Although the Purple Gang was made up of several different factions, the four Burnstein brothers—Abe, Joe, Ray, and Isadore—were always considered to be the leaders. Abe Burnstein often played the underworld diplomat, while Joe and Ray were the main enforcers. Other core Purples of the era included: Joseph "Joe Honeyboy" Miller, Harry "H.F." Fleisher, Louie Fleisher, Sam Fleisher, Harry Keywell, Phil Keywell, Hyman "Two Gun Harry" Altman, Harry Sutton, Sam "Fatty" Bernstein, David "Davey Boy" Feldman, Michael "One Arm Mike" Gelfand, Abe "Abie the Agent" Zussman, Jack "The Enforcer" Budd, Jack "Yonkel the Pollack" Selbin, Zigmund "Ziggie" Selbin, Sam "The Gorilla" Davis, Irving "Little Irv" Shapiro, Isadore "Uncle Izzy" Kaminsky, Sam "Sammy Purple" Cohen, Ben "Benny Purple" Cohen, Sam "Sammy K" Kert, Eddie Fletcher, Abe Axler, Harry Millman, Myron "Young Mikey" Selik, Morris Raider, Harry Kirshenbaum, Sam Soloman, Lou Gellerman, Ben Marcus, Harry "Chinky" Meltzer, Abe "Buffalo Harry" Rosenberg, Jake Levittes, John Wolf, Leo "The Killer" Edelstein, Irv Feldman, Sam Drapkin, Sammy Abramowitz, Lou Jacobs, and Joseph "Monkey Joe" Holtzman.

Some of the aforementioned men were considered "Junior Purples," since they were just teenagers at the start of the gang's reign, working their way up the syndicate's ladder acting as gofers, drivers, and bodyguards before reaching full-member status toward the end of the Prohibition era. Charles "The Professor" Auerbach acted as the gang's primary advisor, and Jacob "Scotty" Silverstein was the Purple Gang's chief financial officer. Sam "Uncle Sammy" Garfield, a close friend of Joe Bernstein's, acted as the gang's go-between with the East Coast mobs, specifically through his relationship with New York Jewish Godfather Meyer Lansky. One of the gang's favorite meeting places was the Oakland Avenue Bath House, known around town until this day as simply "The Schvitz," an establishment owned by Chinky Meltzer. The Schvitz was an ideal place to meet and discuss schemes without having to worry about the people you were doing business with wearing a wire, since everyone was in towels and the humidity prevented government agents from bugging the place.

In 1925, Abe Burnstein teamed up with Francis X. Martel, president of the Detroit Federation of Labor, and formed the racketeer-controlled Wholesale Cleaners and Dyers Association. Every cleaning plant, dyeing plant and tailor shop was invited to join the new association. The argument was that this union would stabilize prices in the Detroit cleaning and dyeing industry. Armed Purple Gang members would attend the monthly association meetings and collect the dues. If a cleaning plant joined the association and paid its dues on a regular basis, there would be no problem. If a plant owner refused to join, things would begin to happen in the plant. Chemicals were put into clothing that would cause the garment to burst into flames when pressed. Truckloads of laundry were hijacked, the drivers sometimes beaten to death. If these tactics failed to work, the cleaning plant owner might disappear or the plant reduced to rubble by dynamite. Sometimes dye was thrown into piles of laundry. Between 1925 and 1928, hundreds of thousands of dollars were extorted from the Detroit area cleaning industry. At least two union business agents were taken for rides and shot in the back of the head. Their bodies were then tossed into the street.

Francis Martel became unhappy with his cut of the profits. He was also fearful that a connection would be made between himself and the Burnstein brothers. Martel persuaded a number of cleaning plant owners who had lost everything to file a complaint with the Wayne County prosecutor. This resulted in the Purple Gang trial of 1928. Thirteen Purples, including several leaders of the gang, were tried for extortion in the Detroit area cleaning and dyeing industry. The trial dragged on through the summer of 1928 and ended with the acquittal of all 13 Purples. Francis "Frank" Martel, who was conveniently out of town when indictments were handed down, returned to Detroit after the trial and was later tried for extortion and acquitted. The reason for the Purple Gang's courtroom victory was that their defense attorneys were better than the state's prosecutors. This courtroom victory, coupled with the machine-gun murders of several gangsters by the Purples a year earlier, gave the gang a veneer of invincibility.

On March 27, 1927, a Chicago gunman named Francis "Frankie the Pollack" Wright and two of his friends were mowed down in the hallway of the Milaflores Apartments in downtown Detroit. Wright had been hired by a freelance hijacker to kill Johnnie Reid, an important Purple Gang liquor distributor. Reid had the audacity to smack around two gunmen who worked for local stickup artist Mike Dipisa. Dipisa had tried to shake down Reid for protection money. Dipisa hired Wright to kill Reid as a result of the insult. Wright killed Reid with a single shotgun blast to the head. He then made the mistake of staying in Detroit. Wright was lured to the Milaflores Apartments to negotiate the ransom of a kidnapped gambler who had been his employer.

It was also in 1927 that legendary Chicago mob boss Al "Scarface" Capone came to Detroit with the idea of setting up a Capone organization liquor franchise. He was called to a meeting with the Purples and representatives of the River Gang at the Pick Fort Shelby Hotel downtown. Here he was told that the Detroit River belonged to the Purples. Any business that Capone wanted to do in Detroit would either be through the Purple Gang or not at all. Capone then contracted with the Purples to purchase shipments of Old Log Cabin, which the Purple Gang would haul to Chicago. This business arrangement lasted approximately two years. Once the shipments arrived in Chicago, Capone sold a consignment of his Purple Gang liquor to George "Bugs" Moran, the leader of the Northside Gang, an Irish-dominated crime syndicate that had always been a thorn in Capone's side. Moran decided to purchase his whisky from a cheaper source. When his customers complained, Capone refused to give back to Moran his Purple Gang liquor consignment out of pure spite. Responding with ferocity, Moran's Northsiders began hijacking truckloads of Purple whisky as they made their way from Michigan to Illinois, sometimes even killing the men who were hauling the barrels of booze. This bold tactic succeeded in starting a gang war that would go down in the annals of infamy around the world.

Scarface Capone saw Moran's aggression as his opportunity to eliminate his major rival and cement his legacy as one of the most fearsome gangsters in American history. Working with the Purples, Capone devised a trap to eliminate Moran once and for all. A phony liquor deal was set up with the Moran Gang to purchase a recently hijacked shipment of Old Log Cabin. The Moran Gang would meet the truck on the morning of February 14, 1929. Several Purples were reportedly used as spotters before, during, and after the crime took place, renting out rooms in boarding houses across the street from the site of the hit. Mistaking another Northsider for Moran, the spotters (named in reports as Louie Fleisher and brothers Phil and Harry Keywell) called in the gunmen. The assassins were dressed as Chicago policemen. They went into the garage and machine-gunned six Moran gangsters and a dentist who hung around with the gang. The murders were never solved, but the event became widely known as the St. Valentine's Day Massacre.

As the new decade dawned, the Purple Gang ruled the Detroit underworld unfettered, achieving heights that far exceeded those of its contemporaries. They centered their operations at the Book Cadillac Hotel, located in a downtown hub of activity at Washington Avenue and Monroe Street. The gang drank in their newfound status, many of them by cavorting with movie stars and dating show-girls. Their success was due to the solid protection they received from city hall, the result of a series of weekly payments made on the doorsteps of certain highly placed government officials, as well as their raw ferocity. Between the years 1927 and 1935, 18 Purples were brutally murdered by their own gang. The self-destruction process was accelerated on September 16, 1931, as the result of an incident known as the Collingwood Manor Massacre.

During the mid-1920s, gangsters from all over the United States flocked to Detroit. About 1925, three Chicago gunmen—Joe "Nigger Joe" Leibowitz, Harold "Hymie" Paul, and Isadore "Izzy the Rat" Sutker—came to the city after being forced out of Chicago by the Capone organization. They had been sticking up Capone-protected speakeasies and essentially given a choice to leave Chicago hor-izontally or vertically. Because of their Jewish heritage, once they arrived in Detroit, they were introduced to the Burnstein brothers. The Purples were rapidly expand-ing their operations and needed muscle. The three Chicago gunmen went to work for the "Little Jewish Navy" faction of the Purple Gang that got its nickname from being in charge of using speedboats to ferry liquor into the county from Canada, up and down the Detroit River.

The three new gunmen quickly became uncontrollable Purple gangsters who would backstab anyone, including their own mentors, to get what they wanted. In September 1931, they were called to a peace meeting after having a falling-out with the Burnstein brothers. The meeting was set for three o'clock on September 16, 1931, at the Collingwood Manor Apartments on Detroit's near West Side. In reality, the peace meeting was an ambush. The three Purple Gang outlaws were shot to death by Harry Fleisher, Irving Milberg, and Harry Keywell. Ray Burnstein drove the getaway car. Burnstein, Keywell, and Milberg were later tried, convicted, and sen-tenced to life terms for first-degree murder. Fleisher escaped prosecution in the murders. The self-destruction of the Purple Gang had begun.

With inter-gang murders and lengthy prison sentences mounting, by 1935, most of the significant leadership of the Purple Gang was either dead or in prison after committing what police say were over 500 murders in a 10-year span. Around this time, a meeting was called between the Detroit area Mafia bosses and the Burnstein brothers. It was agreed at this conference that the Italian mob would take over the former Purple Gang's rackets, including Joe Burnstein's highly valued race wire service. This was a peaceful transition of power. There was very little eth-nic rivalry in the Detroit underworld, the Italian mob in the Motor City being much more willing to cooperate with non-Italian gangsters than was the case in other cities. As the result of this power shift, Abe Burnstein was out of the boss' chair, but he was still a very powerful player in the Detroit underworld, running bookmaking and loan-sharking operations and often looked to as a de facto "consigliere" by ruling mob figures Joe Zerilli and Black Bill Tocco, until he died of a heart attack in 1968. Hotel receipts, recovered by Detroit police after his death, indicated that Zerilli and Tocco had been footing the bill for Burnstein to reside in a penthouse suite at the Book Cadillac since the 1940s. Joe and Izzy Burnstein would both retire to California with their earnings from the gang's glory days and go semi-legit, dying of natural causes in the 1980s. Ray Burnstein was released from prison on his Collingwood Massacre conviction in 1964 and died three years later in a nursing home, debilitated by a stroke he had suffered behind bars.

◇◇◇◇◇◇◇◇◇◇◇◇

Although the Purple Gang controlled the Detroit rackets in the later 1920s, they had no control over other less-organized, renegade outlaw gangs. These notorious bank-robbing and kidnapping mobs refused to pay tribute to any organized crime group. They were based in Hamtramck, Detroit, and the surrounding suburbs. One of the most violent gangs of safecrackers, bank robbers, and heist artists was the infamous Hamtramck mob led by Paul Jaworski. This gang not only operated in southeast Michigan, but in the coalfields of Pennsylvania, where they were known as the Flathead Gang, and they specialized in robbing mine company payrolls. Paul Jaworski would eventually die in the electric chair in 1929 for the murder of a payroll guard, committed during one of the gang's many holdups.

The Jaworski mob was best known for the June 6, 1928 holdup of the downtown business offices of *The Detroit News*. During this robbery, a Detroit police officer was brutally shot to death as he lay wounded on the steps of the Lafayette Street entrance to the building. The murder was committed by Jaworski gang members in front of at least 100 witnesses. Another one of the gang's infamous capers was the dynamiting of an armored car in Coverdale, Pennsylvania, on March 11, 1927, in which $104,000 was taken and a guard murdered. While gangs such as the Jaworski mob, the Shotgun Gang, and the Lizzard Gang robbed banks and individuals, other Detroit area gangs specialized in the "snatch racket" or kidnapping.

One of the most successful kidnapping gangs was the predominantly Irish Joseph "Legs" Laman mob. This gang specialized in kidnapping wealthy Detroit area racketeers and gamblers. From 1926 until it was destroyed by a task force of Detroit and Michigan State Police in late 1929, the gang kidnapped local gamblers and rumrunners at will. They reasoned that underworld characters would quietly pay their ransom without going to the police. This system worked well until the gang became overconfident and greedy, and started kidnapping legitimate businessmen.

Joseph Laman, known as "Legs" because his limbs were out of proportion with the rest of his body, was a career criminal. He once threatened to use a shotgun on Harry Bennett, head of Ford's service department, when Bennett attempted to get information about one of the mob's victims. The gang was composed of more than 20 thugs, and the "snatch racket," as it came to be known, was well organized.

Kidnapping gangs developed their own terminology. A "finger man" was someone who pointed out a potential victim to the gang. Laman would then send "pickup men" to grab or snatch the unsuspecting racketeer at his place of business or near his home. A bag would be pulled over his head, and the prisoner would be picked up and thrown on the floor of a touring car. He would then be taken to the kidnapper's "castle." This was an apartment or house used by the mob to imprison the victim. The Laman mob had castles in Detroit, Dearborn, and Ferndale, Michigan as well as Toledo, Ohio. Waiting at the castle were the "keepers"—gang members who would provide meals for the victim and, if necessary, torture the unfortunate racketeer if he failed to comply with the orders of the mob. The prisoner was bound, blindfolded, and locked in the castle. No one would speak to him for several days. Food would be brought in each day. After several days, a gang member would approach the blindfolded victim, or "package." This thug was called the "voice," as that was all that the kidnapped gangster could identify. The voice would negotiate a ransom and get the victim to name an intermediary, usually another racketeer, to go to the family and pick up the ransom money.

If the package refused to go along with the gang's request, torture was employed. Cigarettes and cigars were placed behind the prisoner's ear or pushed into his body. Eyebrows were plucked out a hair at a time. Sometimes a red-hot poker was used. This method of persuasion was known as "playing poker." "Fancy shooting" involved tying a victim to a tree and taking shots at him with pistols and revolvers. The idea was to come as close to the body as possible without actually wounding the prisoner. With these methods, securing cooperation was not a problem. Ransoms were negotiated according to how much money the gang thought a victim was worth.

In 1929, the Laman mob began kidnapping legitimate businessmen. On July 21st of that year, David Cass, the 23-year-old son of a wealthy real estate dealer, was kidnapped from a Detroit blind pig. The young man's father, Gerson Cass, was contacted by the gang on July 25th and given instructions to meet someone at a West Side Detroit location. The man Cass was supposed to meet was Legs Laman. Gerson Cass did exactly what the kidnappers told him to do. He did not contact the Detroit police. Through an informer, detectives found out about the ransom pickup and were staked out on the scene. When Laman walked up to Cass and took the suitcase full of ransom money, the police appeared and shouted for Laman to stop. The gangster took off running and was felled by several bullets from the detectives' revolvers. Near death, Laman was taken to Detroit Receiving Hospital. To everyone's surprise, the plucky mobster slowly recovered. With Legs in police custody, the kidnapping gang panicked. David Cass was driven out to a field in Lapeer County and executed.

Legs Laman was later tried for extortion in the Cass kidnapping case and sentenced to the maximum two-year sentence. At this point, prosecutors could not prove that Laman had actually participated in the Cass kidnapping. When prosecutors obtained more information, Legs was brought to Detroit on another kidnapping charge and convicted. On December 14, 1929, Laman was sentenced to 30 to 40 years in state prison. Shortly before his conviction, a trapper along the Flint River found the partially decomposed body of David Cass. Ballistics tests were made on the bullets taken from the body of Cass by the Detroit police. The bullets proved to be from the guns of Laman mob thugs Frank Hohfer and Edward Wiles. Both of these men were later positively identified as the slayers of David Cass.

Eventually, Laman was persuaded to become a state witness against his gang in return for a reduced sentence. In June 1930, he and another member of the gang named Henry "Ray" Andrews were brought to Detroit to testify. Laman named Edward Wiles and Frank Hohfer as being two of several gang members who had kidnapped and slain David Cass. By this time, Wiles and Hohfer had been convicted of other crimes and sentenced to long terms in state prison. The testimony of Legs Laman and others destroyed the kidnapping gang. During the trials, it also came out that a plot had actually been formulated by the Laman gang to kidnap the children of Edsel Ford by shooting their bodyguards and snatching the Ford heirs for a hefty ransom.

The Laman mob had always been out of control and deadly. A good example of their cowboy tactics occurred on April 8, 1929, when Andrew Germano, Frank Hohfer, and another Laman mob gunman stole a car at gunpoint from a doctor in Pontiac, Michigan. The thugs then drove to Flint, where they tried to rob a bank and failed. After a shootout with Flint police, they headed back to Detroit by way of Ann Arbor. Driving aimlessly around Ann Arbor at 2:00 a.m., they were pulled over by a local policeman who thought the trio looked suspicious. They promptly shot the officer in the chest when he started asking questions. Fortunately, the policeman was saved because he was wearing a bulletproof vest. Several miles out of Birmingham, Michigan, the drunken thugs rolled the stolen car. Rumpled and bloody, they limped into Birmingham, where they inquired of a policeman where they could get a cab. They explained that they had been in an accident. The gangsters hailed a cab. To the surprise of the Laman gunmen, the officer climbed in after them and told the cab driver to take them to police headquarters to make out an accident report. The gunmen panicked, shot the officer in the arm, and threw him out of the cab. The driver was then thrown out of the vehicle. The car was later found partially submerged in a nearby lake.

Although the Laman mob was put out of business in 1930, several members continued to make the headlines. Early in August 1931, Eddie Wiles died of natural causes in Marquette Prison. Wiles had been one of the Laman gunmen who had shot David Cass. On the morning of August 27th, Andrew Germano, a former Laman mob thug, and two other convicts got into the Marquette Prison sick call line. All of the men carried guns under their shirts. The weapons and ammunition had been shipped into the prison in sealed cans of chicken. When the prison doctor, A.W. Hornbogen, asked Germano to take off his shirt, he pulled a .32 caliber automatic pistol and shot the doctor and a trusty. The doctor was killed immediately, and the trusty died later in the prison hospital. The three convicts tried to shoot their way out of the hospital but were thwarted in their efforts. The prisoners then held off local and state police in the prison's industrial building for several hours before committing suicide.

Another notorious gang that operated in the area around Hamtramck was the Carson-Kozak mob. Jimmy Carson was considered to be the brains behind the gang and Philip "Russian Shorty" Kozak the muscle. This group robbed banks, gas stations, businesses, and even pedestrians. Nobody was safe from these predators. In early 1926, the gang planned to rob a Detroit bank and decided they needed to steal a car that could be used in the heist. On January 11th, Kozak and Carson got into a cab in front of the Ford Motor Company's Highland Park plant. The two gangsters politely waited for a young woman to get out of the cab before they assaulted the driver. Both Kozak and Carson pulled guns and tried to eject the cabbie. The driver put up a ferocious fight until one of the thugs hit him on the head with the butt of his pistol and threw him out of the car. The commotion attracted the attention of a Detroit police officer, Andrew Rusinko. The policeman had just walked out of a nearby bank. Observing the robbery in progress, he ran toward the cab. Both Carson and Kozak fired at the officer, killing him instantly. It was Rusinko's first day on the job after graduating from the police academy. The two gunmen drove off in the cab, which was later found demolished. Carson was eventually convicted of the murder and sentenced to life in prison. Kozak was also convicted and deported.

There were many smaller gangs that terrorized the Detroit area during the Prohibition years. The Green Sedan Gang operated out of a green touring car and stuck up pedestrians and other drivers at stoplights. The Lizzard Gang of Hamtramck, led by Chester Tutha, operated well into the '30s, robbing local banks and cracking safes. These groups of outlaws were even given a wide berth by larger organized gangs such as the Purples and the River Gang. They were considered dangerous and uncontrollable. Because of their cowboy tactics, most of these high-profile gangs lasted less than a year, their leaders ending up dead or in prison.

OAKLAND COUNTY'S NIGHTMARE

Satan's Babysitter

By Ross Maghliese

On February 13, 1976, 12-year-old Mark Stebbins of Ferndale, Michigan went missing. His body was found fully groomed and clothed in a parking lot in Southfield six days later. He was the first in what became a series of child killings in the suburbs of Detroit that shook the entire state. Between February 1976 and March 1977, at least three other children were abducted and found dead days later along various roadways in Oakland County. The body of Jill Robinson, 12, of Royal Oak, was found near Big Beaver Road and I-75 on December 26 1976. According to police reports, she was killed by a shotgun blast to the head. Kristine Mihelich, 10, was taken from the parking lot of a party store near her home in Berkley on January 2, 1977. Her body, like the others, was found days later, neatly positioned on the side of the road, suffocated to death.

The fourth and final victim was 11-year-old Timothy King of Birmingham. King disappeared on December 16, 1977, and was last seen talking to a man in a parking lot. His body was found in a roadside ditch in Livonia nearly a week later. The person responsible for these deaths first became known as "The Babysitter Killer" for the careful, almost fastidious state in which the bodies had been found. Soon, however, the assailant became known as the "Oakland County Child Killer." No defined face has ever been put to this nickname that still haunts the Metro Detroit area, but theories and suspects abound. The evidence indicated that the two male victims were sexually abused before being killed. The abductions were done seamlessly, with virtually no concrete evidence or leads for police to follow. The only details available at the time of the killings were that the predator was a male and was thought to have driven a blue AMC Gremlin with a white stripe.

Some believed there may have been more than one culprit in these crimes and that The Babysitter Killer used candy and other treats to lure the unknowing children into custody. The infamous blue Gremlin was never located, but nonetheless became a symbol of fear in Oakland County.

A special unit, the Michigan Child Murders Task Force, was formed and at one point had as many as 300 people working on the case. Known gay bars and hangouts became sites of stakeouts, and decoy ads were placed in sex magazines in the hope of attracting the killer. Reportedly, although not confirmed by official investigation reports, even grieving fathers from previous child killings were questioned in case one of them might be out to seek some form of vindictive revenge on living children. Local newspapers had a staff of reporters on call in the event that any new developments regarding the killer came to light. Yet over 30 years after the first body was found, the case remains open. Oakland County Executive L. Brooks Patterson, who was the county's lead prosecutor at the time of the killings, is still looking to bring closure to these tragic crimes.

"This case, along with the Jimmy Hoffa case which also happened in Oakland County, is an open wound," Patterson said. "It's important to me both as a parent and as a professional to bring a sense of closure to this county and the families that suffered from these crimes and lost their children."

Patterson said it was not immediately known that the killings were related, but once the third child, Kristine Mihelich, went missing it was clear that a serial killer was roaming the streets of Oakland County: "Nobody connected the dots at first, but the local law enforcement and everyone involved worked feverishly to stop these killings from occurring, and then bring the person responsible to justice," added Patterson. "We lost our comfort zone in our county, which has always been a nice upscale community, but we had to face the fact that it wasn't as safe as we once believed. It changed the way people lived their lives because you just never knew when the son of a bitch was going to strike again."

The original child killer task force shut down on December 15, 1978. Its leader, Dr. Jerry Tobias, passed away in 2005. The task force has since restarted, and although it is smaller than it was during those frightening early months, it is still investigating the case. Patterson and the law enforcement officials and families of the victims are holding out hope that it will one day be closed.

"I know my desire fails in comparison to that of the families involved, but I have a personal and professional interest to put a name on the person responsible," said Patterson, who went on to add that he is not optimistic that the case can be solved.

Perhaps the largest roadblock in solving these killings is that all of the known suspects linked to this case are either in jail, serving life sentences for other crimes, or dead. Yet pieces of evidence were found throughout the course of the investigation, which allowed police to zero in on a few primary suspects. A man identified as David Norberg was at one point thought to be the lead suspect. Police found a cross that was believed to belong to one of the victims in the possession of Norberg during a search of his home, but no DNA evidence was ever found linking him to any of the murders. Norberg died in a car accident in 1981. Another promising suspect pursued by police was Theodore Lamborgine, a native of Parma Heights, Ohio. Lamborgine is currently serving a life sentence for 14 counts for criminal sexual crimes, but like the others, no evidence was found linking him to the case.

Lamborgine's name was disclosed by Michael D. Grant, a previously convicted child killer from Indiana and a fellow suspect in the Oakland County case. Grant coughed up Lamborgine's name after being pressured by investigators. In 1971, Grant was convicted in the stomping death of three-year-old Scott Ingersoll in Mishawaka, Indiana. He served two years in prison and escaped, but was sent to jail again in 2000 for assaulting his son, Chip St. Clair, when Grant was 22. Grant died in September 2010. St. Clair currently lives in Oakland County and has become an advocate for victims of child abuse. He is also an author and motivational speaker. Chip's memoir, *The Butterfly Garden*, discusses his youthful life when he was unknowingly on the run from law enforcement with his father. When Grant died, he was still a suspect in numerous unsolved child murder cases but was nonetheless released from jail after serving his sentenced time. It wasn't until he grew older that St. Clair realized the extent of his father's violent life.

"I had to take one day at a time," St. Clair told *The Oakland Press* after his father died. "Every clue I uncovered only sprouted more questions. Did I have a brother or sister he murdered? Was I kidnapped? I literally had to look in the mirror and ask, 'Who am I?'"

The Michigan State Police declined to release much information or answer direct questions related to the killings, because the case is still considered an open investigation. Yet of all the potential suspects made public in this case, there is one name that government officials are particularly reluctant to discuss. Christopher Busch, the son of former General Motors executive Harold Lee Busch, emerged as a lead and a controversial suspect after the investigation hit an initial lull. At the time of the killings, Busch was a known sex offender and believed to be involved with child pornography. He was questioned by police in 1977, prior to the killing of Timothy King, but was not vigorously pursued as a suspect. Busch eventually pled guilty to sexual misconduct charges involving boys between the ages of 10 and 14, but the crimes were not related to the Oakland County Child Killer case. He then reached a plea deal that entailed two years of probation and an $800 fine. No jail time was given.

Busch was found dead on November 20, 1978 in his bedroom at his parents' home, north of Maple Road and west of Cranbrook Road in Bloomfield Township, with a single gunshot wound to the head. The death was ruled a suicide. At the time of his death, Busch was facing four pending cases of sexual assault, and his probation officer told investigators that Busch had become "despondent" over the four cases against him, according to the original report filed by the Bloomfield Hills police.

In Busch's home, police found drawings of children, one of which closely resembled the first victim in the child killer case, Mark Stebbins. Photographs of the crime scene also displayed bloody ligatures, which could have been used to restrain the victims. Adding to the strangeness of the case was the fact that the ligatures were not processed with the rest of the evidence, and police reports described them as "missing." Presumably, the ligatures could have been used as evidence against Busch in the child killer case because of the blood, and there should be records of a chain of possession to account for where the ligatures ended up. It is unclear whether or not officials even plan to investigate what happened to the ligatures, and the state police will not comment on specifics of the case or identify the person who was involved in handling the evidence. These developments came to light only after inquiries from the parents of Kristine Mihelich into the background of Christopher Busch after learning that he was a suspect. The Mihelich family was shown photos from the suicide scene in Busch's apartment, where they recognized the drawing resembling Mark Stebbins and the bloody ligatures displayed on the floor of the room. Bush's body was on the bed with a shotgun lying next to him. Busch's father, Harold, died in 2002. His mother died in 2003.

"I don't remember his name being on a list of suspects when I was the prosecutor," Patterson said when asked about Christopher Busch. "From my memory, the Busch stuff came up later on and he then emerged as a key suspect. Right now he's still one of the suspects, but he's dead and it's hard to get more information out of that. I don't really know much about him other than what's out there."

Busch's name resurfaced after Barry King, the father of victim Timothy King, brought to light a conversation he had with a polygraph examiner and friend of the King family, Patrick Coffee. According to Barry King, Coffee told one of his children that he had met another polygraph examiner, Lawrence Wesser of Southfield, at a conference in Nevada. Wesser, who had given a polygraph test to Busch, reportedly told Coffee that the results caused him to believe that Busch had killed Timothy King. Barry King said this was the first time he or his family had heard Busch's name in relation to the investigation. Once King learned of Christopher Busch, he said he attempted to get a police report about Busch's prior arrests from the Genesee County Police Department, but was told it was missing. Media reports from that time said the original police report on Busch's suicide was also declared missing. Police later said it had been discovered after being misfiled. King said he shared all the information he got on Busch and other suspects in the case with the state police. He eventually became frustrated with the progress of the investigation.

"I just turned things over to them, 32 years I just turned things over to them and I didn't think twice about it," King said. "I don't think they ever told me about Busch. Every now and then they'd ask if I knew anything about certain people who were suspects, but I don't remember Bush ever being brought up in the original investigation."

Barry King then started to take things into his own hands and filed under the Freedom of Information Act (FOIA) in an attempt to get the state police records on the Busch suicide. King said he was told he'd need to pay upwards of $11,000 to acquire the records on Busch. He then filed a lawsuit against the state police. He also published an open press release sharing his knowledge of the case on *PR Newswire* with the hope of sparking more interest or outrage in the community toward the investigation.

"I just want my questions answered," King said after the lawsuit was filed. "I don't understand why I wasn't given any answers and why our requests to get public files were denied. If they'd answer my questions, then I wouldn't have started this [lawsuit]."

Both the King and Mihelich families met with the task force on November 3, 2009. According to King, there were no representatives from the FBI, the Oakland County Sheriff's Department, or the law enforcement agencies of any municipalities other than Livonia. Timothy King went missing in Berkley. In an updated press release, King said the only agency examining the Busch investigation was the Michigan State Police. The problem with this, however, is that the Michigan State Police may have had a conflict of interest with this case if its investigation of the Busch suicide in 1978 was handled improperly. King said he wanted the governor, the state Attorney General, or the U.S. Attorney to handle the case and determine what truly happened in the Busch investigation.

On December 17, 2009, the King family won its FOIA suit against the Michigan State Police and received 3,400 pages of investigative records dealing with the case and the Busch investigation. Among other information, the files confirmed that Christopher Busch had been convicted four times, in the first three months of 1977, of criminal sexual conduct in four Michigan counties: Oakland, Montmorency, Genesee, and Midland. The reports stated that Busch's father paid a cash bail for his son's release on each of his four arrests. According to a report in *The Detroit News*, one victim assaulted by Busch was offered hush money. Busch's mother reportedly traveled to the victim's Flint neighborhood in a limousine and offered to pay him if he agreed not to say anything to police. This person's identity was not revealed.

After reviewing the records turned over to him in the court case, along with his previous knowledge from his family's conversation with Patrick Coffee, Barry King told reporters in a statement that he was now "more convinced than ever" that Busch was responsible for the death of his son. Attempts to contact both Coffee and Lawrence Wesser failed. In other media reports, however, Wesser denied ever discussing the Busch case. Coffee stood behind what he told the King family. As for the hypothesized conspiracy regarding the case of Christopher Busch, L. Brooks Patterson said he didn't see that as a possibility.

"No way," Patterson maintained. "I have total faith in our justice system and the people we had working on the case then and the people working the case now. I just don't think it's possible. I feel deeply for Barry King and I know this has caused his family a lot of harm. That's why I want to put a name and face to whoever did this, but right now I'm not very optimistic we'll be able to do that."

In 2011, the first DNA match was made in the case when a hair believed to belong to convicted felon James Gunnels, recently released from prison on unrelated charges, was identified as related to a hair found on one of the victims' bodies. Police theorized that Gunnels, 16 years old at the time of the murders, may have been used as a lure by the killer. A connection was discovered in court documents from the 1970s, indicating that Busch was convicted of sexually molesting Gunnels at the Busch family cottage in 1974.

New evidence surfaced in July 2012 when the Oakland County prosecutor's office announced that it had connected a hair found in a vehicle once owned by sex offender Arch Edward Sloan to hairs found on two of the four victims. Sloan, currently serving a life sentence, worked in the area as a mechanic at the time of the abductions.

THE DETROIT CHAIN SAW MASSACRE

Paradise Lost

It was a heinous, gore-ridden scene of raw and brutal violence, the likes of which the city of Detroit had not seen in decades. Three bodies, two which of were mutilated with chainsaws, were strewn across the charred floor of a partially burnt residence in Southwest Detroit, mere blocks from the recently abandoned Tiger Stadium. The date was November 19, 2002, and the triple homicide attained immediate infamy. Catching wind of the gruesome murders on a television newscast, legendary Motor City novelist Elmore Leonard dispatched his research assistant to the scene to gather as many details as possible and soon thereafter included a fictionalized version of the crime in his next book, *Mr. Paradise.*

The trio of victims included Wesam Akrawi, Rany Sharak, and Chris Kasshamoun, three drug dealers alleged to be members of the "Chaldean Mafia," the only all-Arab crime syndicate operating in the United States. Chaldeans are Christian Iraqis. Since the mass migration of Chaldeans to Southeast Michigan in the early 1970s, most of them fleeing the wrath of Saddam Hussein, Chaldean Christians have been big players in the Metro Detroit underworld. Akrawi and Kasshamoun were both mob royalty in the city's Chaldean community, each sharing the syndicate's reputed Godfather, Lou "The Hammerhead" Akrawi, as their uncle. Lou Akrawi's brother, Karim, was Wesam Akrawi's father, and Kasshamoun was a nephew to both Lou and Wesam. Sharak was one of Wesam Akrawi's top lieutenants, a brash and charming young man with a head for numbers.

From the late 1980s into the early 1990s, the Chaldean Mafia was the biggest supplier of cocaine in Michigan, bringing in up to 200 kilos a month of pure Colombian powder. With the imprisonment and murder of the ringleaders of the coke operation, the syndicate was alleged to have shifted its focus to marijuana distribution. By the turn of this century, the Chaldean Mafia was reputed to be the biggest wholesale dealer of marijuana in the city and within the state's prison system.

"The Chaldeans have been a major force since they got here; they adapted to the terrain quickly and made a name for themselves in no time," said Chuck Pappas, a local police officer who was deputized in the Drug Enforcement Administration while working the syndicate beat in the 1980s and '90s. "When I was making cases against them, there was no question that they could hold their own in terms of ferocity and profitability with any group operating on the street."

Lou Akrawi fled Baghdad for the U.S. in late 1968 after personally feuding with Saddam Hussein, a rising figure in the recently elected Baath Party. As a foot soldier in a militant, socialist-backed rebel party opposed to the new Iraqi government, he participated in an unsuccessful assassination attempt on Hussein and was forced to flee the country before his 21st birthday. Arriving with his family in Highland Park, Akrawi soon found himself one of the community leaders of the burgeoning ethnic enclave.

In addition to opening up a number of legitimate businesses—mostly markets, gas stations, and restaurants—Lou Akrawi is alleged to have slowly but surely built himself a formidable and all-encompassing criminal organization that by the late 1970s ruled over the Motor City's Arab underworld with a fierce will and an iron fist. The organization's tight-knit leadership, made up primarily of blood relatives and his strong relationship with the local Italian Mafia, aided Akrawi's cause significantly.

Earning his nickname, "The Hammerhead," due to a penchant for using his patented head-butt in physical altercations, Akrawi successfully evaded major criminal convictions for the first 25 years of his time on the street by utilizing a series of buffers and front men, such as his closeness to a dozen nephews, to insulate himself from law enforcement. As a number of his nephews were either killed or sent to prison with lengthy sentences, Lou Akrawi was the Detroit underworld's "Teflon Don." He was charged with several serious felonies in this time period, including a major narcotics collar he took in the late 1980s, but he beat them all in court.

That was until 1996 when Akrawi and his nephew, Tahrir "Crazy Tommy" Kalasho, were convicted of second-degree murder, stemming from an incident where the pair sent gunmen into a rival's grocery store and an innocent bystander was struck by a stray bullet and killed. The shooting, which took place in the fall of 1993, came in the midst of an internal street war raging in the Chaldean underworld between Akrawi and an offshoot faction of young hotheads led by the younger brothers of former Akrawi lieutenants being backed by the Italians. Prior to the shooting at the grocery store, the rival group had tried on numerous occasions to kill Lou and Tommy in separate unsuccessful shootouts.

"These weren't the type of guys you wanted to mess around with," said Bill Randall, a former FBI agent in Detroit. "They were involved with a lot of drugs, a lot of scams and a lot of violence. Their gambling rackets were very lucrative, and some of them weren't afraid to stand up to the Italian Mafia and hold their ground in the face of being squeezed. The money being made in that community was hand-over-fist."

◇◇◇◇◇◇◇◇◇◇◇◇

Jamale Stewart was a mid-level marijuana dealer who lived and worked in Southwest Detroit. His supply source was the Chaldean Mafia, specifically Akrawi, Sharak, and Kasshamoun. In the weeks leading up to the bloodletting, Stewart had run up a $30,000 debt with his drug suppliers, and he contacted Kasshamoun on the morning of November 18, 2002 about repaying the money he owed and purchasing another few dozen pounds of marijuana.

Stewart lived in a two-unit residential complex at 2315 Vermont Street with his girlfriend, Tuwana Chambers. Three days earlier, DuJuan "Friday the 13th" O'Neal, a onetime live-in boyfriend of Stewart's mother, traveled from New York, where he was living, to Detroit to visit with Stewart, whom he had helped raise as a youth. O'Neal was a veteran of the area's street life and acquired his nickname because of his love of the horror film of the same name and his scary reputation. Other variations of O'Neal's street alias included "Jason," "The Mask," and "The Hockey Mask," all references to the film's main character, a murderous serial killer who stalks his prey wearing a hockey goalie's mask. He even had the name "Jason," the words "Friday the 13th," and a picture of a hockey mask tattooed on his body.

The following day, November 19th, Stewart arranged for Kasshamoun, Akrawi, and Sharak to come by Stewart's place to conduct their transactions. Stewart and O'Neal had traveled earlier to a nearby car dealership to test-drive a red Ford Explorer. While in the middle of the test drive, Stewart received a call from Kasshamoun informing him that he was waiting at his Vermont residence. Opting against returning the Explorer to the dealership, Stewart made his way back to his home to rendezvous with the Chaldeans. Once back at his house, Stewart gave Sharak $30,000 in cash, and Kasshamoun turned over 35 pounds of marijuana stored in a large garbage bag. As Sharak counted the money, Stewart went upstairs to his bedroom to retrieve some marijuana from his personal stash so they all could smoke a joint and O'Neal followed him. According to future court testimony that would be validated by a subsequent conviction, while standing across from each other in Stewart's bedroom, O'Neal stated that he wanted to rob the three Chaldeans of their drugs, jewelry, and money. "Let me lick these niggas," he said.

Not wanting to disturb his business relationship with the Chaldeans, Stewart attempted to dissuade O'Neal from carrying out the robbery. He told him that the Chaldeans had been good friends and had treated him well in their narcotics dealings. They were his people, he said. Totally unconvinced by Stewart's argument, O'Neal responded, "I'm your people!" a terse reminder of where his loyalties should lie. Unsure of what was about to happen, Stewart followed O'Neal back down the stairs where Sharak continued to tabulate the cash in stacked bundles on the kitchen table, and Akrawi and Kasshamoun sat on a couch in the living room, watching television. Taking a seat across from Sharak, Stewart began making small talk, waiting for him to finish his count, as O'Neal took a seat in a chair near Akrawi and Kasshamoun.

This benign scene was merely the calm before the storm. Within seconds, O'Neal jumped out of his chair, grabbed a gun laying on a nearby credenza, and ordered the Chaldeans to get down on their stomachs and interlock their hands behind their heads. Sharak boldly refused, stating, "I'm not getting down on the floor, man. Just take all this shit and leave." Immediately showing the entire room he meant business, O'Neal went over to Sharak and hit him violently on the side of the head with the butt of his weapon. With Sharak still dazed from the blow, O'Neal grasped him by the collar and forced him onto his feet. Guiding him to the top of the stairwell that led to the basement, O'Neal coldly shot Sharak in the back of the head in full view of everyone there, watching his limp body tumble down the stairs with a smile on his face. Akrawi was only a few feet away from the front door, and after seeing O'Neal kill his friend, he made a run for it. Before he reached the door, O'Neal shot him in the head, killing him instantly.

Having just witnessed his uncle and best friend executed in cold blood, Kasshamoun cowered in the corner of the couch, crying and begging for his life. Unfazed, O'Neal forced him at gunpoint to march down the stairs where Sharak's body lay dead at the bottom of the stairwell. Seconds later, O'Neal shot Kasshamoun in the back of the head, leaving the two bodies on the dusty basement floor and returning to the kitchen where Stewart waited in shock. Going into a kitchen drawer, O'Neal got a large plastic kitchen bag and put it over the head of Akrawi, who lay dead in the doorway. Fearing for his own personal safety as well as feeling a sense of loyalty to a man he viewed as a surrogate father, Stewart helped O'Neal move Akrawi's body to the basement where it was thrown on top of the corpses of Sharak and Kasshamoun. At this point, O'Neal left Stewart at the house and went to a suburban Home Depot outlet to secure supplies that would help them get rid of the three dead bodies. Forty-five minutes later, he returned with a vacuum cleaner, garbage bags, cleaning products, gloves, and an electric chainsaw that he intended using to dismember the bodies.

After Stewart and O'Neal finished cleaning the blood from the doorway where Akrawi was shot, O'Neal went downstairs and began cutting up the bodies.

He started by cutting off Kasshamoun's arms and legs. Physically sickened by the scene in front of him, Stewart, who had originally gone into the basement to aid in the dismemberment, had to flee upstairs to throw up. While vomiting in the bathroom from the stench of freshly sawed flesh, Stewart heard a knock at the front door. It was his half-brother, Ramone Johnson, who had just decided to pop in for an impromptu visit. Stewart attempted to get Johnson to leave the residence, but was interrupted by O'Neal, who had emerged from the basement—bloody gloves, garments, and all. He told Johnson what had just happened and requested his help in disposing of the bodies. Seemingly unbothered by the macabre scenario, Johnson agreed with little hesitation.

A few minutes later, O'Neal called Stewart down to the basement where he and Johnson were with the three corpses. When Stewart got there, he saw Kasshamoun's entire body dismembered, with O'Neal and his brother standing in the center of the carnage-strewn chaos. O'Neal put all of his victims' clothes, jewelry, cell phones, and the contents of their wallets, along with the 35 pounds of marijuana and the pistol used in the murders, into several garbage bags and ordered Stewart to get rid of them. As he was loading the Explorer with the garbage bags, Stewart's girlfriend, Tawana Chambers, returned home from work. Informing her of what was going on, Stewart brought her into the house and told her to help O'Neal and Johnson clean up, while he called a friend who was a taxi cab driver to come and help him get rid of the evidence. The taxi arrived within a half hour and Stewart put Chambers in the cab, telling his friend to follow him in the Explorer to a location where he intended to dump the garbage bags and the stolen vehicle.

Unfortunately for Stewart, within minutes of hopping into the stolen vehicle and departing his house, he would find himself getting pulled over by the cops for ignoring a stop sign. Knowing the amount of damning evidence that was stored in the truck, Stewart fled the scene on foot, ducking into a set of neighboring apartment buildings. Upon searching the Explorer, Officer John Furmanski, the driver of the squad car that pulled over the vehicle, discovered five black garbage bags filled with the belongings and blood-stained garments of Wesam Akrawi, Rany Sharak, and Chris Kasshamoun, as well as a bundle of drugs and a semi-automatic Mack 11 pistol.

Returning to his house on foot roughly a half hour after he left, Stewart informed everybody there what had just happened. In the midst of cutting up another body, O'Neal and Johnson immediately stopped what they were doing and started to pack some belongings to go on the run. Chambers was dropped off by the taxi and helped Stewart get everything in order to leave. O'Neal decided it would be best to burn down the residence with the bodies still inside, and he advised the rest of the group to check into a motel. Approximately six hours later, Stewart and Chambers saw the house engulfed in flames on the local television news. It would only be a matter of time before the authorities found out whose home it was and connected it to the bodies and the evidence left behind in the Explorer. There were few choices available. Fearing arrest, Stewart, Johnson, and O'Neal took off for New York, while Chambers fled to Virginia.

On the run for almost a year, Jamale Stewart finally tired of the fugitive life in October 2003, and started negotiations with the Detroit Police Department to turn himself in. Eventually, through his attorney, Stewart worked out a deal with the Wayne County Prosecutor's Office to testify in court to what happened to the three Chaldeans in exchange for a guilty plea to accessory after the fact and felony firearms possession, with a sentencing recommendation of eight to 12 years imprisonment.

Arrested in New York, DuJuan O'Neal was brought to Detroit in early 2004 and questioned regarding his involvement in the triple homicide a little over a year earlier. Under questioning at Detroit police headquarters on the corner of Beaubian Street and Gratiot Avenue, he was advised of his Miranda rights by detective Manuel Guttierez and made the following statements:

Q. Do you recall the incident that occurred on November 19, 2002, involving the murder of three men at 2310 Vermont Street?

A. Yes, I do.

Q. Did you visit the dealership on that day?

A. Yes, I did. I was there with Jamale Stewart; we were looking at cars. Cars are cheaper here than in New York, so I was checking out a Cadillac. I would have bought it but there was something wrong with it.

Q. What happened next?

A. I hadn't been home in a while, so I visited my family. I went to see my brother and I shot craps with him. . . . I got a call from Jamale Stewart, telling me he wanted me to pick up some things from Home Depot. I didn't think a thing of it 'cause his family owns property.

Q. How did you get to your brother's house?

A. In the red Explorer. I asked Jamale if he could find someone else, but he said he left his car at the dealership. So I went to the Home Depot and bought the Shop Vac and chain saw. I was flirting with the lady at the register and everything. Does that seem like something someone would do after they just killed three people?

Q. What happened next?

A. I drove over to Jamale's momma's house on Glendale and gave the truck back to Jamale and Ramone Johnson.

Q. What about the items you purchased at the Home Depot?

A. I gave it to them, also.

Manuel Guttierez testified to these statements made to him at DuJuan O'Neal's trial, noting that O'Neal himself refused to sign the piece of paper on which he had written out the statements. In an attempt to further bolster his alibi, O'Neal's defense lawyer called his wife, Keisha, to testify to the fact that O'Neal had told her in the days leading up to his leaving for Detroit that he was going there to buy a car. The defense for O'Neal was unconvincing, to say the least, and didn't hold up in court. This was especially so when compared to the prosecution's star witness, his own surrogate-son, Jamale Stewart, who got up on the stand and laid out in horrid detail how he witnessed O'Neal slay and then attempt to dismember all three victims. It took little time for the jury to convict DuJuan O'Neal of the triple homicide, followed by the judge issuing a life sentence without the possibility of parole. Unlike the movie franchise of the same name, which started in 1980 and is still going on in one form or another today, Detroit's very own "Friday the 13th" will have no second act.

Interestingly, in the years following O'Neal's conviction, a new theory surfaced regarding the motive for the murders and how they took place—and from more than one source. First, the *Chicago Sun-Times* printed an article in April 2003, examining crime syndicates in the United States with origins in the Middle East, alluding to the fact that the triple homicide in Southwest Detroit could have been a professionally contracted hit. That same year, the National Gang Research Institute, an organization headed by George Knox, a criminal justice professor at Chicago State University, released an analysis of the Chaldean Mafia and declared that the three killings had been the result of a murder contract issued from prison. According to the report, the Chaldean Mafia leadership behind bars, alleged to be led by several of Wesam Akrawi's and Chris Kasshamoun's cousins, was at war with a Muslim-based prison organization. The escalating feud, according to Knox, resulted in the slayings being ordered from "the inside" by the Muslims as a means of gaining leverage on the Chaldeans in their battle for inter-prison supremacy.

Within DuJuan O'Neal's appeal of his triple murder conviction, his appellate attorney points to the fact that his trial counsel never attempted to put into the record the existence of a federal law enforcement report on the killings that states that according to a confidential informant, the murder contract was taken out from prison and given to Jamale Stewart, who then brought in a man named "Rudy" from New York to help with the job.

Contract murders and reports of body dismemberment were nothing new to the Chaldean Mafia. During an internal squabble in the late 1980s, several members of the Chaldean crime syndicate were gunned down execution-style with their respective murder contracts, including cash bonuses for the beheading of the victims.

FROM THE DELTA
TO THE "D"

The Real New Jack City

The rags-to-riches tale of the Chambers brothers, seven siblings who migrated to the Motor City from less-than-meager beginnings in the Deep South, plays out like a Hollywood movie script. The first member of the Chambers family set foot in Detroit in the early 1970s, and they would keep coming until the middle of the next decade. They were ambitious souls in search of prosperity in any form, ready to take it by any means necessary. It took a little while, but by 1985, the Chambers family had gone from growing up dirt poor, without indoor plumping in rural Arkansas, to becoming multi-millionaires living a life of luxury and excess while ruling the Detroit underworld's narcotics industry with almost corporate acumen and efficiency.

Sent to prison in 1988, the Chambers brothers and their gang of Southern recruits, credited by some with being the first group in the city to start selling crack cocaine, left a rich and heavily layered legacy. All bearing an eerie resemblance to one another with their wide foreheads, very dark skin, and short, stout frames, the Chambers boys transcended the drug game to become cultural influences and pseudo-pop culture icons. Anybody who is a fan of the movie *New Jack City* or the New Jack Swing music genre of the early 1990s pays homage to the Chambers crew—primary inspirations for the term "New Jack" itself and everything it represented.

It all started in 1987 when Barry Michael Cooper, at that time an investigative reporter for *The Village Voice*, came to Detroit to do a story on the city's drug trade. He contacted well-known sociologist Carl Taylor, a native Detroiter who taught at Michigan State University and lived in East Lansing, and Taylor pointed him toward the Chambers gang, which he spent several weeks in the Motor City observing first-hand. What Cooper ended up witnessing was documented in an award-winning feature for *The Village Voice* titled, "New Jack City Eats Its Young."

The article spawned a movement, the term "New Jack" going on to represent a substantial shift in urban youth culture and a blending of music, film, dance, and fashion.

Inspired by Cooper's words, Harlem-based recording artist and producer Teddy Riley created the "New Jack Swing" sound, a late-'80s and early-'90s music genre fusing rap, jazz, traditional R&B, and hip hop. Within months, the *Village Voice* piece was optioned for a movie and became the 1991 gangster classic, *New Jack City*, starring Wesley Snipes as flamboyant and diabolical drug kingpin Nino Brown, a character partially based on one of the Chambers brothers and his methods of operation. Although the new sound and the popular film—scripted by Cooper himself—were based in New York, the roots of both were unquestionably seeded in Detroit with the Chambers gang and everything it stood for. A career-making, nationally televised speech by a then-unknown Arkansas governor named Bill Clinton, delivered at the 1988 Democratic Convention, further ingrained the Chambers family into the fabric of that time by citing their rise and fall as an example of the criminal ingenuity being displayed by the nation's youth and the severity of the country's crack epidemic.

"I don't believe that family [the Chambers brothers] came up North to become criminals, but that's what they became," said Carl Taylor. "They came to Detroit to better themselves, get jobs in the plants, find a better life. When they realized that they couldn't sustain that dream or that certain variables prevented them from attaining it, things got twisted real fast and they turned to making a living on the street. Obviously, they were pretty good at it."

Taylor points to the gang's ability to find success in spite of the fact that the Chambers boys and their crew were viewed by most as outsiders, interlopers from the South with a country mentality: "What they did was rare in the sense that these young men were outsiders and they were able to come in without any real help from the Detroit homeboys and basically take over a huge part of the city just for themselves," Taylor noted. "These were country boys and guys around here kind of dismissed them as hayseeds and didn't really give them the time of day at first. But it wasn't long before that all changed and the locals were forced to give them their respect because they [the Chambers brothers] were a force of nature in that once they got going, their operation was rolling and constantly growing."

When the final curtain closed on the gang and its antics, the Chambers brothers' organization was the most lucrative street-level drug-dealing operation in U.S history up until that time. The Chambers family took the whole city by storm. Detroit had never seen anything like this batch of Southern-raised sin-spinners. These young men might not have come to the city thinking they would turn it on its head. But they did. Boy, how they did.

◇◇◇◇◇◇◇◇◇◇◇◇

Curtis and Hazel Chambers were both born in Lee County, Arkansas, a community in the southeastern part of the state, about an hour's drive west of Memphis, that had a long history of cotton farming, economic despair and strict segregation. The couple met when they were teenagers attending school in Marianna, a county center point that exemplified the region's racial divide. Hazel was only 13 years old when she started dating Curtis, who was almost 19 and attending high school later than usual due to spending his earlier teen years working as a sharecropper.

In 1948, Curtis, 22, and Hazel, two months away from turning 17, married and moved onto a family-owned, 44-acre farm and plantation that sat on the borderline between Marianna and La Grange, a mostly black and impoverished farming village on the outskirts of the county. Over the next two decades, the couple would go on to have 16 children—12 boys and four girls. Around 1967, Curtis and Hazel opened up a bar and restaurant on their land, and soon the road leading to the Chambers' property was packed at all hours of the night and early morning with people coming to and going from the county's newest hot spot. Variously referred to as The Tin Top Inn, The Blue Swan, or simply Curt's Place, and in lockstep with the area's customs, it catered to an all-black clientele. The loud and sweaty watering hole became a remarkable learning environment for aspiring criminals. There wasn't anything that couldn't be found there. You name it, they had it: live music, food, booze, dancing, drugs, gambling, pool, dice, prostitution— it was all available for the right price.

However, unlike many future master criminals who are schooled in the way of the underworld by their fathers, it was the Chambers boys' mother, Hazel, who conducted the course in "Hustling 101" for her ambitious offspring. If there was a trick to be turned or a scam to be hatched, Hazel was there in a flash. Such behavior did little to endear her to her husband, who routinely had his wife's public extramarital dalliances flaunted in his face and, in turn, beat her vigorously in private.

One by one, the Chambers boys began getting old enough to fend for themselves, and they started to leave the family nest of their Marianna farm. Curtis Chambers Jr., the eldest son, was the first to leave, going to St. Louis before shipping out to Vietnam to serve his country in the military during the late 1960s. Larry and Danny, the next two eldest boys, wound up in St. Louis as well, an alternative homestead for the family back then since Hazel Chambers' parents had moved there after Hazel had married Curtis in 1948.

As Larry drifted toward an early adult life of petty crime and frequent incarceration, Danny left St. Louis shortly after his arrival and became the first Chambers brother to reach Detroit in 1970, fresh from a six-month stay with his aunt on his father's side in nearby Flint. He went to work in an East Side welding factory and was followed to the Motor City four years later by his brother Willie and sister Delois.

Willie Chambers graduated from Marianna's Lee High School in 1972, spent two years in the Army stationed in San Diego and finally settled in the Motor City in 1974, getting a steady job delivering mail for the post office. Eventually, Danny left his job at the welding factory and went to work at a Dearborn-based plant that manufactured automobile carriages. While working on the assembly line there, he became friends with a fellow Lee County native named L.C. "Big Terry" Colbert, who had a mid-level marijuana distribution network set up on the side. Danny had no idea that in a matter of a few short years, Colbert and his connections in the local drug world would wind up changing his and his whole family's lives.

It wouldn't be Danny Chambers, however, who would facilitate this change in his family's situation and subsequently its bank account. Instead, it would be his baby brother, Billy Joe, a mere 16 years old when he arrived in Michigan in the summer of 1978, ready to take on the world. And he soon would, with the help of practically all his siblings. With Hazel and Curtis divorcing in 1976, there was little keeping Billy Joe Chambers in Marianna. "B.J." as he was known, had a mind for business at an early age and was fast to understand that if he wanted to make big moves, he had to be in the big city. Marianna, he knew, wasn't that place. Before even completing his junior year in high school, B.J. picked up and left Arkansas, traveling to Detroit to live with his two brothers. B.J. enrolled at Detroit Kettering High School in the fall, and although he would never receive his diploma, he used the school's job placement office to land employment at a local shoe store where he went to work as a janitor in the afternoons after class. It was a meager beginning for someone who would go on to become one of the most successful drug kingpins in American history, but B.J. swallowed his pride and did his work diligently.

Along with his new best friend, Jerry "J-Man" Gant, Big Terry Colbert's little brother, B.J. started making some extra money by selling marijuana for Colbert out of "The T and T," a restaurant and convenience store Colbert opened up after getting laid off from his job at the plant. Welcoming a son, Billy Jr., into the world with a girlfriend of his named Niece (pronounced Nee-Cee) in the spring of 1980, B.J. quit his job at the shoe store and decided not to go back to Kettering for his senior year, opting instead to take an unofficial apprenticeship under Colbert at The T and T and start fending for his soon-to-be growing family.

Adding a daughter to the abode with Niece in 1981, B.J. was schooled in the ways of the narcotics trade by Colbert, who took an immediate liking to the young and hungry fledgling street pharmacist. Proving a smart pupil, B.J. branched off on his own in the drug world in 1982, setting up a base of operations at "Willie's Retail Store," a virtual clone of The T and T opened by him and his brother Willie at the corner of St. Clair and Kerchival on the far East Side of the city. The store and a neighboring car wash were in Willie's name and on property he had purchased with savings from his nearly 10 years on the job as a postman.

Displaying his well-honed business sense, B.J. used the dual properties to launch his own drug empire, pushing marijuana and heroin out of both the store and the car wash. With a steady supply line of drugs coming from Big Terry Colbert and surrounded by a close-knit crew of lieutenants made up of family members and trusted associates, the aspiring kingpin was off and running. B.J. kept his inner circle relatively small. Besides himself, there was his identical twin, Little Joe (also known as "Yo-Yo"); his older brothers Danny, Willie, and David; his best friend Jerry Gant; Big Terry's son, Little Terry, and two of his girlfriend's brothers, Perry "P-Boy" Coleman and Willie "Boogaloo" Driscoll.

Then there was his workforce, an ever-expanding group of teenagers and young adults that, as soon as the Chambers organization was up and operating, started relocating en masse from Arkansas, looking to make money in the Detroit drug game. DEA documents from the era estimate that over 300 young men and woman from Marianna and the surrounding areas of the Delta migrated to the Motor City and went to work selling drugs for the Chambers gang. The seeds of success had been planted. They would soon blossom into a garden of riches the likes of which were well beyond any of the brothers' wildest dreams. Diminutive in size—barely five-feet-five in height—B.J. made up for his lack of physical stature with an ironclad will, a natural business sense, and a gigantic ambition. Once he got started in business for himself, he wasted little time imposing all three on the city he called his adopted hometown.

◇◇◇◇◇◇◇◇◇◇◇◇

By the early part of 1984, B.J. Chambers had already become one of the biggest drug dealers in the city, operating out of Willie's Retail Store on St. Clair and Kerchival—which by that time had been renamed "B.J.'s Party Store"—and several local residences across the East Side that he purchased and converted into fully functional product factories and sale houses. And things were about to get much, much bigger. Around this time, B.J. was introduced to crack cocaine by Perry Coleman, his girlfriend Niece's older brother. Back when B.J. first arrived in Detroit, Coleman was someone who had taken him under his wing and showed him the ropes around the local streets. As the years went on, B.J. began tapping Coleman as an alternate source for marijuana, if Big Terry Colbert was ever running low, and going to him for counsel on business strategy. Coleman had recently started selling crack, the newly created super drug—cocaine in smokeable rock form, and was eager to promote its merits to his former street protégé. Soon, B.J. was including rocks of cocaine in the menu of products being sold out of his party store, and within a matter of weeks it replaced marijuana and heroin as his primary source of illegal income.

Up until the summer of 1984, B.J. and his family were not even remotely on the radar of area law enforcement. Then came the month of August when word on the street had reached a fevered pitch about the Chambers boys and their prowess moving crack. The cops could no longer ignore them. Within weeks, by Labor Day in fact, the brothers and their drug organization were smack dab in the middle of that radar, and squarely in the government's crosshairs. A few months of heavy crack dealing had made the Chambers brothers and their laidback yet lurid leader a top priority. Crack cocaine and those who peddled it were targeted by the city, state and federal authorities as "Public Enemy No. 1," and as soon as police started culling information from their widely placed snitches, the name they kept hearing was B.J. Chambers. Old school dealers who sold "junk" and "weed" were shuffled to the back burner, and a freshly convened task force of Detroit police, and DEA and FBI agents set their sights on finding out everything they could uncover on the mysterious out-of-towners who were flying up the ladder of the local underworld.

"They were really the first group in the city to start moving crack cocaine at a major level," said Robert De Fauw, the head of the DEA in Detroit from 1978 to 1987. "We became aware of the Chambers brothers at the same time the crack epidemic hit. Both took the city by storm."

The task force's top street unit dubbed itself the "No Crack Crew" and was made up of grit-laced, adrenaline-junkie cops, all ready to roll 24 hours a day, seven days a week and at a second's notice. Pounding the pavement at a relentless pace, gathering information and raiding suspected drug houses, these guys worked hard and partied even harder. Most interestingly, even though nearly all of the criminals they were trying to take down were black, practically all of the members of the task force and 100 percent of the No Crack Crew were white.

The undisputed leader of the No Crack Crew, composed primarily of DPD narco squad detectives, was Gerard "Mick the Bronco" Biernacki. His nickname said it all. For good and for bad, Biernacki was an animal on the job, exhibiting unbridled intensity and aggression and manic-like compulsion in pursuit of his targets. An ex-Marine who served on the front lines in Vietnam, Bronco Biernacki became a drug cop in 1973 and ended up serving more than two decades on the job, participating in over 1,000 arrests and convictions. The No Crack Crew developed a reputation for high-profile arrests and for being fixtures on the local nightly news broadcasts, but some of its members became known for their questionable views on race relations.

"Detroit was a great place to work narcotics until the blacks became bosses," said Greg Woods, a No Crack Crew member from a long line of Detroit police officers. He was quoted in William Adler's book, *Land of Opportunity*, which chronicled the Chambers brothers' organizations and the men in law enforcement who tried to lock them up. "But I'll be honest, I'm a racist. Fuck them niggers."

Having operated for over two years without so much as a sniff in their direc-tion from the police, August and September 1984 put an end to any form of ano-nymity the Chambers clan thought they might have possessed. Between mid-August and early September, B.J. had four busts, resulting in two arrests. The first was a charge of assault on a police officer, lodged against B.J. and Little Joe, that stemmed from a street brawl between the pair of twins and two DPD patrolmen who had made a traffic stop of B.J. in front of his house. The incident, although not drug-related, would serve as the impetus for a vendetta forged by the federal task force, specifically Biernacki and the No Crack Crew, against the Chambers family, and it set into motion a nearly five-year cat-and-mouse game that they vowed to win at all costs.

B.J.'s second arrest came on Labor Day and as a result of a raid of his residence on Gray Street, which uncovered nearly 2,000 small packets of rock cocaine. It was on the Labor Day 1984 raid—the second the brothers had faced in two weeks, and one of many in a long line of them dating from 1984 until 1988—that B.J. Chambers was positively identified for the first time in person by police. Going to great lengths over the previous two years to keep his appearance a secret to law enforcement, the pint-sized drug don's cover was officially blown when an infor-mant pointed him out to surveillance agents who were watching the house prior to the raid. One member of the task force was so surprised by B.J.'s young age that he commented, "Nigger, I thought you was an old man."

The No Crack Crew was so overjoyed that they were finally able to pinpoint who the gang's leader actually was that the members of the rough and rugged police battalion started chanting "Billy Joe, Billy Joe, Billy Joe" as the brothers and their associates were rounded up outside the house. Handcuffed and chained together in a line, those placed under arrest—including B.J.'s brother, Danny, and his first cousin, Alvin "Frog" Chambers—were forced to announce "We sell dope, we sell dope, we sell dope" as they were paraded around a crowded street corner on which neighborhood residents had assembled to witness the siren-filled commo-tion. They were then placed in a DPD paddy wagon that had been called to the scene to haul them away.

Although the drug bust would not stick due to a technicality, the incident dealt a severe blow to B.J. and his whole organization. First, it placed a giant target on B.J.'s back, but second and more importantly, it would serve as a predicate offense for a massive narcotics indictment years down the road. On September 10, 1984, B.J. and Danny had their house on Gray Street raided for the third time in three weeks, this time with Big Terry Colbert inside. Nobody was arrested, but B.J., Danny, and Big Terry were all cuffed, placed in the back of a police vehicle, and taken by the No Crack Crew on a raid of one of their competitors' drug houses a few blocks away. The tactic was one of general harassment and was used as a means of making B.J. and his crew look bad to other dealers by making it appear that they tipped off the cops about the whereabouts of their rivals' place of business.

B.J. was no dummy. The heat was being heavily applied, and there would be no escaping its wrath if he kept to his routine. He needed to make some changes. And so, as the rest of the city was preparing for the first trip to the playoffs in 12 years by its beloved Detroit Tigers, B.J. Chambers vanished from sight, taking refuge on the family farm in Arkansas for the next 10 months, hundreds of miles away from the tight scrutiny he was facing up north.

◇◇◇◇◇◇◇◇◇◇◇◇◇

Of all the Chambers brothers, the only one with a significant criminal record prior to the family's entrance into the drug trade was Larry, the third eldest sibling. "Marlow," as he was sometimes called, was highly intelligent—a prison psychiatrist once tested his I.Q. at well over 140—yet he didn't want a regular nine-to-five job as a young adult, instead finding himself drawn to the jolt he got from living a life on the wrong side of the law. While the rest of his brothers dabbled in some form of legitimate employment before turning to narcotics to make their living, Larry knew from an early age that being a crook was the only existence he ever wanted.

Unlike his younger brother, B.J., however, Larry didn't find his criminal calling until he was practically middle-aged. And as a result of a rigorous and mostly failure-ridden trial-and-error process on the street early in life, his road to the top of the heap was considerably bumpier, filled with crater-sized potholes and a flair for drama worthy of an old Clint Eastwood movie. For a man who would go on to have one of the most memorable careers of any American gangster in the latter half of the 20th century, Larry's career in the underworld got off to quite an inauspicious start: 15 years of arrests, incarcerations, and living on the run as a fugitive with a laundry list of escapes, felonies, and frauds perpetrated along the way.

It wasn't more than a few months after Larry and his brother Danny had left Marianna in the late 1960s and landed in St. Louis that he had his first major arrest. On the day before Christmas Eve 1969, after returning to Arkansas to spend the holiday season with his family, Larry was caught stealing a couple of cars for joyriding with a friend from his boyhood days. After spending Christmas behind bars in the Lee County Jail, he staged an escape on New Year's Eve, springing himself from custody by causing a backup of the toilet in his cell and then overpowering the guard who had come in to fix it.

Hiding out in a nearby church for the night, Larry stole the minister's car in the morning and fled the county. Embarking on a two-day binge of armed robberies—seven in all—he was finally caught along a highway in Ouachita County, in the south central part of the state, as a result of a routine traffic stop by the Arkansas

State Highway Patrol. Living up to his reputation as the "wild card" of the family, Larry wouldn't do down without a fight, and he shot one of the officers coming to his car to request identification. Taking off on foot in below-freezing temperatures, he was apprehended the following morning after a county-wide manhunt and landed himself a 40-year state prison sentence for assault with intent to kill.

Five months into his sentence, Larry escaped and made it all the way to Phoenix before being caught and shipped back home to Arkansas where his prison term was extended to 200 years. It didn't take long for the cagey criminal to work his magic, and he once again escaped by burying himself in a field during chain gang duty and bribing a guard to miscount when the caravan of prisoners was returned to their cells. Waiting a sufficient amount of time for everybody to leave, Larry emerged from the earth and went on another crime spree, robbing several gas stations and stealing a car on his way to visit a prison acquaintance in Pittsburgh. A few weeks later, on his way back to Marianna to try to sneak in a visit with his family, he was caught in a botched attempt to rob a jewelry store in Wynne, in northeastern Arkansas.

Luckily for Larry, the state parole board showed mercy on him and he was released from prison in 1976 after serving only five years. Unluckily for Larry, his taste of freedom would be short-lived, and a mere 30 days after being paroled, he was arrested for robbing a post office in Helena, Arkansas, roughly 15 miles outside of Marianna. While awaiting trial in the local police station jail, Larry escaped three more times; he was tracked down after short stints on the run each time before finally being convicted of the robbery and sentenced to three years in prison.

Almost exactly one year later, in the summer of 1977, Larry had his conviction reversed by the state supreme court as the result of a lengthy, handwritten appeal prepared by Larry himself, and he returned to Marianna to try to live a reformed life. Like many of his earlier endeavors, his time trying to go straight didn't last long. By Thanksgiving 1977, Larry had resorted to his past behavior and resumed his old habits, carrying out another string of robberies. In the fall of 1979, he was arrested for possessing half a dozen firearms stolen from a Marianna area gun shop and was returned to prison for eight months.

Starting in the spring of 1980, Larry hit an unusual hot streak. Upon his release from incarceration, he went on a run of nearly a year and a half of uninterrupted success, robbing jewelry stores in small towns across the state of Arkansas. Larry himself estimated that he robbed over 100 stores in that time period, usually by drilling a hole in the ceiling in the middle of the night and clearing out the place before morning. The hot streak came to an abrupt end in late 1981 when Larry was brought down by authorities in Detroit, ironically the city where in only a few short years his fortunes in the criminal world would reach a crescendo. Wanted by numerous law enforcement bureaus in the South, Larry came to Detroit that October to take refuge and hide out with his brothers. The previous month

Larry and a friend he had met in prison had stolen a money order machine from an Arkansas post office and the pair had been making a steady amount of cash selling the orders from the machine on the black market. While at his younger brother Willie's house one afternoon, he received a phone call from his accomplice in Arkansas who said he had an uncle of his in Detroit who wanted to purchase some money orders. It was a setup.

Meeting at a Highland Park motel off Woodward to make the transaction, Larry was surprised to find out that the accomplice's alleged uncle was in fact an undercover U.S. Postal Inspector. His former prison buddy had ratted him out. Arrested for theft of government property, among some other back charges levied by the state of Arkansas, Larry was sentenced to four years, most of it to be served at the federal penitentiary at Leavenworth, Kansas.

Larry's time locked up at Leavenworth—a prison with a long history of housing some of the nation's most notorious and dangerous hoodlums—didn't go to waste. Within weeks of entering the facility, he underwent a complete mind and body transformation, laying a solid foundation for what he would be able to accomplish in the years to come. He swore off drugs, alcohol, caffeine, and tobacco—four of his most cherished vices—and became a devout advocate of yoga and spiritual meditation, which he promoted vigorously and taught to his fellow inmates. Never before interested in physical fitness or personal health, Larry became a vegetarian and workout fanatic, lifting weights and running for hours at a time around the width of the fenced-in yard. Faced with many hours of solitude in his cell, he began reading dozens of books about philosophy, politics, and business strategy. Proving the consummate opportunist, Larry utilized his general criminal savvy and what he learned from his reading and opened up a series of prison rackets ranging from gambling and loansharking to contraband smuggling and extortion.

In just over three years, Larry's business interests in prison netted him approximately $50,000 in cash, a nest egg that he planned to hatch the minute he was free. Once known for his unpredictability and a quirky disposition, Larry Chambers became completely transfixed by self-discipline and regimentation. For a little while at least, it would serve him very well. And the nest egg he cultivated would grow to be very large.

◇◇◇◇◇◇◇◇◇◇◇◇

Released on April 29, 1985, after nearly 40 months behind bars, Larry was quick to reunite with his younger brothers. Larry knew that B.J., at that time hiding out in Arkansas, was making major money dealing drugs in Detroit, and he wanted in on the new family business. Having always admired his older brother, even though most of his contact with him was in prison visiting rooms, B.J. offered to bring Larry into his operation without hesitation, encouraged by how transformative the years in prison had been for him. The pair hooked up at the family farm in Marianna and spent a few months getting to know each other—sharing ideas, good times and a stream of beautiful women whom B.J. always had on tap no matter where he was.

Although in self-imposed exile in Marianna for almost a year, B.J. kept tabs on his interests in Detroit through Jerry Gant and his brother David, both of whom he had left in charge of his organization while he was away. This new "hands-off" approach to his drug operations, while allowing B.J. to relax at the Chambers family homestead without the worry of police harassment, proved bad for business. The suitcases and garbage bags filled with cash being delivered on a monthly basis to B.J. in Arkansas got ever smaller. Being out of town was severely cutting into his bottom line. The numbers didn't lie and he couldn't ignore them.

"J-Man" and David were not up to the task and failed to maintain the status quo while their boss was away. As the summer of 1985 went into full swing, B.J. had no other choice but to head back to Detroit with Larry in tow to recharge the battery of the family business himself. Little did he know just how much his big brother would help out in the process and how epic their collaboration would be when it was all said and done. When B.J. and Larry reached Detroit in July, they immediately set about getting the organization back in order. Disappointed with his underlings' lack of drive and self-motivation, B.J. broomed his entire staff—with the exception of Gant and his brothers, Joe, David, Willie, and Danny—and decided to start fresh. Things were not up to par and he largely blamed those who surrounded him. His siblings got a pass because they were blood. Because Gant was practically a brother to him, he was exempted, too. Everyone else got the axe.

Little Terry Colbert and Boogaloo Driscoll were let go because they would often neglect their work duties in favor of smoking the cocaine they were being paid to sell. They thought they could hide their increasingly troublesome habits, but B.J. was well aware of what was going on. He had no time for slackers. Business was business and time was money. Both were gone the minute B.J. returned to town. Giving Larry his own wing of the family business to run by himself, B.J. assembled a new group of foot soldiers made up mostly of young Arkansas-bred teenagers sent north to manufacture and sell crack on his behalf in what started out as half a dozen different houses, but soon swelled to well over 50. He replaced Colbert and Driscoll in his inner circle with Anthony "Tony the Tiger" Alexander and Eric "Fats" Wilkins, two 19-year-old Detroiters who were loyal, hungry, and hot-tempered, and used them as his conduits to the streets for day-to-day control of business operations. A fellow Marianna native, Marshall "Cadillac Mario" Glenn, established himself as the main go-between for B.J.'s and Larry's personal entourages and became a key liaison to things back on the home front in Arkansas.

There was little time for Larry to adjust. From almost the moment he hit the city, he was thrust into the thick of things, but there was no other way Larry would have liked it. Despite the fact that he had been locked up for the better part of 15 years, B.J. had tremendous faith in his big brother and entrusted him with a large amount of responsibility right away. Larry was a fast learner, quickly thriving in his new role as drug lord. He hit the ground running and never looked back.

Just like B.J., Larry grabbed a handful of Arkansas transplants as workers, got a pair of formidable top lieutenants in Roderick "Hot Rod" Byrd and William "Jack Frost" Jackson, and immediately took over control of several of the family's drug houses. Eager to stay busy in his free time away from the narcotics business and to keep feeding his mind the way he did in prison, Larry started taking weekday classes in Spanish and music history at Wayne State University. He also enrolled in classes at the university to learn to play the clarinet and saxophone.

Soon after arriving in the Motor City, Larry began dating Belinda Lumpkin, a local girl of 15 and some two decades his junior. As he amassed money in his first months on the job, Larry had Belinda move in with him in the downstairs flat of a two-home residence owned by his brother David near Knodell and Gratiot. It was a modest place, but only the beginning. The best of what life had to offer was just on the horizon. There was no rush; Larry had become a patient man. While he was once haphazard in his movements, he became deliberate and calculated. These newfound virtues were about to be rewarded.

◇◇◇◇◇◇◇◇◇◇◇◇◇

Within months of B.J.'s and Larry's return to Detroit, the Chambers brothers' drug organization was expanding at a tremendous rate. While at the organization's previous peak, it owned and operated half a dozen manufacturing and sales locations, by the mid-fall of 1985, the number was well into the double figures. Old-time connections like Perry Coleman and Big Terry Colbert could no longer handle B.J.'s and Larry's supply demands, so B.J. went directly to their source, Sam "Doc" Curry and Art Derrick: the biggest wholesale suppliers of pure Colombian cocaine in the whole Detroit area. The pair might have appeared odd at first glance—Curry was black, slick, and well-manicured, while Derrick was white, slovenly, and middle-aged with the look of a used car salesman—but their success in moving mass amounts of drugs more than made up for any visible shortcomings they might have exhibited. Derrick, who later died of a drug overdose after serving a 10-year federal prison sentence, once estimated that he and Curry were bringing in $100,000 per day in profits for close to three years.

Using an introduction provided by Perry Coleman, B.J., Larry, Curry, and Derrick consummated a lucrative partnership. In a series of interviews before his death, Derrick—who was known on the street as "AD" and lived in a mansion in Harper Woods—declared that the two siblings were easily his operation's biggest customer. While for a short while prior to B.J.'s 10-month sabbatical from the drug game, the Chambers brothers' organization was one of the city's largest street distributors of cocaine, for much of the late 1980s, it was the largest by far.

Although Larry respected his brother and the way he did business and would never forget the fact that B.J. gave him his start in the drug world, he didn't agree with the way B.J. ran his crew. It was clear from very early on in their business relationship that the two brothers had two very different and distinct styles of leadership. B.J.'s command was loose, non-authoritative, and very employee-friendly. Larry's demeanor as a boss was strict, highly organized, and designed to strike fear in every single one of his subordinates. While B.J. might take his crew on an all-expense-paid trip down to Florida or out to Las Vegas and was prone to impromptu jaunts to nearby Ohio amusement parks like Cedar Point in Sandusky and Kings Island in Cincinnati, Larry could often be seen putting his crew through rigorous physical training and constant drilling on security procedures out in front of his places of business. In some ways the two bosses worked well together; in other ways they butted heads. The more comfortable Larry became in the narcotics business, the further he distanced his day-to-day operations from those of his little brother. The newspapers, television newscasts, and police may have portrayed them to the public as a single entity, but by early 1986, B.J. and Larry were running two separate organizations that, while loosely connected by sheer convenience, were in essence competing against each other in the ultimate game of sibling one-upmanship.

"They pushed each other and motivated one another to grow the business," Robert De Fauw said of the two siblings. "Larry got to town and adapted to his surroundings very quickly. He had new ideas and influenced B.J. to think about shaking up the original business model. The further they pushed the envelope, though, the easier they became to combat in that our marching orders increased and so did our budget. Once Larry got in the picture, they really put themselves front and center on everybody's radar. I mean it was impossible to ignore them and what they were doing."

After a little under a year overseeing the operations of a handful of crack houses, Larry desired to expand—and in a major way. He wanted to carve out his own niche in the local underworld, separate from that of the one B.J. originally created for the family three years earlier and the one he was currently helping to improve. Larry fancied himself a gangland innovator. He had big plans and big dreams. The drug empire his younger brother had built was a good start, but he still wanted more. That's where the nest egg of cash from prison days came in. Larry took that $50,000 sum and along with some money he had stashed away in his first few months of dealing crack, he bought himself an entire apartment building. He intended to turn the apartment complex into a 24-hour emporium of vice the likes of which the Motor City hadn't seen since the racket-filled Prohibition era. In a lot of ways, it mirrored the business tactics once employed by his mother at her Marianna watering hole.

Scouting several locations for his flagship drug superstore, in early March 1986, Larry finally decided to purchase The Broadmoor, a four-story, horseshoe-shaped complex at 1350 East Grand Boulevard that was constructed as luxury living quarters for the city's elite back in the 1920s, but that had since become a victim of extreme urban decay and housed a variety of low-income residents. The outward appearance of the red brick building meant little to Larry. He knew that the clientele he wanted would care considerably more about the services they were being provided than the manner in which the property was decorated and maintained.

Like a wartime rebel force, Larry and his crew invaded and took over the whole block. Owners of neighboring residences were forced to relinquish their homes for use as stash spots or security posts. Those who resided in The Broadmoor were strong-armed into letting their apartments be used for the production and sale of crack cocaine. Apartment owners were enticed with reductions in rent and cash bonuses for making their residences available to Larry's staff of workers. The building's longtime manager, David Havard, had his pay doubled to look the other way and keep his mouth shut. Havard's live-in girlfriend, Patricia Middleton, was hired by Larry to help calculate his weekly payroll and act as a general den mother, looking after the building's upkeep and managing the stove in the backroom eatery.

Quickly gaining the street moniker "Rambo" for his militant intensity in running his crew at The Broadmoor, Larry structured his one-of-a-kind business like a corporation. As soon as customers entered the building's first floor, they were greeted by an employee who escorted them to their desired location. For instance, different-sized rocks of cocaine were sold on different floors with the most expensive being found in the "penthouse," which served as a VIP area of sorts. In the back part of the first floor, Larry set up a pawnshop and a makeshift bar and grill. The second floor housed a lounge, complete with couches, card tables, and a big-screen television, where customers were encouraged to indulge in their purchases right there on the premises. The third and fourth floors were slightly higher-class, with powdered cocaine being sold and the quality of the furnishings somewhat better (leather couches and recliners, cable TV, a closed-circuit feed for all the major professional boxing matches of the day). The third and fourth floors also featured a selection of prostitutes supplied by Larry and a number of rooms set aside for them to ply their trade.

Like any manager of a successful business, Larry was compulsive when it came to customer service. He instructed all of his employees to treat everyone who sought to purchase drugs from them, whether they were the lowest junkie or the best-dressed kingpin, with the utmost respect, courtesy, and kindness. During his busiest days, which normally came on the weekends, Larry would send around free shots of tequila and offer special "two-for-one" deals. Even those employees who worked as security staff and toted submachine guns were told to be personable and as non-threatening as possible when dealing with customers, police, or potential troublemakers.

The expenditure Larry put out to buy the building, eventually dubbed simply "The Boulevard," was soon paying astronomical dividends. Once up and running—a process that took less than a month—the full-service house of hedonism was taking in close to $100,000 a day of cash profit. Taking advantage of his newfound riches, Larry moved from his brother's house to a nicer residence, which he bought on Buffalo Street near the intersection of Six Mile and Mound, and then to one on Albion that looked from the outside like a modest, two-story abode, but was in fact outfitted with opulent furnishings and accessories in nearly every part. Eventually, he would purchase multiple pieces of real estate, both across the city of Detroit and in Jamaica; a trove of jewelry, cars, and furs; and a slew of entertainment toys. Larry still ran a few scattered crack houses on the side, but he consolidated most of his operation under the roof of The Boulevard. B.J, Willie, and David began joking one day that their brother should shell out some money and shoot a commercial advertising the fact that you can find anything you want under one roof at The Boulevard. Allegedly, Larry chimed in and said he would call it "Marlow's One-Stop." Nino Brown's takeover of the Carter Housing Project in *New Jack City* was clearly inspired by Marlow's One-Stop at The Boulevard.

If you were diligent and well-intentioned, working for Larry was a pleasure, far from the thankless and often hazardous work environment experienced by most in the lower regions of the drug trade. Larry was a strong believer in the concept of meritocracy and incentive-based employment. Every worker had a quota to meet for the job they were assigned, and those who exceeded their quota were rewarded with cash bonuses. Extra money was always offered and promptly delivered to workers who clocked overtime on their shifts, brought in new customers and/or other employees, and helped with any menial chores that needed to be done around the sales locations. Those who showed loyalty to the organization were looked after and compensated tremendously well. Larry's employees were showered with perks and fringe benefits. Food, lodging, child day care, laundry service, and legal counsel were all provided free of charge to those under Larry's command.

Posted on a wall in every one of Larry's crack houses, including a larger-sized, laminated version in the front hall of The Boulevard, was a typewritten list of rules and fines for all of his workers that came to be known as "The Crack Commandments." The list of regulations was strictly adhered to and enforced, and it told its readers everything they needed to know about Larry's meticulous and ardent nature as a commander-in-chief.

Please Read
- With hard work and dedication you will be rich within 12 months.
- Your success in this organization will depend on how well you follow instructions.
- Employees will be graded and promoted according to their work and conduct.
- If you are planning on getting rich, forget about your girlfriend and family and expect to have very little time for parties and concerts.
- You are "on call" 24 hours a day.
- No chains or gaudy jewelry are to be worn while working.
- All money must be picked up from ALL of the houses before 6 a.m.
- You are never to ride with drugs and money at the same time.
- Drop-offs should be done in segments (do not ride with all the drugs in your car at the same time).
- If you recommend a worker who ends up stealing from the organization, you are responsible for paying for the loss out of your own pocket.

Fines
- Stealing Money or Drugs – $300
- Fighting – $100
- Neglecting ones duties – $100
- Getting high on the job – $300
- Failing to follow instructions – $100
- Talking out of school (revealing secrets about the organization to outsiders) – $500
- Playing loud music during drop-offs and pick-ups – $50
- Bringing outsiders (unauthorized personnel) into your place of work – $500
- If you are caught riding by yourself (pick-ups and drop-offs must be done in pairs) – $100
- Stopping for personal affairs while "riding dirty" – $400
- Lying – $500
- Intentionally causing confusion amongst the staff – $200
- Speeding while making drop-offs and pick-ups – $100

It is rumored that "The 10 Crack Commandments," the drug game anthem of slain rap legend Christopher "Notorious B.I.G." Wallace, was inspired by Larry Chambers himself, at that time almost a decade removed from his heyday on the streets. The story goes that Wallace was told of the Chambers brothers' exploits in the Motor City underworld, specifically the sheet of rules Larry posted on the walls of all his crack houses, by one of his friends from Detroit, and wrote the future classic in homage to Larry's ingenuity.

The dream had been achieved. Larry was the king of crack, and accordingly he was treated like a god. His arrival at The Boulevard was as if an international head of state was arriving for a public appearance. Prior to getting out of his car, Larry's men made sure all nearby streets and alleyways underwent security sweeps. Flanked by bodyguards and his top lieutenant, Rod Byrd, a sharp-minded college grad he had met while taking classes at Wayne State, Larry strutted from his Mercedes Benz into his ever-busy cathedral of sin. He then made his rounds, half inspecting the premises for any breach of protocol by his staff, and half glad-handing and schmoozing with his diverse clientele. As soon as word that Larry was in the building started to spread, kids from around the neighborhood scurried to The Boulevard and stopped at his feet, eager to be the beneficiary of one of Marlow Chambers' famous $100 handshakes or, better yet, to be offered a job working in his organization. Besides running The Boulevard, Larry oversaw the operations of close to 50 of the gang's 150 crack houses spread across the city. The real Nino Brown was born.

◇◇◇◇◇◇◇◇◇◇◇◇◇

Almost as soon as the Chambers brothers' gang reached the top of the drug food chain in Detroit, a six-month streak of bad luck put in motion a series of events that would eventually lead to the organization's downfall. The doom-filled half-year started on March 29, 1986, just a mere three weeks following Larry's opening of The Boulevard, when Little Joe Chambers was killed in Marianna. B.J.'s twin brother died in a brutal automobile accident, getting hit by an oncoming freight train while trying to beat it across the tracks. This was only a month after his release from serving a two-year federal prison sentence for stealing food stamps and postal money order slips back in Michigan. With a few stragglers left behind to tend to the family business, practically the entire Chambers brothers workforce followed B.J. and Larry down to Arkansas in a caravan of expensive cars for Little Joe's funeral, which was held on April 4th. After partying the night away following the interment, toasting copious glasses of cognac and champagne to his honor, the Chambers brothers and their convoy returned to Detroit and got back to work. Included in the organization's caravan back up north were close to two dozen new recruits from their hometown, mostly underage youths between the ages of 12 and 16, that B.J. and Larry had brought back with them with the intention of opening a pair of new crack houses in Little Joe's honor. Trying to honor their deceased brother became a major priority in the month of April. Prior to leaving for the funeral, both siblings bought new, flashy cars for the ride down home, each of a specific variety that their little brother was known to favor. Once they returned, B.J. instructed his entire crew to start referring to him on the streets as "Yo Yo," Little Joe's former alias, as a way to further commemorate his passing.

Then came a brief but much-celebrated and audaciously announced return to Marianna by the group a few weeks later in May for their baby brother Otis' high school graduation. This was highlighted by their arrival in town and appearance at the graduation in a fleet of stretch limousines. On their return to Detroit, they brought even more recruits to work in the family's narcotics empire. The recruit with the most expectations attached to his arrival in the Motor City was Otis himself, immediately tapped by B.J. and Larry to head the gang's security staff and enforcement unit. Otis, whose hair-trigger demeanor was considerably more reminiscent of Larry than B.J., gladly accepted the appointment and was quick to earn a reputation around his new neighborhood as someone who was capable, conniving, and fast to shoot.

The beginning of the end for the Chambers brothers came in August 1986, courtesy of three significant occurrences. In the first week of the month, Patricia Middleton, Larry's den mother at The Boulevard, contacted the No Crack Crew and started providing inside intelligence on the organization's workings. These intelligence briefings would lead to a series of raids that uncovered evidence proving lethal to the siblings' operation. Secondly, sometime in the middle of the month, in an attempt to impress a couple of neighborhood girls they had brought back to Larry's house, he and his lieutenant, "Jack Frost" Jackson, decided to tape themselves clowning around with the mountains of cash they had made that day selling drugs. This would be one incident recorded in a series of videotapes that highlighted the luxurious, crime-ridden, and excess-filled life being led by Marlow Chambers. To his ultimate detriment, he decided to keep and store these tapes in a home movie library. The third and final nail hammered in the brothers' coffins that August was a raid of two of the organization's drug houses by the No Crack Crew, the first pair in what would end up as a series of successful raids that the ambitious narco unit would conduct over the next three months. Both raids took place simultaneously at 1:30 in the afternoon on Monday, August 25th, and they yielded stashes of powdered cocaine and bundles of cash. The organization was under siege, barely providing any time for the Chambers brothers to enjoy their time on the throne.

"Bronco" Biernacki and the No Crack Crew sewed up their case against the massive and multi-layered drug syndicate in early October by gaining the cooperation of Little Terry Colbert, the onetime insider in B.J.'s crew, who had since been relegated to the outskirts of the gang as punishment for a bothersome drug habit he had developed. Colbert might have been on the outer edges of the Chambers brothers' organization, but he still had a good deal of access to the gang's inner workings because of his father. Days after garnering Colbert's help, the No Crack Crew executed its third raid in as many weeks, hitting Larry's house on Albion Street with a full ground and air battalion, as well as up-and-coming local investigative TV reporter Chris Hansen, with cameras in tow.

At first glance, it looked like a big flameout. In the first 45 minutes of their search of the residence, the police and television cameras had failed to find one piece of incriminating evidence. There were no drugs, sales or manufacturing paraphernalia, nor any signs of hidden stashes of illicit cash. Then, suddenly, they struck gold and uncovered the "Holy Grail." The find would net the government's number-one piece of evidence at trial, promotions and commendations for the No Crack Crew, and huge ratings and an eventual promotion to major network news for Hansen. Stored in a set of drawers located in a plush entertainment room on the top floor of the house, Biernacki and his fellow cops found a collection of eight home videotapes, each containing raw and uncut footage of Larry, his brothers and their crew of soldiers living the lives of drug kingpins and flaunting it to the extreme. The video recordings spanned a five-month period of time, beginning in the spring of 1986, and were all shot on a top-of-the-line Panasonic camcorder that Larry had purchased on one of his infamous spending sprees. The footage, highlights of which eventually made their way onto local and national television, showed the Chambers boys at a series of amusement parks and vacation spots, toting rifles and demonstrating their marksmanship on homemade targets and Larry himself taking the camera on self-narrated tours of his opulent house in Detroit, a boat he owned in Jamaica and a new garage he had constructed to store his fleet of expensive automobiles. It was damning and there was much, much more.

All in all, Larry recorded some 30 hours of clips ranging from the mundane—counting endless bundles of cash, Larry displaying a variety of yoga poses for the camera and teaching his pitbull, "Pancho," tricks and commands—to the maddening: Larry giving a series of soapbox testimonials on any number of subjects from politics to pimping, Larry bullying his subordinates and outlandish flouting of authority by taunting the police assigned to catch them by name on camera. Most crushing to the Chambers' cause was the segment filmed back in August at the residence on Buffalo when Larry and Jack Jackson taped themselves carelessly throwing cash around like it was tissue paper while showing off for a couple of female companions they had just picked up.

"Money, money, money! We rich, goddammit!" proclaimed Jackson with a wide grin, preening for the camera as he tossed cash from a laundry basket up in the air. "Fifty thousand here; ain't no telling how much upstairs. I'm gonna buy me three cars tomorrow and a Jeep."

Later on in the segment, Jackson turned to Larry, who was seated at the kitchen table, and asked, "Should we give some of this stuff [cash] away, since we got five hundred thousand dollars up in here right now?"

"I'll tell you what we can do," Larry replied. "We can give it to the poor. We can send it over to South Africa where brothers and sisters need it the most. Either way, we still got like a million dollars upstairs for ourselves."

And then to top it all off, Larry wandered with the camera onto the porch and, in an act of extreme stupidity, exposed the address and location where he was shooting. The proverbial ship was sunk at that very moment. For the task force, it was priceless. For the Chambers brothers, it was a death blow and meant their freedom was in grave jeopardy. The castle was about to come tumbling down.

Although B.J. was minimally featured throughout the collection of tapes, it was guilt by association. It might have appeared unfair to B.J. at the time, but his brother's actions were speaking for him and speaking loudly. And what they were saying wasn't good for his chances to avoid the government's wrath. Two days later, the No Crack Crew raided a "cook house" of Larry's on Knodell and found his infamous "Crack Commandments" list pinned to a wall in the basement, which they immediately confiscated and added to the mounting cache of incriminating evidence against the organization.

Most of 1987 was uneventful, a calm before the massive rush of a storm. As federal grand juries convened throughout the year, B.J., Larry, and the No Crack Crew went about their business as usual. B.J. opened more crack houses and just as fast as they were up and running, the No Crack Crew raided them and shut them down. The Boulevard was clocking at optimum capacity, and Larry began spending more and more time in Jamaica, even striking up a close friendship with the mayor of the popular resort town of Ochos Rios.

In the middle of the year, Little Terry Colbert and Patricia Middleton were both tagged as informants by B.J. and Larry. Colbert was attacked with gunfire by Otis and his enforcement posse, barely surviving the shooting, and Middleton was accosted and threatened by Larry and Roderick Byrd at gunpoint. Fortunately for the government, neither strong-arm tactic deterred their cooperation, and both Colbert and Middleton eventually made it to court to testify about those incidents as well as many more while working for the Chambers boys.

The month of September 1987 set the tone for the siblings' foreseeable future when at the start of the month the Chambers family again buried one of its own. B.J.'s and Larry's older brother, David, died on September 12th of complications resulting from contracting the AIDS virus. When fall turned into winter, the case against the Chambers boys was finally completed, and to the government's great satisfaction, it was air-tight. The first of two mammoth federal grand jury indictments was unsealed in December, exactly one week prior to Christmas, and it took down Larry and most of his crew. Unlike the year before when he and his inner circle spent New Year's Eve on a luxury cruise ship in Jamaica, Larry spent New Year's Eve 1987 in the Wayne County Jail, denied bail due to being assessed as a flight risk.

The month of January concluded with the No Crack Crew completing its 48th and final raid on the Chambers organization. While most of the rest of the city sat down in front of their television sets to watch the Washington Redskins defeat the Denver Broncos in the Super Bowl that Sunday evening, January 31, 1988, the No Crack Crew arrested B.J. at one of his houses on Beaconsfield with seven ounces of cocaine, thousands of dollars in cash, and a gun under his belt. After reigning atop the city's crack industry for four years, the Chambers brothers gang was officially dismantled by a second, more extensive, superseding federal indictment that came down on February 26th and charged B.J., Willie, Otis, and 18 other members of their organization with 15 separate counts of conspiracy to sell narcotics. The four brothers were all tried together in a month-long courtroom drama that concluded with guilty convictions across the board for virtually the entire gang in October.

Larry, a habitual offender, got life without the possibility of parole. B.J., Willie, and Otis all got sentences of 25 years to life, but with the chance of being paroled after 20 years of incarceration. The family's rags-to-riches story was officially over, the siblings trading in the matching Nike tracksuits they favored, and they were paraded in front of the local press corps during their arraignment in prison uniforms.

"At first, I think we may have underestimated those guys because they weren't from around here, but they sure changed that perception very quickly," Robert De Fauw commented. "They didn't look like much either; I'm talking a bunch of tiny little fellas who just kind of blended in. You wouldn't think twice about these guys if you saw them walking down the street. However, at the end of the day, they made a name for themselves and did a lot of damage. I don't know of a single organization that sold more crack during that era than the Chambers [brothers] did."

◇◇◇◇◇◇◇◇◇◇◇◇

Within days of Larry's incarceration, The Boulevard was vacant. Some junkies and vagrants still squatted there for shelter, but The Broadmore was no more by early 1988. What grew to be the symbol of the gang's innovative thinking and superior salesmanship stood as a decaying and abandoned structure until it was finally condemned by the city and torn down in 1992.

Willie was the first of the brothers to emerge from prison, gaining his freedom in August 2007. B.J. earned his release in December 2010, after penning a novel he called *Prodigy Hustler* and releasing it from behind bars in 2006. Baby brother Otis was the last of the siblings to hit the streets, walking out of lockup in November 2011 at age 43. Already in his 60s, Larry is doing his time in a federal penitentiary in Terre Haute, Indiana, at peace with the fact that he will never again see the light of day as a free man. In 2008, the gang's exploits were showcased in an episode of the hit BET show, *American Gangster*. Its title was "The Chambers Brothers and the 10 Crack Commandments."

DAY OF THE DON

Team America vs. Team Tocco

When Joseph "Joe Uno" Zerilli, the long-anointed patriarch of organized crime in the Detroit area, was laid to rest in November 1977 at the ripe old age of 81, some experts thought that there might be confusion and turmoil within the leadership of the Detroit Mafia. True followers of the Detroit branch of La Cosa Nostra, however, knew that notion couldn't be further from the truth. The bloodletting that might erupt in other American Mafia crime families as a result of the power void would never happen in the Motor City. It's not their style. First and foremost because the crime family in Detroit is a family in the most literal sense of the word—practically every member was related either through blood or marriage to every other member.

"The Detroit crime family has been generations ahead of other families around the country for years," famed Mafia expert and best-selling author Nick Pileggi was once quoted as saying. "After Prohibition, they stopped fighting internally, intermarried and put their dirty money into legitimate businesses. Meanwhile, the nation's other families were out there killing each other. That's why Detroit is where it's at today and most of the rest of the families are falling apart."

Since the 1930s, Joseph Zerilli had been overseeing the local Mafia, a paragon of stability in organized crime circles nationwide. The reason for the city's unprecedented run of relative peace and quiet was Don Joe Uno's willingness to share power and a penchant for delegating authority. These leadership traits elicited great trust and loyalty from his lieutenants and severely cut down on disharmony among the rank and file. After Zerilli and his best friend and brother-in-law, William "Black Bill" Tocco, seized control of the area underworld in the days following Prohibition, they set up a "Ruling Council" made up of leaders of different factions of the syndicate as a method to deter intra-gang violence. With very few exceptions it worked perfectly, and Zerilli would die having ruled unfettered for over four decades, never having spent any significant time behind bars or faced any "palace coups"—both extreme rarities in the pantheon of American mob dons throughout history.

"Joe Zerilli was one of this country's most prominent Bosses of his era," retired U.S. prosecutor Keith Corbett noted. "He was revered in those circles. And he was the one that set the tone for everybody else in that he always carried himself in a very low-key, understated manner, and that's the way the entire Family in Detroit has always operated."

In the years leading up to his death, Joe Uno had named his nephew Giacomo "Black Jack" Tocco, eldest son of Black Bill, his successor. From early in the decade, Black Jack had been running the ship for his uncle on a day-to-day basis, tagged as the syndicate's "Acting Boss" sometime in 1973. Although the decision would be honored and go unchallenged, it didn't come without controversy. In fact, it caused some major waves. Prior to Jack Tocco's ascension to heir apparent, Joe Zerilli had been grooming his son, Anthony "Tony Z" Zerilli, to eventually take his place atop the throne. Federal authorities were reporting as early as 1965 that Joe Uno had tapped Tony Z as Acting Boss and was spending more time than usual at his vacation home in Florida as a means of letting his son get his feet wet in the job. Then, as would prove a problem for the entirety of his career in the mob, Tony Zerilli talked his way into trouble with the government on an FBI-authorized wiretap and fell out of favor with his dad. A bust for skimming six million dollars from the Frontier Hotel and Casino in Las Vegas made his father lose faith in him and turn his attention to Jack Tocco as the new face of the family business. It was a vicious blow to Tony Z's ego and a snub he would not soon overcome.

Tony Z was the opposite of his father. He was loud and garish, and the way he carried himself emitted an air of overconfidence and entitlement. Raised as a mob prince, he viewed it as only a matter of time before he succeeded his father and had the reins to the Mafia in Detroit all to himself. When he married Rosalie Profaci, daughter of legendary East Coast Godfather Joseph Profaci of New York, his status in national gangland circles was further solidified. Being passed over didn't sit well with the portly and prematurely balding mafioso.

"One thing I always noticed that I think is interesting is that Tony Zerilli and Jack Tocco both took on the personalities of their uncles, not their fathers," Keith Corbett observed. "Tony is just like Black Bill Tocco, brash, bullish, more extrovert than introvert, and Jack is exactly like Joe Zerilli, very reserved and quietly calculating."

The younger Zerilli and Tocco were raised side by side in an exclusive, tree-lined enclave in the posh suburb of Grosse Pointe Woods. Living across the street from each other as young boys, the two first cousins were practically inseparable in everything they did. They both received business degrees from the University of Detroit in 1949, the same year they were alleged by federal authorities to have been initiated into the Mafia after "making their bones" two years earlier by jointly strangling to death a recalcitrant Greek numbers operator named Gus Andromolous. There was no question as they rose up the ladder in the crime family that they were the future. But originally, Tony Z had been assured that he would be Boss and Black Jack would be his right-hand man. Now the tables were turned and Zerilli was being asked to be subservient to his onetime subordinate. It was a trying and delicate transition for everyone involved.

"Tony Z was real upset about being snubbed, but he had no other alternative but to accept his father's decision and get in line with the new order of things," Corbett stated. "There was never any question that what the old man [Joe Zerilli] wanted was going to be the way it was. Decisions like that aren't questioned in that family. I know things were pretty cold between Tony and Jack for a while after that whole ordeal played out. The feeling from Tony's perspective was that the Boss' chair was rightfully his and that Jack stabbed him in the back by taking the promotion and allowing him to be passed over."

In contrast to Tony Z, Tocco was intelligent and stealthy in his demeanor. He was considerably more reserved than his cousin, and his appearance begged comparison more to a banker or accountant than an aspiring crime czar. For over 20 years, he had been president and principal shareholder in the Hazel Park Race Track, with Tony Z as his vice president, until Zerilli's Frontier conviction forced the Detroit mob out of ownership and management of the cash cow of a facility. Besides the racetrack, Tocco had ownership interests in a wide variety of legitimate businesses, ranging from construction companies and linen distributors to golf courses and restaurants. Due to his placement and stature in the overall American mob hierarchy, for years he reputedly collected "skim" profits stemming from the Mafia's control over the Las Vegas hotel and gaming industry that were alleged by the federal government to be in the range of several hundreds of thousands of dollars.

Identified by federal officials as early as 1960 as a crew leader of the Detroit Mafia and a proxy of his father, who was in semi-retirement in Miami Beach, Tocco followed protocol and married the daughter of family underboss Angelo "The Chairman" Meli. Extremely cautious in his movements, dating back to his youngest days in the crime family, he went to great lengths to avoid any suspicions that he engaged in illegal activity. This portion of an FBI wiretap, recorded in the 1990s, reveals a local mob soldier expounding on Tocco's reputation for being overly judicious in his dealings:

"Jack is triple fucking cautious," he said. "It used to be a big inside joke, if you wanna get rid of Jack, just tell him you're getting heat and you'll never see him again. Ya know, if you didn't want to be bothered by him or you wanted to get him off a score, that's what you said and you were home free."

One former FBI agent pegs Jack Tocco as a hands-off type of wiseguy:

"If you had to categorize him, he would definitely be considered a boardroom gangster, as opposed to his uncle and father, who both had pretty lethal reputations as blue collar hoodlums," he said. "He's a very good delegator and not opposed to letting others, those very far removed from him, do most of his heavy lifting."

That didn't mean that Tocco wouldn't get his hands dirty when he had to. Besides his being implicated as a participant in the Gus Andromolous murder, Vincent Piersante, former head of the Michigan organized crime task force, testified at U.S. Congressional hearings in the 1960s that one time after an associate tried to blackmail Jack Tocco, the Detroit mob went on to have him killed as punishment. FBI documents would tie Tocco to several gangland-related beatings and other murders too, including pegging him as most likely one of the planners of the Jimmy Hoffa assassination. This was the man who would be the new don.

"He got named Boss by his uncle for a good reason," said Mike Carone, a retired FBI agent who worked in the Detroit office's organized crime unit for over 20 years. "Jack was well educated and had the right demeanor for the job. He didn't act like a gangster, and he was very shrewd and even-keeled. The old timers felt safe leaving the future of the Family in his hands. I don't know if you could say that same thing about Tony Z."

With Joe Zerilli's death in 1977, his longtime consigliere and third-in-charge, Giovanni "Papa John" Priziola, became the titular head of the Detroit mob. On the street, though, it was widely known that Black Jack Tocco had actually grabbed the mantle of power and was already in the midst of shoring up his administrative hierarchy.

"Out of respect for Papa John, I think they waited to officially install Jack as Boss until after he passed away," Keith Corbett suggested. "Papa John was never named don, but they wanted to give him his time in the sun. For all intents and purposes, though, Jack was Boss of the Family from the time Joe Zerilli took his last breath."

In the spring of 1979, John Priziola died of natural causes. That left Pete Licavoli as the only remaining founding father of the Family still alive: Angelo Meli passed away in 1969 and Black Bill Tocco had died in 1972. But Licavoli, although officially the syndicate's underboss at the time, wasn't really a plausible candidate for the Boss' chair, in that he was currently in the process of serving a short prison sentence and by then had already moved his base of operations out of Michigan and into Arizona years before.

The road was paved for Jack Tocco to assume the throne. After Licavoli sent word from behind bars that he gave his blessing, the preparations started to be made by the crime family to inaugurate its first boss in over four decades. It was a colossal event that would require top secret planning. Somewhere along the line, however, things went awry. A security breakdown of massive proportions followed by a critical intelligence leak eventually led to the lid being blown off the most sensitive of crime family operations. Nobody outside a small circle of federal agents and attorneys would know it for another 17 years, but the day Black Jack became don would live in infamy as a red letter day and a monumental victory in the government's longstanding fight against the Mafia.

The day was certainly one of the proudest of Jack Tocco's life. Like his father before him, he would be joining a fraternity of the highest order in the nation's underworld. One could even excuse the normally stone-faced gangster for cracking a grin or two on such a cherished occasion. It was a good thing Tocco was smiling on that sunny afternoon in 1979, because he was getting his picture taken quite a bit. And not just from within the confines of the hunting lodge where the ceremony anointing him boss was taking place, but courtesy of a nearby government-issued surveillance camera pointed directly at everyone in attendance. Keeping the photos and forthcoming information that the meeting was held to elect Jack Tocco Godfather of the Detroit Mafia in their back pocket for the better half of the next two decades, the feds bided their time in playing their trump card. When that time finally did come, it would be center stage for everyone to see and would serve as Tocco's official unmasking as a gangland titan.

◇◇◇◇◇◇◇◇◇◇◇◇

The morning of June 11, 1979 started innocently enough with several sets of FBI surveillance teams following their usual routine and shadowing their assigned crime family members around town as they did a series of mundane errands. Neither the FBI agents involved nor the mobsters they were tracking knew that in a matter of hours they were all about to make history.

"From our end, it was a very fortuitous situation," said Greg Stejeskal, one of the FBI agents on security detail that day. "All the planets were aligned for something very special and unique to happen, and it resulted in an important piece of history being accomplished in the government's war against organized crime."

Late that morning, Vito "Billy Jack" Giacalone, at that time considered to be the "acting street boss" of the Detroit mob in place of his older brother, longtime day-to-day syndicate leader Anthony "Tony Jack" Giacalone—away serving a prison term — was seen arriving at Motor City Barber Supply in Roseville, which was the headquarters of Raffeale "Jimmy Q" Quasarano, a protégé of Papa John Priziola and the crime family's new consigliere. This was significant because Giacalone and Quasarano represented opposite sides of the syndicate, and although both held important leadership positions, they weren't normally known to interact with each other. Within only minutes, Frank "Frankie the Bomb" Bommarito, Billy Jack's right-hand man, showed up in the parking lot driving a van. Immediately the agents following Billy Jack and Jimmy Q sensed that something was brewing.

"It was surprising to see them meeting together, especially so early in the day," Stejeskal remarked. "My partner, Keith Cordes, and I were working Jimmy Q and followed him to Motor City Barber Supply. The next thing we know, Billy Jack shows up and then Frankie Bommarito is there a couple minutes later. At that point, we knew something was up; we just didn't know exactly what it was."

The Giacalone brothers were the face of the Detroit Mafia on the street and had been for close to a quarter century. Frankie the Bomb was one of their most reliable leg-breakers, an enforcer with an impeccable reputation for evoking fear and obedience from everyone he encountered.

"If there was trouble, Frankie would usually find his way around it," Mike Carone recalled. "He's a pretty rough individual, not someone to mess around with. They [the mob] go to him for some of their grimiest stuff. He was dealing with some real nasty people."

Flanked by the menacing Bommarito, the Giacalones were the Family's top strong-arms, enforcing the edicts of the administration with ruthless efficiency. Rough around the edges but aligned very closely from a young age with Joe Zerilli and Bill Tocco, the Giacalone brothers rose through the ranks due to pure viciousness and earning potential as opposed to lineage. Bommarito, whose cousins were local mob royalty, hitched his trailer to the Giacalones' rising star and as they ascended up the ladder, so did he. Over a period of 50 years, the Giacalone brothers and their two crews were linked to at least 25 mob murders and were indicted multiple times for loansharking, illegal possession of weapons, gambling, and tax evasion.

"Unlike Jack Tocco, the Giacalone brothers craved notoriety," Keith Corbett reported. "They courted the image as the faces of organized crime in Detroit. Tony Jack was John Gotti—before John Gotti. He fit the bill as the quintessential Mafia don, like something out of a movie. He looked the part with his expensive suits and constant scowls for the cameras, and he reveled in his reputation and the limelight that came with it. His stare could cut glass. Billy Jack was more affable. He was more of a politician and would act as a buffer between his brother and those whose heads he butted. I don't know if I would say it was a 'good cop, bad cop' routine, but it was something along those lines. Maybe you could have called it 'bad cop, a little less bad cop.'"

Tony Giacalone and Jack Tocco were not the best of friends. In fact, the feeling most people got was that the two didn't much care for each other at all. There was a distinct coolness and standoffish quality to their relationship that was impossible to hide. Some of the animosity stemmed from Tocco's jealousy of Tony Jack's close relationship with his father and uncle. Some of it came from Giacalone's disdain for Tocco's surpassing him on the Family food chain, despite never really having to pay his dues on the street as he and his brother had.

"There was a lot of resentment between them that never boiled over but always kind of festered and simmered underneath the surface," said one former federal agent. "I think Tony Jack resented the fact that Tocco was born with a proverbial silver spoon in his mouth and was anointed without having to really put in his time grinding. Tocco always kind of looked down at Tony Jack for being from the street, or at least that's how Tony Jack perceived it, anyway. The situation could have really gotten out of hand if Jack Tocco hadn't handled it properly. Jack was a pragmatist. He knew he might lose a street war with the Giacalones. But if he petted them and let them do their own thing, he could use them to his advantage."

Because of his stature in the Family, Tony Giacalone also had to sign off on Jack Tocco's selection as Boss. An FBI informant at the time revealed that the previous December, as Tony Jack prepared to go away to prison for seven years, he attended a sit-down meeting with Tocco brokered by Papa John Priziola, which was called to discuss the changeover in power. According to the informant, Priziola preached a peaceful coexistence between the two men and an extension of the agreement that had been in place prior to Joe Zerilli's death, giving Giacalone control of the street on a daily basis and Tocco final say on all major decisions and any crucial policy-making. For the good of the crime family, the two agreed to put their differences aside and create an alliance.

"Jack was smart and avoided a lot of headaches by letting the Giacalones be autonomous and kind of do their own thing," Mike Carone remembered. "He chimed in when he had to, but he really just wanted to sit back and collect an envelope at the end of every week. If his cut was there on time and wasn't ever short, Tony Jack and his brother could run around and act like Don Corleone all they wanted to in his eyes. He was perfectly fine deferring to them, letting them get the headlines and letting the whole city think they were running things. I think he saw their behavior as a benefit to him in that it put him further and further in the background of the public consciousness."

Greg Stejeskal and Keith Cordes watched and snapped photos as Billy Giacalone, a more than adequate replacement for his brother as the Family's front boss, Frankie Bommarito, and Jimmy Quasarano, met and talked shop for a good 20 minutes in the parking lot of Motor City Beauty Supply.

"Those guys were always worried about bugs inside their hangouts and were known to talk business outside on walk-and-talk sessions, especially in the summertime, so we knew they had to be discussing something important when we were watching them chop it up outside Jimmy Q's place," Stejeskal recalled. "We were communicating with the surveillance units that were tailing Giacalone and just kind of waiting to see what their next move would be."

At about 11:30, Quasarano departed the premises in his car, while Giacalone and Bommarito sat in Giacalone's vehicle at Motor City Beauty Supply, apparently making small talk. Jimmy Q returned with Michael "Big Mike" Polizzi and Anthony "Tony the Champ" Abate, two more high-ranking local mafiosi, in tow and everyone but Bommarito, who left by himself in Giacalone's car, piled into the van and started driving toward the nearest expressway ramp. Their destination was an hour-long drive west to Dexter, a small suburb of Ann Arbor, and the

Timberland Game Ranch, an upscale hunting lodge owned by reputed Detroit Mafia capo, Luigi "Louie the Bulldog" Ruggirello. He was the son of Antonino "Big Tony" Ruggirello, an elderly local mobster who was at one time Black Bill Tocco's personal driver and bodyguard. Big Tony had been acquitted of a gangland murder that took place in 1921. Louie Ruggirello and his two brothers, Antonino "Tony the Exterminator" Ruggirello Jr. and Antonio "Toto" Ruggirello, were alleged to oversee all crime family rackets being conducted in Washtenaw and Genesee Counties.

"We were following them on the expressway and the longer we drove and couldn't figure out where they were going, the more suspicious we became," Greg Stejeskal recounted. "The further west we got made us think they were heading to Chicago. Then we started getting communications from the other units that they were all heading the same way we were. The whole thing was happening very quickly, and I think it surprised all of us because we were just expecting a regular day on the job. All of a sudden we realized we had this huge event on our hands. Outside of weddings and funerals, these types of men didn't congregate. Now we got a bunch of them carpooling out of the area together."

Also known as "Jimmy the Goon" for his ice-cold stare, thuggish antics, and reputation for never cracking a smile, Quasarano was Papa John's longtime number-one lieutenant and like Priziola himself, a suspected major narcotics trafficker and reputed hit man. FBI documents reveal that Jimmy Quasarano was suspected by authorities of being involved in close to two dozen gangland homicides. An FBI informant claimed that Central Sanitation, a garbage collection company he owned in Hamtramck, had been used to dispose of at least 10 Mafia victims before it was burned to the ground in a suspicious fire.

Big Mike Polizzi was Papa John's son-in-law and the Family's unofficial chief finance officer, having acquired an accounting degree from Syracuse University in 1947. Tony the Champ Abate, who earned his nickname because he used to be a boxer, was acquitted of a gangland murder when he was 26 and acted as a top proxy for the imprisoned Pete Licavoli, being related to him through the marriage of their children. Polizzi gained early infamy in the eyes of law enforcement when he was just 31 years old, and his home phone number was found on a piece of paper in the woods behind the house that was raided in the infamous Appalachian mob conference in 1957.

The van being driven by Billy Giacalone and containing Jimmy Quasarano, Mike Polizzi, and Tony Abate, pulled up to the Timberland Game Ranch at around 1:00 p.m., where they linked up with several others. Discreetly following them, always keeping a safe distance in traffic, Agent Stejeskal's surveillance unit set up shop outside the property. Soon several additional vehicles showed up at the ranch. Stejeskal and the FBI had hit pay dirt in a monumental way.

"The next thing we knew, we were in Dexter at the Timberland Game Ranch and within minutes of us arriving, a bunch more cars show up carrying a lot more top guys," Stejeskal recollected. "At this point, there's no doubt in our minds, we've stumbled on to something big. We didn't know everyone who was there because some of the fellas had slipped the agents we had trailing them, but we knew at least more than half of the entire administration were conducting some sort of important meeting inside."

Entering the sprawling wooded estate by jumping a rear fence, which was located to the far west of the main lodge where everybody was congregating, Stejeskal found a nicely guarded hiding place behind an archery range that backed up to a set of tall bushes. Nestled in between a pair of canvassed targets, he had a direct view of the lodge's balcony, which was soon filled with virtually the entire Detroit mob hierarchy enjoying the beautiful afternoon and toasting their new don.

"I got as close as I could, close enough where I could hear voices coming from the main building, and very quietly started snapping photos of the people who were there," Stejeskal remembered. "There was some nice coverage where I was hiding, so I was relatively safe from detection. Fortunately, some of the shots I got were of Jack Tocco himself."

The self-professed "Men of Honor" stayed and celebrated at the ranch for several hours. The first car to depart was driven by Anthony "Tony T" Tocco, Jack's younger brother and like his first cousin Tony Zerilli, a son-in-law to New York City Mafia legend Joe Profaci. Tony Tocco left with an unidentified person in his passenger's seat at 3:30. Two hours later, the rest of the group began leaving. At approximately 5:30 p.m., a car driven by Anthony "Tony the Bull" Corrado, a top capo in the Family, was seen by an FBI surveillance squad ferrying Jack Tocco away from the ranch and heading back to Detroit. A few minutes later, another squad of agents saw another car, this one being driven by Dominic "Fats" Corrado, Tony the Bull's older brother and fellow capo, leaving Timberland. Inside Fats Corrado's car were Carlo Licata, Jack and Tony Tocco's brother-in-law; Greektown capo Peter "Bozzi" Vitale, and Salvatore "Sammy Rocks" Misuraca, believed to be the syndicate's representative in Canada, who also held residence in Chicago. Billy Giacalone, Mike Polizzi, Jimmy Quasarano, and Tony Abate left in Frankie Bommarito's van, meeting back up with Frankie the Bomb in Roseville at Jimmy Q's headquarters and exchanging vehicles. Staying behind at the ranch were the Ruggirello brothers and their dad, who at that time was dying of cancer.

"Once we got all got back together at the office and started comparing notes, we couldn't believe what we had uncovered," Stejeskal recalled. "My photos and what all the different surveillance units witnessed painted quite a picture. In fact, at that point, we still didn't know exactly what it was that we had stumbled upon."

Things would get clearer in the coming days. Less than a week later, Jack Tocco's driver, a federal informant, told the FBI that the event, held up at Timberland Game Ranch on June 11th, was called for the sole purpose of officially electing Tocco the crime family's new Godfather. The photos that Stejeskal had taken, the best of which showed Tocco in conversation with Billy Giacalone and Tony Corrado, were the icing on the cake.

"What we gleaned from Jack's driver shed a lot of light on the situation for us," he said. "Really, it served to confirm most of our suspicions. The only thing we hadn't known for sure was that Tocco had surpassed Tony Zerilli. When we started to list all the people we knew for sure were in attendance, it was a true rogues' gallery. These were all the highest-placed guys, getting together to commemorate the passing of the torch. The fact that we were there to see it transpire is pretty amazing."

Known for sure to be at Jack Tocco's inauguration that summer day in 1979 were Jack Tocco, Tony Tocco, Dominic Corrado, Anthony Corrado, Carlo Licata, Peter Vitale, Jimmy Quasarano, Tony Ruggirello Sr., Tony Ruggirello Jr., Luigi Ruggirello, Mike Polizzi, Tony Abate, and Billy Giacalone. The government believes another two, possibly three, more high-ranking individuals from the organization were there at the ranch that day as well. FBI documents reveal the names of long-known local mobsters Paul Vitale, Peter's older brother; Salvatore "Little Sammy" Finazzo, Joe Zerilli's brother-in-law; Vincent "Little Vince" Meli, Angelo Meli's nephew; and Salvatore "Sammy Lou" Lucido, the son-in-law of Angelo Meli, as possible additional attendees.

Tony Tocco was Jack's most trusted confidant and advisor. When Jack became Acting Boss back in the mid-1970s, Tony, who also had a business degree from the University of Detroit, was alleged to have taken over as capo of his crew. Known as more approachable than his older brother, Tony T, sometimes referred to as "Tawn" or "Tic Toc Tony," had always been a big earner on the street and had a reputation as someone who never wanted to rely on his last name as a ticket for advancement.

The Corrado boys were the sons of legendary Motor City mobster Pietro "Machine Gun Pete" Corrado and the nephews of Joe Zerilli. Machine Gun Pete, who got his street moniker during Prohibition for his favored form of firearm, ran the numbers racket in Detroit until his death from a sudden heart attack while vacationing in Florida in 1957. A local numbers operator who worked under Corrado once told journalists that Machine Gun Pete had "killed probably a dozen people in order to take control of the illegal lottery racket for the Detroit mob." With the long list of known gangland-style murders and disappearances in the 1940s and '50s attributed by police to the Mafia's hostile takeover of the numbers industry from the city's black kingpins, this does not seem like an exaggeration.

Fats Corrado, Machine Gun Pete's eldest son, took over his father's crew and business operations upon his death and a few years later, his younger brother Tony would join him in the ranks of the crime family as a fellow crew leader and captain, being named by his uncle, Joe Zerilli, as head of the syndicate's collection branch. Second cousins to Jack Tocco, Fats and Tony the Bull Corrado were tightly entwined in his inner circle.

Carlo Licata was Jack and Tony Tocco's brother-in-law and the son of deceased California mob don Nick Licata. He was initiated into the Los Angeles Mafia in 1950 and then transferred to the Detroit family when he married Josephine Tocco, Black Bill's daughter, in 1952 as a means of quashing a longstanding beef between his father and Joe Zerilli.

Pete Vitale was a longtime mob lieutenant, who along with his older brother Paul, ran all rackets taking place in Greektown from the 1950s until the 1990s. The Vitale brothers were best friends with Jimmy Quasarano—they co-owned Central Sanitation in Hamtramck—and ran their joint operations out of the Grecian Gardens restaurant, located on the far east end of Monroe Street in the heart of the area's nightlife district. In the 1960s, a much-publicized police raid of the popular eatery netted a black leather ledger notebook, detailing payoffs to numerous police officers and public officials. It was long speculated by authorities that Pete Vitale was a partner with Jimmy Q and Papa John in their drug business.

Although not related by blood, the Ruggirello brothers were as close as family to Jack Tocco. They had practically been raised together due to the extremely close relationship between their fathers. Tony the Exterminator got his nickname because he co-owned a pest extermination business with Tony Giacalone. Some might say it held a double meaning. Tony's wife, Judith, disappeared in 1968, FBI records report, on the afternoon she had intended to file for divorce. Her car was found in the parking lot of Darby's, a popular delicatessen of its day on Six Mile Road, but she would never be seen again alive or dead. In the years following the disappearance, highly placed Greek Detroit mob associate Peter Lazaros, an alleged bagman for area politicians and policemen who became a government informant, publicly accused Mafia member Joe Barbara Jr. of putting Ruggirello's wife "down a drain" during an altercation in the hallway of the federal courthouse downtown.

Louie Ruggirello got his nickname, "The Bulldog," because people used to claim that in his younger days the short, stout, and pug-faced hood resembled in looks and behavior the wrinkly and fearsome canine. It was Louie who conceived and built the Timberland Game Ranch in 1971. In strange contrast to their tough reputations, the Ruggirellos were known to be avid gardeners and conservationists. At the time of Jack Tocco's inauguration, Big Tony Ruggirello was dying of cancer, but he attended out of a sense of paternal loyalty in Black Bill's stead.

Salvatore Misuraca was and remains a bit of a mystery. In an attempt to identify him, FBI agents stopped the car driven by Dominic Corrado for supposed traffic violations. After showing their identification, it was discovered that Misuraca was 79 years old and resided in the Chicago area, but also had Canadian citizenship papers on his person. Although no definite links between the Mafia in Michigan and Misuraca could be unearthed, FBI agents would later receive information that he may have been in attendance representing Detroit mob interests in Illinois, Canada, or both.

Conspicuously absent from Jack Tocco's coronation as the Midwest's newest Godfather was his former best friend Tony Zerilli, whose reasons for not attending were out of pure spite. Despite the snub, Tocco named the bitter Zerilli as his underboss and number two in charge in a peace offering that Tony eventually accepted. Relations between Black Jack and Tony Z remained frigid for a good couple of years. Still bristling from being passed over, Zerilli allegedly turned down an invitation by Tocco to travel to the East Coast to officially introduce himself as the city's new don to Philadelphia Mafia leader Angelo Bruno and New York mob boss Tony Salerno, and then a few months later skipped out on attending Tocco's ritzy 25th anniversary party.

By the mid-1980s, the cavernous rift between Tocco and Zerilli had been bridged and the two were once again on good terms. But the harmony and open discourse between the boyhood chums wouldn't last long. The future was bleak for both Mafia czars. Further hazardous behavior by Tony Z would send both the Detroit Mafia and Black Jack personally reeling into a multi-year tailspin that did considerable damage to the vice conglomerate their fathers had built from the ground up and concluded with both of them serving time in a federal penitentiary. The ensuing second rift between Tocco and Zerilli would prove permanent.

◇◇◇◇◇◇◇◇◇◇◇◇

For the better part of two decades, Jack Tocco prided himself on being one of the most elusive crime lords in the United States. Despite numerous tries, the government had not been able to nail Black Jack for anything bigger than a citation in the 1960s for attending an illegal cockfight. As a result, any time news outlets or law enforcement spokesmen went on record accusing him of being a Mafia boss, Tocco hit them with a lawsuit—over half a dozen when all tallied up. Tocco's battle with the government, purported by him to be based solely on his last name and the reputations of his father and uncle, was the inspiration for the hit 1981 movie *Absence of Malice*, written by Oscar-winning screenwriter Kurt Luedtke, a native Detroiter, and featuring a central character played by Paul Newman that Luedtke admitted was loosely based on Tocco himself.

Black Jack went to great lengths to parade himself as a respectable member of high society in Metro Detroit, and he scoffed at any notion that he was a leader of the city's Italian organized crime faction. A cultured man, he was often seen downtown attending plays, operas, and museum openings. On his tax returns, Tocco routinely declared hundreds of thousands of dollars of donations to local charities and the Holy Family Church. Privately, it was a different matter. FBI surveillance tapes reveal the old-school don wanted everyone on the street to kiss his ring and pay tribute to his regime with both undying loyalty and hefty compensation.

"I was called to a meeting with Jack and Tony Tocco and I was told, 'This is our town and you're gonna do what we tell ya to, plain and simple.' That's exactly what they said to me point-blank."

His rivals in the government had a high opinion of their target—at least professionally—as they tirelessly worked to put him away.

"Jack's a real strong boss, and he was a very tough adversary," Keith Corbett stated. "He knows how to make money and he runs a tight ship. In that world, that's really the bottom line. He might not be overly popular like his dad and uncle were, but there's no doubt he's respected and feared and that ultimately beats likeability in that line of work. The investigation into his activities was long and arduous. It wasn't an easy nut to crack because he knew how to insulate himself and had a very strong base of knowledge with how to successfully veil his movements and affairs."

Any semblance of legitimacy Tocco's cries of innocence and unfair mislabeling had came crashing down in the late 1990s when the feds capped an investigation called "Operation Gametax"—in the works for over a decade—by arresting and convicting Tocco and practically his entire mob administration of a widespread racketeering conspiracy.

"They say the Mafia has a long memory, well so does the FBI, and we worked around the clock for over 15 years making that case," Greg Stejeskal noted. "We put the intelligence we got from the mob summit up at Timberland away in a safe place and kept plodding away, pounding the streets, running down our leads and documenting everything we could for use in the future. When everything paid off with convictions, it gave me and a heck of a lot of other people in law enforcement an incredible sense of satisfaction."

Announcing the multi-tiered, 50-count indictment against the leadership of the Detroit Mafia in March 1996, the U.S. Justice Department put out a statement saying the takedown of Jack Tocco was the FBI's most significant bust of an American mob figure since New York's "Teflon Don" John Gotti because Tocco was "one of the most powerful Mafia bosses walking the streets of our country." The charges levied and eventually proved in court against the continuing criminal enterprise included loansharking, extortion, illegal gambling, conspiracy to commit murder, and violence in furtherance of the enterprise and former hidden ownership in two Nevada-based casinos. Besides the surveillance materials gathered from Tocco's inauguration meeting in 1979—headlined by the photo Stejeskal snapped of Black Jack, Billy Giacalone, and Tony Corrado—the feds had hundreds of hours of audiotapes acquired from a bug in Tony Zerilli's nephew's car, which recounted in vivid detail life in the Detroit Mafia under the rule of Jack Tocco.

"All those years before his conviction, Jack dodged the dreaded label of mob boss in the public and wanted the city to view him as some kind of misunderstood victim," Corbett remarked. "That was fine because I knew we would have the last laugh. Today, he can say what he wants, but the truth is that he is a convicted racketeer and felon and was head of one of the biggest Mafia families in the country. That's not speculation or innuendo, that's a certifiable fact."

To add insult to injury, Zerilli's nephew, Nove Tocco, a low-level street soldier, and Tocco's godson, Angelo Polizzi, a syndicate attorney whose father was Big Mike Polizzi, both became government informants and testified against the crime family in multiple court proceedings. Amazingly, Nove Tocco's defection to the federal government following his conviction in the case is the only time a made member of the notoriously ultra-secretive Detroit Mafia has ever flipped and spilled the beans about the Family in court.

It looked to be a crippling blow to Jack Tocco and his inner circle. And to his inner circle it was. For him, however, it wasn't anywhere close. After U.S. Federal Judge John Corbett O'Meara issued his sentences in early spring 1998, it was obvious that Tocco had gotten off with a mere slap on the wrist. While his most trusted lieutenants, like Billy Giacalone, Tony Zerilli, and Tony Corrado, would all get hit with stiff prison terms, O'Meara gave Tocco, the convicted ringleader of the violent, multi-million-dollar organized crime empire, only a year and a day of jail time. Although prosecutors would end up successfully appealing O'Meara's sentence and getting the convicted mob boss to do an additional 14 months behind bars, some believe it was a sign of just how high and far Tocco's hand could reach.

"Something clearly wasn't right with that sentence; it was very suspicious," Stejeskal maintained. "There was no question it was not standard operating procedure. Now what caused the decision to diverge from normal sentencing requirements is something that will always kind of hang over that case. A lot of people, myself included, have some very strong opinions about what went down there." Corbett, who retired from the U.S. Prosecutor's Office in 2009, concurred:

"The sentencing was just downright outrageous. It was inexplicable and definitely raised a lot of questions. That type of conviction should carry at the minimum a 15-year term. The crux of the entire case that the jury came back with guilty verdicts for was that Jack Tocco was the ringleader, the head of all organized crime in Detroit. Sentence-wise, he was treated as if he was some sort of petty thief. The whole thing was baffling."

◇◇◇◇◇◇◇◇◇◇◇◇

Jack Tocco walked out of his federal prison cell in early 2002, and according to federal authorities, he reassumed command of the Detroit Mafia, intent on ruling well into his 80s and beyond. Informants tell the FBI that since Tocco's release from prison, there have been at least two initiation ceremonies held as a means of infusing the Family with fresh, young blood.

"He's going to hold onto the mantle of power until his last dying breath, that's one thing I can guarantee," said one former federal agent. "Jack has a vested interest in seeing the Family continue to flourish after he passes. This is literally his family business. His dad and uncle started this family back in the Prohibition days. He wants to do everything in his power to make sure things are in the right shape when he leaves this earth so that the legacy and name will live on in infamy."

As for the other men known to have been in attendance at the Timberland Game Ranch that day, only Tony Ruggirello Jr. remains alive at this writing. In 1998, Billy Jack completed a plea deal following his arrest in the Operation Gametax case by admitting in open court the existence of an organization known as the "Detroit Mafia" and his membership in it. He was released from prison in 2004 and became the Family's underboss, replacing a deposed Tony Zerilli until health issues pushed him out of the job in 2008 and he died in 2012.

Jimmy Quasarano was sent to prison himself in 1981 for extorting a Wisconsin-based cheese company, and was forced to relinquish his consigliere position to Big Mike Polizzi. Released from prison in 1987, Jimmy Q continued to be a valued and much-used counselor to Jack Tocco until his death in 2001 at the age of 90. Polizzi, whose father was a close ally of Black Bill Tocco and Joe Zerilli during the early days of the crime family, died in isolation in 1997, shunned by his former friends and relatives in the mob after his son, Angelo, became a government witness. Polizzi passed away of a heart attack in Pennsylvania, stripped of his consigliere post—replaced by Tony Tocco—and booted out of the state by the organization he helped run for the previous 50 years.

Carlo Licata died under suspicious circumstances in his Bloomfield Hills residence in the summer of 1981, his passing officially ruled a suicide. Dominic Corrado died of heart failure in 1985, and Tony Corrado died in prison of cancer in 2002, serving out his sentence from the Operation Gametax bust. Paul Vitale died in 1988 and Peter in 1997. Salvatore Misuraca passed away in 1984. In a situation that mirrored what happened with Big Mike Polizzi, Tony Zerilli was ostracized from the organization as a result of his nephew Nove Tocco's defection to the feds. He has been living in virtual solitude since release from prison in 2009, not allowed to take back his position as the Family's official number-two guy and allegedly forced into retirement by his cousin for his continued gaffes.

With Jack Tocco getting up in age—he turned 85 in 2012—the Detroit Mafia began bracing itself for another transition of power, identical to the one Tocco rode into the boss' seat back in 1979. Following the lead of his uncle and predecessor,

Black Jack is said to have named his own replacement. The name most associated with being tagged as the Family's new heir apparent is Jack "Jackie the Kid" Giacalone, a 61-year-old capo who is Billy Giacalone's son. Black Jack Tocco himself might be on his way out, but few think the Family is going anywhere anytime soon.

"We're talking about a pretty sophisticated group here, so I don't think the future is dim at all for the Mafia in the city of Detroit and its surrounding regions," Stejeskal stated. "They are very adept at changing with the times, molding to the terrain that presents itself and integrating new rackets into the fold as they become available. These aren't your average mobsters. I think that's been shown by the level of success these guys have attained and their ability to stay below the radar for the most part. As a guy who spent a good portion of time trying to dismantle this organization, I can tell you that I always felt like I was dealing with a much sharper criminal mind than you would face on a regular basis."

THE LOST LEGACY

A Gentleman's Gangster

The outfit said it all. It told you about the man he was and the man he was soon going to be. In the most simplistic of terms, Eddie Jackson's wardrobe while in New York City, attending the classic March 1971 boxing match between Muhammad Ali and Joe Frazier, exuded an aura of power, pride, excess, and class. To be even more specific, he was sporting an ensemble that cost close to a quarter of a million dollars, more than half of which was accounted for by the jewelry he wore on his hands and around his neck and wrist.

Not even knowing who he was, *Ebony* magazine snapped a photo of Jackson for an article they were doing on the best-dressed people attending the fight. The picture was included in a collection from the event that, besides Jackson, spotlighted only well-recognized celebrities from the sports and entertainment world. It was the perfect metaphor for Detroit's ultimate gentleman gangster and a figure in the annals of the city's underworld with few equals—comfortable living lavishly in the shadows, unfazed that others got headlines when he quietly crafted his luminous legacy. Unassuming he was not.

"The Fat Man" or "The Crowd Pleaser," as Eddie Jackson was affectionately referred to on the streets of the Motor City, was taking the Big Apple by storm, ready to cement a place for himself as a genuine player on a nationwide scale. He wasn't comfortable with his current status as a successful mid-level narcotics distributor, and he knew that infiltrating the drug scene in New York was the answer to all of his prayers. Taking his seat in the fifth row to watch the Ali-Frazier fight, Eddie scanned the crowd, intent on finding himself a steady connection, someone who could provide him large quantities of high-quality heroin at a reasonable price. What he didn't know was that he had already found that connection, sitting right next to him.

◇◇◇◇◇◇◇◇◇◇◇◇

Henry Bell, Eddie Jackson's father, was born and raised in Arkansas. Taking off on an early life of petty street crime, Henry was forced to flee the South in the late 1920s after having a warrant issued for his arrest stemming from a shootout at a local tavern where he had killed a couple of guys following a heated dice game. Settling in Detroit around Thanksgiving 1926, Henry changed his last name to Jackson and immediately turned away from a life of crime and instead started off slowly but steadily building a career in real estate. Before long, Henry Jackson had worked his way up from stock boy at a grocery store to the owner of multiple businesses in Paradise Valley, the city's all-black entertainment and nightlife district. Already in his forties, Henry married a beautiful young woman who worked in one of his establishments and had two sons. The couple's first son, Elijah, was born in 1942, and two years later in 1944, they had Eddie. Tragedy struck the burgeoning new family a couple of years later when Eddie's mother died while giving birth to a baby sister.

Using his keen natural instinct, Henry parlayed his pair of small properties into a sizeable real estate portfolio, which came to include a restaurant, pool hall, bar, apartment buildings, and industrial warehouses all across southeastern Michigan. Left to raise his two boys alone, the stern and calculating man of rigid self-discipline did the best that he could. His reaction to his wife's passing was to spoil his sons, making sure they wanted for nothing in their early lives. The family lived in a large, two-story house in one of the city's nicer residential areas on the West Side and had a live-in maid. Living near the Jackson brothers was a young boy around the same age as Eddie. His name was Courtney Brown, and he would go on to become Eddie's best friend and business partner. Brown and the Jackson boys were practically inseparable during their childhood.

Despite the fact that he came from affluence, Eddie drifted toward a life on the street from an early age. By the time he was 12, Eddie and his older brother Elijah had both quit going to school and spent their days running around with older troublemakers from the neighborhood. They hung out mostly in their dad's pool hall, where a rogues' gallery of local underworld characters would gather to get in on the high-stakes action. While Courtney stayed in high school and got his diploma, Eddie and Elijah got an early start in the hustler's lifestyle, and they developed quite a taste for it. Racked with guilt over the fact that his sons grew up without a mother, Henry allowed this behavior by basically ignoring it, turning his head and in some cases pleading ignorance to those who inquired as to why his two boys weren't in school. As Courtney acquired the knowledge and book smarts needed for their future endeavors together, it was Eddie and Elijah who cut their teeth learning the ways of the Motor City underworld.

In 1965, when Eddie was 21, his father died of a heart attack and left him and his brother a quarter-million-dollar inheritance. The brothers lived lavishly off the unexpected windfall for almost three years, using the money to party and travel, all the while binging on a steady diet of women, alcohol, and drugs. However, by the start of 1968, the cash had run out and the Jacksons were broke.

Forced to join the workforce for the first time in their lives, Eddie took two jobs—one driving a taxicab around the city on the late-night shift and the other working in an auto plant during the daytime. With the new decade dawning, Eddie and his brother found themselves practically destitute, barely able to pay their monthly bills. It was quite a fall, and not a place where Eddie intended to stay for very long. Having little taste for the common man's existence, Eddie Jackson used the squandering of his inheritance and the subsequent repercussions as motivation to build back his family's wealth by any means necessary. A man of prodigious weight, he also had prodigious ambitions, and the idea of driving a cab for the rest of his life simply wouldn't do. Eddie fancied himself in some ways urban royalty, and to live anything else but the good life was unacceptable.

Roughly six months into his career as a moonlighting cab driver, Jackson had a chance encounter with "Gentleman John" Claxton, one of Detroit's biggest wholesale narcotics distributors. This fateful introduction would go on to change his life. It was spring 1968, and Claxton stopped into the family pool hall, at that time being run by Elijah, for a drink. After taking a few shots of whisky, he requested that Elijah call him a taxi to drive him to the city's West Side. Elijah told Claxton that his brother drove a taxi and called upon Eddie to drive Claxton to his desired destination.

The pair got into the taxi and Claxton told him he wanted to make two stops, both at hotels, before being driven home. While Eddie drove Claxton from a hotel at one end of the city to a hotel at the other, the two struck up a casual conversation and immediately hit it off. There was something about Jackson's demeanor and natural intelligence that made Claxton trust him from the start. When the cab finally reached Claxton's driveway at a mansion in Sherwood Forest, a strictly upper-class white neighborhood, Eddie was blown away. He didn't understand how a black man, not much older than himself, could afford to live in such luxury. Before exiting the vehicle, Claxton gave Jackson two crisp 100-dollar bills and asked him if he would return the following morning and take him back to the two hotels they had just visited so he could do some more business. Not even knowing what Claxton's profession was or why he had taken such a liking to him, Jackson accepted the request for the sole reason that he thought he could make a nice stack of cash for his troubles. He was right.

Eddie quickly figured out that Gentlemen John was in the dope game. And not just in it, but on top of it. And just as quickly, he decided he would do everything in his power to become exactly what his future underworld mentor was and more. After Jackson picked Claxton up, drove him to his meeting and then back to his house for the second time in as many days, he was asked if he could repeat this same routine every day. Another $200 fee didn't hurt the pitch either, but his decision would have been the same. It was a no-brainer. Eddie was in, and ready to work, wiggle, and hustle his way all the way to the top. For the next three months, every day at 7:00 a.m., Eddie Jackson fetched John Claxton at his residence, drove him to his two "meetings" and returned him home. Men of fine taste and an appetite for indulgence, they clicked from the very start. Soon Claxton requested that Eddie make the trips by himself each day. He explained that at each stop, he was to drop off the daily package of drugs, which would be concealed in a suitcase.

Just as Gentlemen John suspected would happen, upon being given the opportunity to get more involved with the drug game, Jackson was cool and calm as ever. This instilled even more faith in Claxton's new protégé. Accepting the job offer, he shook Claxton's hand. Their newfound friendship had just become a business relationship. Never had Eddie been so eager to get to work. Making the daily drop-off on behalf of Gentlemen John was a minor, almost menial job when compared to his future riches as a boss in the drug industry, but it proved a tipping point. The fast, easy money was too appealing for the broke former rich kid to turn down, and it would quickly open a door to much bigger and better things.

◇◇◇◇◇◇◇◇◇◇◇◇◇

John Claxton was part of the Motor City's so-called Black Mafia, second-in-command to Henry "Blaze" Marzette, Detroit's first-ever urban Godfather. Marzette ruled over much of the region's narcotics industry throughout the 1960s and early '70s, and he carved out a legacy for himself as the area's original ghetto kingpin. Claxton met Marzette as a teenager in the months after Claxton and his mother had relocated to Detroit from South Carolina. In fact, his real last name wasn't Claxton at all: it was Classen, a name he got from his dad, who had died in combat. Almost as soon as he got to Detroit with his mom to live with an uncle on the city's West Side in the 1940s, the boys from the neighborhood began mispronouncing his name and calling him Claxton. It stuck, and the legend of John Claxton was born.

Building a friendship based on their love of sports, shooting pool, and chasing girls, Claxton and Marzette were thick as thieves until the early 1950s when Marzette joined the military and went off to fight in Korea. At that point, the pair drifted apart. While Marzette went off and became a war hero, Claxton headed into the life of a street hustler and con artist, specializing in selling illegal moonshine throughout the city's housing projects. For the next several years, the two would see little of each other. They weren't supposed to. Returning home as a highly decorated officer in the Marines, Marzette joined the Detroit Police Department and became an instant celebrity in the city's law enforcement community. Claxton, on the other hand, was a common crook.

Detroit Mafia capos Peter "Bozzi" Vitale and Raffeale "Jimmy Q" Quasarano seen together in an FBI surveillance photo from 1978.

A mid-1970s FBI mug shot of longtime Detroit mob street boss Anthony "Tony Jack" Giacalone, the face of the crime family on the streets from 1960 until his death in 2001.

Former Detroit FBI field agent Greg Stejeskal snapped this hazy photo on June 11, 1979 at Jack Tocco's secret inauguration as don. The photo shows Tocco (center), flanked by capo Vito "Billy Jack" Giacalone (left) and Anthony "Tony the Bull" Corrado.

An FBI surveillance photo taken at the November 2, 1977 funeral of longtime Detroit mob Godfather Joseph Zerilli at Bagnasco's Funeral Home in St. Claire Shores.

A Detroit Police Department photo of local Mafia leaders and gangland pioneers Joseph "Joe Uno" Zerilli and William "Black Bill" Tocco from the early 1930s.
(Courtesy of the Paul Kavieff collection)

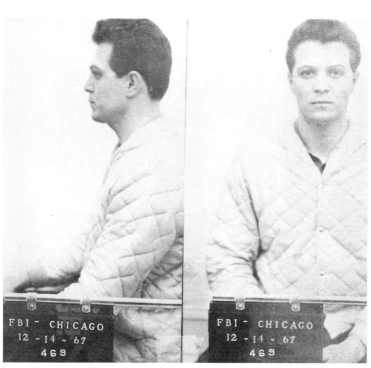

A Chicago FBI mug shot of Anthony "Chicago Tony" La Piana from 1967.

Mob soldier and hit man Nick "The Executioner" Ditta in a Detroit Police Department mug shot from the 1960s. (Courtesy of the Paul Kavieff collection)

The Detroit mob's Canadian capo, Joseph "Cockeyed Joe" Catalanotte, in a DPD mug shot from the late 1950s. (Courtesy of the Paul Kavieff collection)

A Detroit Police Department mug shot of Jimmy Hoffa as a young man. (Courtesy of the Paul Kavieff collection)

A recent photo of 680 West Long Lake Road in Bloomfield Hills, a house suspected by some former members of the FBI as the site of the murder of Jimmy Hoffa in July 1975.

A 1940s DPD mug shot of longtime Detroit mob consigliere Giovanni "Papa John" Priziola.
(Courtesy of the Paul Kavieff collection)

A press photo of Detroit's first and only Jewish Godfather, Abe Burnstein, who along with his three brothers founded and ran the Purple Gang.
(Courtesy of the Paul Kavieff collection)

Infamous Motor City hit man Chester Campbell, one of the most feared underworld assassins in American history.

Detroit drug kingpin Eddie "The Fat Man" Jackson and his partner, Courtney "The Field Marshal" Brown, in the 1970s.

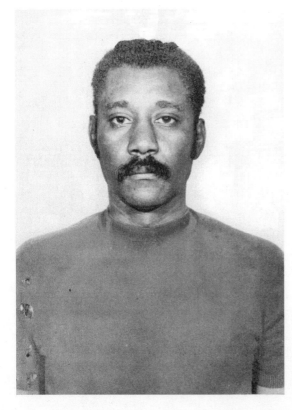

Early 1970s drug kingpin "Gentleman John" Claxton, who skipped bail in 1974, fled Detroit and has never been seen again.

A large crew of Young Boys, Inc. members, at the peak of the drug conglomerate's power, as they appeared at the Pontiac Silverdome in 1980 for a Parliament Funkadelic concert.

Detroit Godfather Giacomo "Black Jack" Tocco in an FBI photo from the late 1980s.

Detroit Mafia lieutenant Peter "Fast Pete" Cavataio in an FBI mug shot from the 1970s.

A family photo of brothers and longtime Detroit Mafia capos Anthony "Tony Jack" Giacalone (left) and Vito "Billy Jack" Giacalone with their wives at a formal gathering in the 1990s.

Flamboyant 1980s drug kingpin Richard "Maserati Rick" Carter.

In keeping with department policy, Marzette could not socialize with his old friend as it was a clear conflict of interest. Early in his career, this distinction between cop and crook was an important one to him. Later on, that distinction would blur and Gentlemen John would re-enter the picture. Originally assigned to the department's exclusive undercover unit, Marzette earned the nickname "Blaze" from his fellow police officers for the rapid rate at which he churned out drug busts. In fact, by the end of his first year on the force, he had broken the DPD's record by racking up the most arrests and convictions in the shortest amount of time.

Marzette's exploits on the streets were just as legendary. After Blaze was kicked off the force in 1956 and served a short prison term for corruption, he remerged in his old stomping grounds, but on the other side of the law. He took what he had learned from acting as a drug dealer in an undercover capacity and made himself into a kingpin. More importantly, Marzette became the first African-American trafficker in the Detroit underworld to separate himself and his operation from the city's Italian organized crime faction, the area's traditional narcotics supplier since the 1930s. This move by Blaze Marzette wound up laying the foundation for independence on behalf of practically every drug kingpin and urban crime syndicate in Detroit that followed him—an equally staggering and dubious distinction to say the least.

"Henry Marzette was really one of a kind," said sociologist and author Carl Taylor. "He was a true original. The city had never seen a black man from the streets with such power and swagger before. African-American criminals had always been subservient in the pecking order of the Detroit underworld. Marzette changed that. He set his own path and followed his own set of rules."

Blasting his way onto the scene in the local dope game by allegedly killing one of the city's biggest dealers, a man named "Mississippi Red," and forcefully seizing control of his sprawling heroin network, Marzette was never one to do things quietly. After first getting his drugs from the Italians just like everyone else, Marzette traveled to Malaysia to secure his own supply source. The Mafia and Marzette had always gotten along very well, often socializing together at area nightclubs and restaurants. But business was business, and Blaze wasn't happy towing the company line.

By the late 1960s, Marzette had constructed a pipeline of heroin of the highest quality that ran unfettered from Southeast Asia's Golden Triangle directly to the Motor City. He also built up a colossal-sized narcotics ring that was dubbed "The West Side Seven," or simply "The Seven." Marzette's move to Malaysia to secure his drugs was no coincidence; the floodgates to Asia's premium heroin market had recently been opened by some of his peers in New York and the rush was on to head to the Far East and get rich on powder. The knowledge that most of those on the East Coast were receiving backing from the Italians in these endeavors didn't dissuade Marzette from setting out to do the same thing in Detroit, without his former partners in the Mafia.

Simply being associated with Henry Marzette gave anyone instant status and credibility. Being Blaze's right-hand man, John Claxton was his eyes and ears on a day-to-day basis. And naturally, as Marzette's star rose to astronomic heights throughout the 1960s, so did his own. Claxton controlled the delivery of the "daily package" early in the day and oversaw the pickup of the profits late at night. When Marzette gave an order, it was Gentleman John who was doling out the instructions. Marzette and Claxton had become very tight once again, reconnecting after Blaze got out of jail. Together they set out to rule the streets. Once they did, the ostentatious pair were often seen cavorting around town, enjoying themselves at the area's most elite restaurants and clubs. They traveled the world together, wheeling and dealing from one end of the globe to the other. Hand in hand, they oversaw the drug trade in Detroit's black community and raked in the cash, prestige, and power at an epic rate. Claxton was quite impressed with himself and what he had become, and he acted accordingly. People called started calling him "Gentlemen John" for his generous tipping policy, or "Diamond Tooth John" for the four-karat diamond he wore in one of his front teeth. To put it mildly, he liked to show off.

"He certainly was an ostentatious figure," said former Detroit Police Chief and Gang Squad captain Ike McKinnon. "I knew him as Classen. His real name was Classen, but on the street they called him Claxton. He drove a big, chocolate-brown Cadillac. I happened to live down the street from him back then, and one day I was walking by his flat and saw him counting these huge stacks of cash in the window with the blinds wide open. I think that kind of speaks to his mindset."

Within weeks of meeting John Claxton and being exposed to his lifestyle, Eddie Jackson was convinced that he wanted to emulate him and his boss Blaze Marzette in every way possible. Soon he would do just that.

◇◇◇◇◇◇◇◇◇◇◇◇◇

Around the same time Eddie Jackson started to make his drop-offs for John Claxton, he lost half of his left index finger in an accident at the auto plant he worked at during the day. As a result of the accident, Eddie quit his job at the plant and decided to jump full-time into the dope game. The unfortunate incident served as an easy excuse to abandon his life on the straight and narrow and transition into a life of crime. Like a fish in water, Eddie was a natural. In no time he had graduated from running errands for Gentlemen John to opening up shop for himself. Recovering a substantial worker's compensation claim in the following months, Jackson used it as seed money to jumpstart his own drug operation. Getting a steady stream of top-quality heroin from Claxton, his burgeoning narcotics empire was off and running.

Proving a fast study, Jackson shot up the ranks. Four months into his new-found profession, he was already Marzette's and Claxton's biggest earner with a growing reputation of being able to dispense drugs almost as fast as his new bosses could supply them to him. In no time, Eddie Jackson, or as he came to be called on the streets, "The Fat Man" for his girth, was making more money than he had ever seen before in his life. His dad had achieved moderate wealth, but Eddie was becoming rich. And because he was so good at his job, those he was working for, specifically Marzette and Claxton, were getting richer.

The first thing Eddie bought for himself with his new surplus of cash was a candy-apple-red Cadillac Fleetwood, the ultimate sign of success in the inner city. Then, with enough cash stashed away to establish a payroll, he put together a skilled crew of soldiers and lieutenants to help maintain and grow his business operations. At the top of the food chain were Eddie's brother Elijah and his child-hood best friend Courtney Brown, who left his job as a city bus driver and labor union representative to enter the drug world with the Jackson brothers. Eddie called Brown "The Field Marshal," because of his pal's love of military history, or "Birmingham Brown," a reference to a comic strip character from their youth. He would be the organization's de facto consigliere and chief financial officer for the next decade and a half. Always a phone call away, and often utilized by both Jackson and Brown as a go-to advisor, was an old-timer named Richard "The Penguin" Wakefield, whose knowledge of the local underworld was unparalleled.

Underneath them were top street lieutenants like Ronald "Five-O" Garrett, Charles "The Great Dolph" Rudolph, and Russell "Rango" Clayton, and enforcers like Thomas "Black Butch" Sharpe, Eddie's bodyguard and most trusted strong arm, and William "Big Willie" Kilpatrick. The Fat Man's crew was complete. It was a fearsome bunch with brains, brawn, and guts. Interestingly enough, Courtney Brown, who would go on to be Eddie's longtime right-hand man and number-two guy in the organization, was the last to come on board—the final holdout from a group of childhood friends who had slowly turned their backs on living a legiti-mate life. Up until 1970, a good year into Jackson's rise up the underworld ladder, Brown had resisted the temptation, counseling Eddie and Elijah on business affairs, but never fully embracing their new endeavor and certainly not asking to be a part of it.

That all changed in the fall of 1970, when frustrated by the bureaucracy and politics of his job with the city and exhausted from working his fingers to the bone for little pay as a bus driver, Brown went to Eddie and asked to come on board full-time. Having already helped his best friend tremendously as a part-time sounding board and business counselor, it was a no-brainer to bring The Field Marshal officially into the fold. Jackson, Brown, Garrett, Rudolph, and Clayton called themselves "The Fabulous Five," and the organization they were building was dubbed "The Empire." The group of like-minded young and street-savvy men took off with reckless abandon. Brown, Garrett, Rudolph and Clayton followed the lead of their boss, The Fat Man, who had already made all the crucial inroads and connections in the game prior to the formation of their crew.

Inspired by his father's love of real estate, Eddie and The Empire started acquiring property and securing territory all over the city. Their reputation was solidified when Eddie, wanting to expand his operations and with the help of Courtney's keen eye, purchased an apartment building on Hancock and John R Road, right off the service drive of the I-75 expressway. The Hancock location became the organization's base of operations, and the immediate success the tight-knit crew experienced there further tagged Eddie as an up-and-coming power player on the streets of Detroit. Using the top floors to manufacture his product and the bottom floors to sell it, Jackson's red-brick, colonial-style building became a 24-hour drug den that racked up a steady flow of daily profits due to the quality and cheapness of the drugs being sold. Celebrating their good fortunes and soaring business prospects, Eddie and Courtney bought neighboring estates in an upscale subdivision of houses in Southfield, the city that borders Detroit directly to the north. They raised their families side by side in Caucasian- dominated suburbia, instead of in the city where they were plying their illicit trade. Elaborate vacations and impromptu excursions to sporting events and music concerts became the norm for the pair and their families.

"Eddie Jackson really epitomized the post-riot underworld in the city," Ike McKinnon commented. "Overnight, this guy went from a nobody to a millionaire. It was literally in a matter of months. He was just a kid from the neighborhood with a lot of ambition and street smarts. Before the riots in 1967, a young man like that might have gone the other way and become a real success in the legitimate world. But the kids got disillusioned and people were moving out of the city just as fast as the hustlers and big-time dealers were coming in. They looked up to people like Marzette and Claxton, not the guy working the line shift at Ford."

Everything seemed perfect and as 1971 began, it was. Then, like a sudden earthquake, the ground beneath Eddie became unstable, and the way he made a living was put in jeopardy. Some of the cause of this instability had to do with Eddie personally, but most of it didn't. No matter what the cause, the fact was that the streets were engulfed in a war. Eddie and Courtney, although for all intents and purposes neutral in the dispute, were about to experience some collateral damage. And things were going to get worse before they got better.

◇◇◇◇◇◇◇◇◇◇◇◇

A man of short temper who had a penchant for holding grudges for even the smallest perceived slight, John Claxton was angered by how close Eddie had become to Henry Marzette. In Claxton's mind, he had brought Jackson into the game and it was at his doorstep that Jackson's loyalty should lay. The fact that Marzette had swooped in and claimed Jackson as his own protégé incensed him. The fact that Jackson was encroaching upon his territory as Marzette's favorite social companion drove him downright crazy. Instead of Gentlemen John sitting next to Marzette at his table in The Safari Room, a popular lounge and bar on Dexter, it was now Eddie Jackson. Instead of Claxton accompanying Marzette on his bicoastal jaunts, it was Eddie and Courtney.

The tension built steadily, based primarily on the fact that Claxton resented Eddie's rise and saw him as a threat to his own position within Marzette's kingdom. These suspicions were further solidified in Claxton's mind when he saw Eddie starting to become the apple of the boss' eye as an earner and a social companion. The first sign that things were going south came when Claxton stopped returning Eddie's phone calls. Next, he stopped showing up in person at their weekly "sales meeting," sending a crony instead. It wasn't long before Gentlemen John had cut him and his crew off altogether, refusing to sell their organization any heroin.

What started as a minor rift due to petty jealousy had developed into a full-blown feud between the two drug bosses. Under normal circumstances, this type of beef would immediately be sorted out and mediated by Marzette. But the reputed Godfather of the Motor City's Black Mafia had more pressing concerns to deal with than the schoolyard spat going on between his two top lieutenants. For the previous few months, the Marzette organization was under siege. It was in the midst of a street war raging out of control for supremacy in Detroit's inner-city drug market, a war that Marzette himself had started. On top of that, the 44-year-old kingpin was dealing with serious health issues related to a failing kidney.

The early 1970s were tumultuous times for everyone involved in the Detroit underworld. Sides were being chosen and the battle promised to be intense and bloody. Eddie Jackson saw the unrest among his peers as an opportunity to make an eventual power grab. He planned and plotted stealthily, sitting back in the shadows as those around him fought among themselves for the top spot in the local narcotics market—a spot he desired and knew could be his if he played his cards just right.

◇◇◇◇◇◇◇◇◇◇◇

It was an idea as dangerous as it was ambitious. Henry Marzette wanted to shut the Italians out of the inner-city drug industry and create a city-wide conglomerate of African-American crime bosses which he would oversee. The endeavor was the definition of a "high-risk, high-reward" gamble. Never one to shy away from a risky challenge, Marzette seized upon the idea and tried to make it a reality. In mid-1970, he invited nearly 30 of the city's most respected wholesale dealers to a meeting at the 20 Grand Motel on Gratiot in order to make his pitch. The 20 Grand was owned by a longtime local underworld figure and friend of

Marzette's named Edward "Big Foot Eddie" Wingate. Making an early fortune in the numbers business, Wingate owned a moderately successful R&B music label and partnered with several Italian mobsters over the years in a variety of gambling ventures until his death in 2008.

Greeting everyone personally as they walked through the door to the suite he had reserved for the gathering, Marzette tried his best to play the role of politician, rather than ruthless drug lord. As the meeting commenced, Blaze stood in the front of the room, ready to hold court. His inner circle—Eddie; Gentlemen John Claxton; Arnold "Pretty Ricky" Wright, his third in command; and James "Jimmy the Killer" Moody, his personal bodyguard, enforcer, and assassin—sat in folding chairs to each side of him. Men with nicknames such as "Cincinnati Black," "Mr. Clean," "Texas Slim," and "Big Son," among an equally colorful brigade of others, were seated in several plush couches adorning the brightly decorated suite.

Getting straight to the point, Marzette asked those in attendance to come under his umbrella and turn their backs on their Italian supply connections. He offered a very enticing bottom line price for their product, as a result of recent deals he had struck in Malaysia, as well as protection if the Mafia chose to protest and declare war. In closing, he noted that the Italians were making all the big bucks on their collective drug transactions and that those present had the leverage to change that. Since they were the ones putting in most of the work, he suggested to them, they were the ones who deserved to be getting the lion's share of the spoils.

When Marzette was finished, the room went silent for a couple of moments. While most of the men he invited appeared ready to acquiesce, if only out of pure fear, one man made it more than obvious that he would not. That man's name was Nual Steel, a ruthless independent drug lord who was known on the local streets for his reckless behavior and indignant attitude. Steel stood up and charged to the front of the room, trying to attack Marzette. Met by Moody before he could lay a hand on his boss, the pair scuffled for a second or two before Steel composed himself and readied to leave. In one last gesture of disdain, he spat in the direction of Moody and Marzette, declaring, "I ain't taking orders from nobody, especially no old man like you!" Never one to enter or exit a room without letting everyone know about it, he stomped out the door of the motel suite in a huff, muttering threats and insults until well out of earshot.

The mini crime conference had backfired. For whatever reason, Marzette couldn't sell his vision. And it wasn't just Steel who was balking. Almost immediately after the kingpin summit, word began to filter out that a number of other attendees, although not nearly as vocal as Steel, were also unhappy with what was presented to them. What was pitched as a cooperative alliance to increase profits for everyone was perceived, at least in part, as a greed-driven power grab. A man of keen instinct, Blaze Marzette knew full well that his actions had just incited a war.

Teaming with a group known as the "East Side 12," it's alleged in police reports that Steel and his new allies approached members of the Detroit Mafia, informed them of what was going on and requested backing in the simmering street battle. Several leaders of the East Side 12 were in attendance at the 20 Grand meeting and when they joined forces with Steel, they introduced him to their contacts in the mob. Impressed by the brash and sharp-minded Steel and realistically having no other choice without risking the loss of their stranglehold on the city's wholesale drug market, the Italians are alleged to have signed off on their war against Marzette.

Unfortunately for Nual Steel, his participation in this blood feud would be short-lived. On August 27, 1970, a mere seven weeks after the fateful get-together at the 20 Grand, James Moody and two of his henchmen gunned down Steel and his bodyguard as they sat having a drink at LaPlayer's Lounge on Joy Road. One of the bar's patrons that night, a man named Charles Perkins, identified Moody to police as the man who murdered Steel, and Jimmy the Killer was soon arrested and charged with the crime. Released on $25,000 bond pending trial, Moody made sure the case would never reach the courtroom—within weeks Perkins disappeared, never to be seen again.

The first salvo had been fired and the violence between the two factions would not cease for another two years. Roaring back on behalf of Steel, the East Side 12 started killing off Marzette's men and firebombing his various drug houses. In retaliation, Moody killed a pair of East Side 12 lieutenants as well as a former Marzette enforcer named Robert "Bobby the Bopper" Martin, who had shifted his loyalty to the Eastsiders, and Joe Graves, a fellow kingfish and participant in the 20 Grand conference, who Marzette felt was too quiet in his support of the Westsiders' cause.

As 1971 began, things got worse and blood was flowing heavily on both sides of the heated gangland dispute. Newspaper accounts of the day put the body count at two gangland-related deaths per week. Police reports indicated that Moody was reputed to have executed 15 people personally between Christmas 1970 and July 1971, all on behalf of the Marzette organization. This included his helping to orchestrate and carry out the infamous Flag Day Massacre, a bloodletting of eight of Marzette's enemies on June 14, 1971.

Despite the casualties that both groups were taking, neither side was backing down and the death toll continued to rise. In what would end up being the most violent and carnage-strewn street war in the city's rich criminal history, close to 75 murders were attributed to the combat engaged in by Marzette's West Side contingent and the East Side 12 for over a year and a half.

"Things were pretty unstable there for a while," said Robert De Fauw, agent in charge of the DEA in Detroit in the 1970s and '80s. "There was a patch there where bodies were dropping at a pretty hefty rate. It was all over who was going to control the heroin in the city. The Italians had always had the power dating back to Prohibition. In the '70s, guys like Marzette wanted to break off and find their own supply connections. They felt stifled. When you mix that with ambition, which Marzette and those people had, it can be combustible and it was."

Implored by the mayor's office and his former associates in the police force and to call off the war, if only to quell increasing public fears stoked by the incessant media coverage of the endless brutality, Marzette did his best, but it proved futile. At the behest of the East Side 12 as a means of ending the dispute, he ordered the murder of his trusted confidant and most-utilized executioner, "Jimmy the Killer" Moody, who was found dead in the trunk of his Cadillac El Dorado at Metropolitan Airport in Romulus in September 1971. Betraying his trust, the Eastsiders extended their assault on the Marzette organization, killing six more of his lieutenants in the next three months.

Meanwhile, Eddie Jackson was content to sit in the background while the two warring drug factions slugged it out and killed each other, keeping out of the way of any and all flying bullets. Although officially he was under Blaze Marzette's banner and sided with the West Side Seven, the Fat Man was always more of a diplomat than a dissident. He didn't believe in extreme violence, feeling it was bad for everybody's bottom line, and preferred negotiation and compromise as methods of resolution. Nevertheless, Jackson was a pragmatist. He understood that violence was inherently intertwined throughout the world where he did business. He also realized that he could spin the situation to his advantage by scooping up all the territory left in the wake of the dozens of dealers who were killed off in the war. The only lingering problems for Eddie were a steady supply connection and his own personal beef with John Claxton. Eddie and Gentleman John had grown to hate each other. It's alleged that Claxton went to Marzette for permission to have Jackson murdered, but Marzette refused. Before things could come to a head, and in a stroke of good luck for Jackson, Claxton was jailed for income tax evasion.

In early 1971, Eddie found a stopgap source for his dope in Denard "Devil" Jackson, a highly feared and well-respected independent wholesaler, whose days on the street were numbered since he was out on an appeal bond, facing impending incarceration for a previous narcotics-related conviction. The drugs were still coming in, but not nearly at the rate Eddie desired. He knew that his relationship with Devil Jackson was only temporary, given Jackson's legal problems. Whether or not Eddie's boss won or lost his current street war was of little consequence. The word was out that Blaze Marzette was living on borrowed time. His kidneys were getting worse, and doctors told him there wasn't much chance of his surviving more than another year or two. There would soon be a void at the top of the city's drug hierarchy. And The Fat Man was intent on filling it.

◇◇◇◇◇◇◇◇◇◇◇◇◇

Eddie Jackson needed a new drug connection. He couldn't go through the Italians because of their ties to the East Side 12, and he couldn't go directly through Henry Marzette because he had practically folded up shop to focus all of his attention on waging war with his enemies and dealing with his health concerns. Resourceful as he was ambitious, Jackson set his sights on New York City as the location where he could find what he needed. Knowing that any underworld player worth his weight in powder would be attending the "Fight of the Century," the first in the trilogy of ring classics between legendary pro boxers Muhammad Ali and Joe Frazier, scheduled for March 8, 1971 at Madison Square Garden, he decided that was the date he would make his mark on the East Coast.

With nothing but the clothes on his back and the money in his wallet, Eddie headed out to Manhattan to find himself a wholesale supplier of heroin. Taking along almost his entire bankroll, which at that time was about $300,000, and renting a fleet of Rolls Royces, Eddie and a small entourage drove from Detroit to New York. Checking into the ritzy Park Plaza Hotel on the morning of the fight, he and his crew took off for an afternoon on the town. As fate would have it, their choice of a clothing store to visit that afternoon would prove fortuitous. While perusing the suits and sport jackets of an upscale Greenwich Village clothier, Eddie struck up a conversation about the fight with a nicely dressed Italian, who was being fitted for a tuxedo. The two men made a wager of $10,000 dollars on the fight with Jackson taking Ali and the other man, who introduced himself only as "Doc," putting his money on "Smokin' Joe." Impressed with Eddie's taste in clothes and boldness in wagering, Doc offered Jackson a ticket to watch the fight with him at ringside. Accepting with a smile and a handshake, Eddie had a hint that there might be more to the friendly gesture than met the eye. The pair sat together at the much-hyped prizefight and watched Ali drop a unanimous decision to Frazier. Leaving Madison Square Garden that night, Eddie and Doc ducked into Doc's limo around the corner from the arena to settle up. Thanking him for his hospitality, Eddie forked over the $10,000 in cash and started to exit the vehicle. Doc grabbed him by the coattail and asked that he sit back down for a second.

"You know, Eddie, you don't have to leave here tonight a loser," he said. Eddie shot Doc an inquisitive look and then asked him what he meant. "I think you and I are in the same business," Doc explained. "And if we are in the same business like I think we are, I think you and I could make some nice money together out there where you live in Motown."

It didn't take Eddie Jackson more than a second to realize he had stumbled upon exactly what he had been looking for. Doc, as it would turn out, was Carmine "The Doctor" Lombardozi, a top narcotics lieutenant in the Gambino crime family, one of the most prominent of the five New York Mafia syndicates. After exchanging numbers, Doc told Eddie he would call him in Detroit in a few days with more details of how they could consummate a transaction. For Eddie and his crew, it was the beginning of a glorious and lucrative relationship. "The Empire" was about to fulfill its name. Returning to the Motor City in good spirits, Eddie was ready to embark on his own and leave the stifling environs of Blaze Marzette's West Side Seven. With the exception of losing his bet on the fight and the gunshot wound his brother Elijah sustained in an altercation with a Harlem pimp in the hours after leaving Madison Square Garden, Eddie's trip had been quite fruitful. If the New York connection turned out as good as he thought it was, he was about to go big time. The jump from well off to wealthy was imminent.

In the following weeks, Jackson sent Charles Rudolph and Ronnie Garrett to Manhattan with $100,000 and instructed them to meet with one of Doc's men on Mulberry Street in Little Italy. Rudolph and Garrett exchanged the cash for a large package of heroin and came back to Detroit to test it. The quality of the drugs was off the chart. After Eddie called to inform Doc of his satisfaction and his desire to get as much heroin as possible, the pair cemented a business relationship from which both would benefit greatly in the coming years. Nobody in Detroit, let alone the Midwest, had heroin so pure. Once processed with the proper cutting agent, Jackson could sell the heroin more cheaply than anyone else in the city. Being of such premium quality and providing such a superior high, the drugs would practically sell themselves. Eddie would be able to undercut and outsell every dealer in town. And that's precisely what he did. Jackson called the special blend of heroin he sold "mixed jive," and it was the biggest hit in town with all the junkies. The money started flowing in faster than he could count it. However, almost as fast as things started to sail off the ground, Eddie and the Empire hit a few bumps in the road. None of these would be immediately damaging, nor would any undercut Jackson's ultimate plan of ascension. But almost all would wind up coming back to haunt him in the end.

◇◇◇◇◇◇◇◇◇◇◇◇

The first piece of bad fortune Eddie experienced was in June 1971, when his brother Elijah overdosed on cocaine. Elijah and Eddie were exceptionally tight and the loss hurt Eddie gravely, sending him into a brief but consuming depression. It got worse. In September, one of Eddie's couriers, a woman he dated on the side named Farrah Lee Riggins, aroused the suspicion of a security officer at the Detroit Metropolitan Airport when she dropped her purse, revealing several stacks of cash, while in the process of boarding a flight to New York City. Airport security informed the Drug Enforcement Administration and Riggins and her two companions, both Jackson employees, were followed when they arrived on the East Coast and traveled to meet their Mafia drug contact. When Riggins went to board her flight back to Detroit, she was detained and eventually arrested after DEA officials found 2,000 grams of uncut, high-grade heroin and $5,000 in cash in her luggage.

Although Riggins never cooperated with the government, the DEA was able to identify her and one of her traveling companions, Big Willie Kilpatrick, as members of the Jackson crew. A case file was immediately opened on Eddie Jackson, with agents in Detroit noting that the Fat Man had branched off from underneath Marzette and Claxton's wing and gone into business for himself. It didn't take long before they had found a weak link in the barrier of soldiers separating Jackson from the street. That weak link ended up being a close associate of Eddie's named George "The Pimp" Blair. As one might be able to deduct from his nickname, Blair was a former pimp turned drug dealer. Jackson had known George for a long time and trusted him fully. But Blair's instincts on who to trust proved faulty, and that is where the problem arose.

During the opening weeks of the DEA's investigation into the Jackson organization, in a sheer stroke of luck for the feds, one of Blair's lieutenants, Roosevelt Nabors, got arrested on an assault charge. The Detroit Police Department, which had custody of Nabors following the arrest, knew that he was a drug runner and soldier in the Fat Man's army and alerted the DEA of his presence. Agents went directly to the city lockup, pulled Nabors out and started trying to get him to flip on his boss, George Blair, and on Blair's boss and the government's ultimate target, Eddie Jackson. Far from a model of strong-mindedness, Nabors folded like a cheap suit.

Using Roosevelt Nabors to gather highly sensitive intelligence on Jackson and his operation, the DEA worked the case for three months, getting court-authorized wiretaps, and setting up round-the-clock surveillance on Eddie and his crew. The feds hit paydirt when Nabors tipped them off about a shipment of heroin coming from New York to Detroit, intended for the Jackson organization. Swooping in on Eddie, Courtney, and Joe and Reggie Weaver, a pair of brothers who were their lieutenants, on December 15, 1971 as they sat around a table in a Jackson-run stash house on Hubbell Street in Northwest Detroit, the DEA agents arrested everyone on the premises and seized 22 kilos of uncut heroin, over $5,000 in cash, and several firearms. No more than a month later, in mid-January 1972, Eddie Jackson, Courtney Brown, and 30 of their underlings were indicted by the federal government.

This was a time period when the city's urban underworld was in the process of undergoing a monumental shift in power. The throne of the kingdom was vacated when Henry Marzette finally lost his battle with kidney disease on April 4, 1972, dying quietly at his residence in Highland Park, surrounded by his family and under indictment on tax evasion charges he would never live to face in court. Eddie wanted the brass ring, and he took it.

Despite his recent legal setback, the Fat Man was a natural choice to fill the top spot. Eddie and Courtney had both posted bail following their indictment and retained two of the best criminal defense attorneys in the country, H. Ross Black of New York City and Milton Henry of Detroit, to fight the case. John Claxton, expected to get out of prison soon, was considered too much of a wild card for the job. In addition, both he and Pretty Ricky Wright were facing mounting problems of their own regarding fallout from investigations into their activities while working under Marzette. Strongly opposed to going back behind bars, Claxton was out of jail and on the streets for less than six months when he jumped bail after being indicted on more charges. To this day, he has never been found.

Before Eddie Jackson could assume the throne and start to flood the streets of Detroit with more pure heroin than the city had ever seen, he had to straighten things out with the Italians back in New York. The Gambinos had heard that Jackson's operation had been raided and that he was facing major jail time if convicted. They wanted assurances of his trustworthiness. Eddie had something he wanted to discuss with his mob contacts as well, since he had recently been informed by some associates that Doc and his men had been overcharging him for his product. Taking his lieutenant Black Butch with him as protection, Eddie boarded a plane for New York and readied himself for a confrontation.

Instructed to meet with Doc and his men at a bakery in Little Italy, Eddie and Black Butch arrived 10 minutes early to find the Gambino clan already there waiting for them. Putting to ease their fears that he would betray them, Eddie explained that his legal problems were in good hands with his lawyers and that the Detroit drug market was opening up for the taking with the untimely death of Blaze Marzette. Pleased by the news he was given, Doc perked up and smiled in Eddie's direction from across a table in the back room. It was then that Jackson broached the subject of the price discrepancy in what he was being asked to pay for his drugs. Doc was not pleased with the line of questioning and quickly changed his tone. In turn, Eddie was offended that the Italians were unmoved by his concerns and believed he was not being taken seriously. Never one to hold his tongue, he minced no words in telling Doc how he felt. With nothing left to be said between the two, Eddie motioned to Black Butch and they stormed out of the bakery and took the first plane back to Detroit. After a couple of days, Doc's people phoned Eddie's home in Southfield and requested another meeting to resolve the situation. Eddie returned to New York and Doc's bakery with Black Butch in tow. Doc greeted the pair at the door and got straight to the point.

"You were right to be angry, Mr. Jackson, and I want to make it up to you," he said. "But at the same time, you have to know speaking to me the way you did was unacceptable."

Agreeing to let bygones be bygones, Eddie apologized and told Doc that the way he could make it up to him was to start filling larger orders. He explained the current scenario in Detroit with Marzette out of the picture and a void at the top of the city's drug supply line that needed to be filled.

"I'm going to give you what you ask for," Doc said to Eddie. "I'm going to give you what you ask for because I respect you as a businessman and think you can make us all a lot of money."

Before ending the meeting, Doc left Eddie and Butch with one final thought to ponder as they were about to depart: "My hand reaches far and wide in this country and I can touch anyone, anywhere, anytime," he said, extending his right hand in a sweeping motion. "Try to remember that, Mr. Jackson, as we continue to do business together and it will serve you well."

Nodding his head in assent, Eddie shook Doc's hand and returned to the Motor City with all the necessary tools to build his organization to new heights. He might have been facing one federal indictment—and although he didn't know it yet, he would soon face another—but Eddie Jackson was about to hit the prime of his career as a drug czar. Ironically, he would make more money and achieve more success with the numerous legal hassles hanging over his head than he ever did when he was not in trouble. According to those who knew Eddie at that point in his life, the irony was not lost on him.

"He became The Man, the biggest dealer in the city all the while he was facing all those charges," said Jackson's son and namesake, Eddie Jr. "That was always funny to him. It was like he needed to work out some of the kinks before things could really get cooking."

◇◇◇◇◇◇◇◇◇◇◇

Life was good for everyone in "The Empire" in 1973. It was practically perfect for childhood best friends Eddie Jackson and Courtney Brown, raising their families side-by-side in a beautiful, tree-lined suburban neighborhood, miles away from the dirt-filled streets and alleyways where they made their fortunes. The two sprawling residences formed a mini-compound, often hosting a cast of characters straight out of the early-'70s blaxploitation flick, *Super Fly*. In the shadow of their husbands' nefarious activities, Octavia Jackson and Theresa Brown did their best to make living in the midst of a thriving crime conglomerate as normal as possible for their children.

"We'd be playing in the yard every afternoon after school when I was a kid and we'd see the FBI surveillance cars driving by at the same time every day," said Eddie Jr. "Other than that, we had a real normal childhood. But even that whole thing was normal for us because we didn't know any better. I thought all people had dads that acted like my father."

The money was coming in faster than they had ever seen. Overwhelmed by the deluge of cash careening through their pockets, Eddie and Courtney went on epic spending sprees and began piling up legitimate side businesses to launder their profits. Later on, when the government was analyzing Eddie's financial records and asset holdings, it was discovered that he owned several million dollars in real estate and Wall Street investments. Only able to dump so much of their money into banks without raising the suspicions of the Internal Revenue agents assigned to track all of their cash deposits, Eddie and Courtney bought a half-dozen residential homes to be used strictly for storing their illegal proceeds. Ditching his Caddy for a sterling new Rolls Royce, Eddie proclaimed himself "The Crowd Pleaser." Living up to his new nickname, Jackson would drive through the ghetto in his Rolls and throw cash out the window to screaming kids. He would do the same at the night clubs he liked to frequent, cementing later claims by local dealers and kingpins that Detroit was the city that invented the hip hop culture phenomenon of "making it rain."

"Eddie Jackson was old school and represents that whole era right before things kind of went crazy in the '80s," Carl Taylor commented. "People were drawn to him and he ran with a fast, celebrity-filled crowd. He was cool and calm, not a hothead and not someone who wanted to start chopping people up like some of his successors. Making money and having fun was what he got off on, not death and destruction. He was the last of that kind in a lot of ways."

The larger Eddie's name became on the streets, the more high-profile company he started to keep. Word quickly spread after Henry Marzette's passing that the best place to get your stuff was with Eddie Jackson and "The Empire." And it wasn't just within the city's drug world. Practically all of Detroit's black celebrities who used drugs beat a path to Eddie's doorstep. Motown Records stars David Ruffin, Eddie Kendricks, and Marvin Gaye were frequent social companions of Eddie and Courtney, and some of his best customers. When comedians Richard Pryor and Red Foxx came to town for gigs, Eddie's house was often their first stop after they touched down at the airport.

It was at this time that Eddie developed a very close relationship with iconic black author Donald Goines, a born-and-bred Detroiter himself. Goines, who made a legendary reputation in the African-American community writing fictional stories of street life, was fascinated by Jackson, his profession and position in the underworld, and the fact that the Fat Man lived the stories he wrote about. They would spend days on end holed up in luxury hotel suites together, snorting cocaine and exchanging stories. Often Eddie would take Goines with him on business trips to New York or on vacations to California to see the concerts of the men he was supplying back in Michigan. Rumor has it that one of Goines' most celebrated novels, *Dopefiend*, as well as several others, had central characters based on Eddie Jackson and instances depicted in the storylines plucked straight from their friendship.

Eddie and The Empire hit their full stride in the fall of 1973. The top of the mountain brought in more money than was imaginable by today's standards. Unfortunately, as was the case with much of his success, it was accompanied by a series of bitter legal setbacks.

"When I arrived in Detroit in the 1970s, it was evident that Eddie Jackson out in Southfield was controlling most of the drugs flowing into the city," Mike Carone recalled. "I was advised that he had taken over operations from Henry Marzette.

Not a lot of people remember or talk about Jackson today, maybe because he didn't have the flashy nickname or wasn't spread all over the headlines, ordering killings and stuff. But he was as big as they got in that world in Detroit for a good chunk of time."

Earlier that year, Eddie, Courtney, and nearly three dozen of their lieutenants were convicted in federal court on drug conspiracy charges. The government's evidence was too damning to overcome. Roosevelt Nabors' testimony, combined with the wiretap transcripts and the surprise testimony of George Blair's wife Ruth, who told of life inside the Jackson-Brown compound and inner circle, simply blew the jury away and led to a fast guilty verdict. It continued to get worse as Jackson and Ronnie Garrett were convicted of further federal charges spawning from a routine June 1972 traffic stop on the Pennsylvania Turnpike where police found 11 kilos of heroin and three kilos of cocaine in their vehicle. Bonded out on both charges by mob-connected bail bondsman Charles "Chuckie G" Goldfarb," Eddie went about business as usual. And business was more than good. From October until December, The Empire cleared a staggering $50 million, taking in nearly a million dollars a day of gross profit.

The good times lasted for another four years until April 1977, when with all of his appeals exhausted, Eddie Jackson was sentenced to 30 years in federal prison, ordered to be served concurrently between the Detroit and Pennsylvania convictions. The judge in the Detroit case wasn't much easier on Courtney, hitting him with 21 years. Released on an appeal bond in 1983, Jackson went back to work in the drug game for 15 months before being jailed on another narcotics conviction. He died of natural causes in April 1995 in a federal prison in Colorado. Following his release, Courtney Brown also drifted back into the world of illicit powder. He was caught in a federal drug bust and sent back to jail in 2002. Brown was released from prison in 2011 and is reported to have gone straight.

"Most people don't remember Eddie Jackson these days," Carl Taylor noted. "But he is an important figure from that time period. Men like him and Marzette blazed a trail for all the guys, like YBI, Pony Down, and Best Friends, who came after him. Jackson represented a mentality, a level of empowerment that people around Detroit had never been exposed to before. The fact that all the characters that most people know of that followed him in the game had that same mentality at the core, a mindset that 'Hey, I'm gonna go for mine and not bow down to anyone,' is no coincidence."

UNION WARS

Three the Hard Way

Hoffa's Last Stand

Waiting inside the foyer of the Machus Red Fox restaurant on the corner of Maple and Telegraph in Bloomfield Township, Jimmy Hoffa was furious. Scheduled to attend a lunch meeting with high-profile mob leaders Anthony "Tony Jack" Giacalone and Anthony "Tony Pro" Provenzano at 2:00 p.m., it was after 2:45 and there was no sign of either of them. The former union czar had been stood up. Seething with anger over being disrespected, Hoffa, a long-established icon of the organized labor movement, stormed out of the restaurant and made his way to a pay phone outside a nearby hardware store. Calling his wife of nearly 40 years, Josephine, at his cottage on Lake Orion, he told her what had happened and added that he would be back home in less than an hour to start grilling steaks for dinner. He never made it there.

At approximately 3:00 p.m. on July 30, 1975, witnesses saw Hoffa getting into a maroon-colored Lincoln Mercury occupied by three other men and leaving the restaurant parking lot. After that, Jimmy Hoffa disappeared, never to be seen again. Over 35 years later, Hoffa's disappearance has gone down as the most notorious unsolved crime in American history. In 1982, the state of Michigan officially issued a death certificate to his family and legally declared him deceased, yet the civic formality did little to quell the unquenchable thirst for information on the specific circumstances that ended with Hoffa's almost certainly violent demise. Theories and explanations for what actually happened to Jimmy Hoffa have ranged from the absurd to the logical. However, it remains an open case with no charges having been filed against anyone. One thing that was known for sure at the time Hoffa went missing was that he had a lot of powerful enemies who all had a lot of reasons to want him out of the way. For all of his good qualities, possibly Hoffa's biggest flaw was his outright stubbornness and his penchant for challenging authority of any kind. In the end, it is without a doubt the flaw that got him killed.

◇◇◇◇◇◇◇◇◇◇◇◇

James Riddle Hoffa was born on Valentine's Day, February 14, 1913, in Brazil, Indiana, where his father was a coal miner and his mother washed laundry for a living. After his dad died of lung cancer when he was seven, Hoffa's mother took him and his four brothers and sisters for a two-year stay in Clinton, Indiana before coming to Detroit in 1924, following Jimmy's 11th birthday. Dropping out of school in the ninth grade, Hoffa made a name for himself around his working-class West Side neighborhood as a tough kid with a magnetic yet very aggressive personality. Wandering around the city's pool rooms and back alleys for a couple of years, he finally landed a job unloading boxes of produce at the Kroger Grocery and Bakery Company when he was 16. Hoffa's natural leadership ability and knack for confrontation were soon in evidence, and by the time he was 18 in 1931, he had organized a headline-grabbing labor stoppage at Kroger dubbed "The Strawberry Strike." The action eventually led to union representation and a raise for the strikers.

Hoffa's gutsy maneuver gained him much notoriety in the press and in the world of organized labor, and within a year he was hired as an official organizer by the International Brotherhood of Teamsters, a union that specialized in protecting the rights of the nation's truck drivers. Hoffa brought with him several of his co-workers from Kroger, a number of whom would go on to become the anchors of his future power base, Local 299 in the heart of Southwest Detroit. In the coming years, Hoffa rose rapidly in the union ranks, cementing his status by forging deep ties with members of the Mafia. He was introduced to shady underworld characters, including Frank "Frankie Three Fingers" Coppola, Santo "Cockeyed Sam" Perrone, and Angelo "The Chairman" Meli, by his longtime girlfriend, Sylvia Pagano, one of the city's most famous gun molls. Hoffa and his friends in the mob built the once lowly trucker's union into a juggernaut in the labor world with few if any equals.

The shadowy relationship between the mob and the Teamsters was a long-standing one. The mob gave the Teamsters protection from strikes and an intimidation factor at the negotiating table, and in return the union provided the Mafia with incredible influence inside its own ranks, not to mention nearly unlimited access to its robust coffers. Seizing on the Teamsters' previously embedded underworld connections, Hoffa cultivated increased activity between the two groups and used the ties to guide the union to epic heights.

In 1952, at the age of 39, Hoffa became the youngest man ever to be elected to the Teamsters vice presidency. Five years later in 1957, after President Dave Beck was convicted on federal charges of embezzlement, larceny, and tax evasion, Hoffa was elected president, starting a reign of more than a decade that would make him one of the most recognized public figures in America and the Brotherhood of Teamsters the largest, most powerful labor union in the world. Hounded by constant rumors of corruption within his administration and rampant speculation about his links to organized crime, Hoffa tiptoed through the minefields for a while, but he was eventually taken down by an aggressive full-court press from the federal government. In 1967, he was convicted of jury tampering, fraud, and conspiracy in the handling of his union's benefits fund.

Defiant to the bitter end, Hoffa refused to relinquish his presidency when he was shipped off to serve a 13-year sentence at Lewisburg Federal Penitentiary in Pennsylvania. Instead, he had his vice president and right-hand man Frank Fitzsimmons run things on his behalf while he was locked up. Like an imprisoned mob boss, Hoffa ran his regime from behind bars. His indignant attitude and lack of contrition significantly undermined his chances of an early release. In June 1971, Hoffa finally acquiesced and surrendered his leadership post, paving the way for Fitzsimmons to be elected the new head of the Teamsters later that summer and securing his own ticket to freedom before the end of the year. With the aid of Fitzsimmons and other powerful allies, Hoffa was able to finagle himself a presidential pardon, and by December he was spending Christmas at home with his family. Unbeknownst to him at the time, his plan to reclaim his seat atop the Teamsters' hierarchy was dead in the water even before he stepped out of his Pennsylvania prison cell.

The Mafia didn't want Hoffa back in the union presidency. He was a high-maintenance ally, causing too many headaches for their liking and often refusing to take orders. They preferred Fitzsimmons, a mild-mannered bureaucrat who was easily influenced and didn't question instructions. Without Hoffa's knowledge, the mob had Fitzsimmons negotiate a clause in his former boss' sentencing commutation stipulating that he would be barred from holding any official union leadership positions until 1980. Informed of the restriction in the days after his release from prison, Hoffa was incensed. He was immediately aware of what was going on: the Mafia and his former top lieutenant were trying to push him out of the picture altogether. Never one to back down from a fight, Hoffa would declare an all-out war against Fitzsimmons and the same mobsters he had relied on so heavily during his rise to power. It was a bitter feud that lasted over three years, escalated as it progressed, and didn't end until Hoffa was taken out of the picture permanently.

◇◇◇◇◇◇◇◇◇◇◇◇

Jimmy Hoffa's return to Detroit in early 1972 was big news. His star-studded homecoming party was held on the day after New Year's at the Raleigh House on Franklin Road and Telegraph in Southfield, at that time a very popular restaurant and banquet hall. The occasion was covered by all the local newspapers and television channels. Surrounded by family, friends, and reporters, Hoffa made it clear to everyone in attendance that his first and only priority from that point forward would be to fight his commutation's restrictions and regain the Teamsters presidency at any and all costs in the 1976 election. Keeping a relatively low profile for the next year or so until his parole ended, Hoffa then took his fight public, doing a series of interviews in which he stated his case and bad-mouthed Frank Fitzsimmons and his rivals in the mob. He spoke about turning over a new leaf and wanting to rid the union of the influence of organized crime. These words didn't sit well with his old compatriots, and several messages were sent through intermediaries warning Hoffa to watch what he was saying to the press.

After a year of politicking and publicly making his case at every opportunity, Hoffa was starting to make significant headway. Word was spreading as early as spring 1974 that plans were in the works to have Hoffa's ban on running for office lifted by the court. The beefs he had with the mob did little to affect his popularity. Despite the fact that he was convicted of federal corruption charges related to his tenure in office, Hoffa's popularity with the Teamsters never waned. Everyone knew that if the restrictions were lifted and Hoffa ran in the 1976 union presidential election, he would defeat Fitzsimmons in a landslide.

The mob couldn't, and more importantly wouldn't, let that happen. They had too much invested in their relationship with the Teamsters to have it threatened, especially the lucrative financial interests in Las Vegas tied directly to control over the union's hefty pension fund. It was feared that Hoffa, with his intimate knowledge of these shady dealings, would agree to sever the relationship between the Teamsters and the mob if the government allowed him to take back his post as union president. Furthermore, many worried that Hoffa was already attempting to curry favor and sway the court's decision on whether or not the clause in his pardon was constitutional by feeding the FBI information on both his friends and enemies throughout the nation's criminal underworld. Friends instantly became enemies in this heated conflict that eventually became front-page news and engulfed the lives of many in both camps for over two years. Violence and intimidation tactics were widespread across the board, neither side willing to give an inch and each always looking to gain leverage over the other whenever possible.

The biggest and most vocal adversary Hoffa faced in his quest to defeat Frank Fitzsimmons and the mob and reclaim the Teamsters' empire for himself was Anthony "Tony Pro" Provenzano, a New Jersey-based organized crime figure and labor union boss who was at one time a close confidant of Hoffa's but had since turned into a fervent enemy. Besides his legal fight with Uncle Sam over his candidate status in the upcoming union election, the bad blood that had developed between Hoffa and Provenzano, who was capo in the Genovese crime family in New York and who, ironically, gained his position in the union power structure due to an appointment by Hoffa a decade earlier, was the biggest hurdle for Hoffa to overcome.

Serving prison time together in Lewisburg back in the late 1960s, Hoffa and Provenzano started as workout companions and bridge partners and wound up nearly killing each other in the penitentiary mess hall, coming to blows one day over money Provenzano felt he was entitled to from the union during his stay behind bars. Upon release from incarceration and back on the warpath, Hoffa was quick to understand that he would need to squash the beef if he wanted to return to the Teamsters presidency. Unlike in prison, where Hoffa had a leg up in the dispute since he was still running the union and oversaw Provenzano's activity with the Teamsters, once back on the street, Tony Pro held all the cards. He controlled the East Coast delegates that Hoffa needed in his pocket to beat Fitzsimmons in an election. Without Provenzano's backing, Hoffa's chances of winning his seat took a major hit. Hoping that bygones could be bygones, Hoffa requested a meeting with Tony Pro in Miami to settle their differences. The sit-down only made things worse. Similar to what had happened back in Lewisburg, the two strong-minded and volatile men had to be separated inside a plush suite at a Miami hotel. Volleying threats back in fourth, the altercation concluded with Provenzano threatening to kidnap and kill Hoffa's grandchildren and storming out of the room.

After Hoffa went on television in February 1974 and trashed Fitzsimmons and Provenzano, saying that the entire sitting Teamsters leadership was controlled by organized crime, the mob had Fitzsimmons strike back by systematically eliminating Hoffa loyalists from the union ranks. His wife, son, and countless close associates and supporters were fired from their jobs. Federal documents allege that Fitzsimmons and Provenzano created an entire squad of Teamster strong-arms headed by Roland "Big Mac" McMasters, the union's most feared enforcer, to make it their daily mission to block Hoffa from returning to power.

One of Hoffa's closest allies was Dave Johnson, president of the old Local 299 on Trumbull Avenue in Detroit. Johnson wouldn't give in to pressure from Fitzsimmons' mob-backed contingent to step down so he could be replaced by Richard "Little Fitz" Fitzsimmons, Frank's son. McMasters and his crew of henchmen then started making Johnson's life a living hell. He began to get hang-up phone calls at all hours of the night; he had his office riddled with shotgun fire while he sat at his desk; and in the summer of 1975, he had his luxury sailboat, docked on the Detroit River, blown to pieces by an explosive device. Although Johnson would make a deal to spare himself more violence by agreeing to let "Little Fitz" become his vice president, the assault on Hoffa continued.

Things reached a crescendo in the heated battle of wills in the spring and summer of 1975. According to FBI documents, at the beginning of that year, Hoffa attended several meetings with ranking members of the Mafia in Detroit and Chicago, where he was ordered to retire from his pursuit of re-election. Unfazed, he responded by spewing more threats and refusing to stop campaigning in an attempt to retrieve his old job. That was the first nail in Hoffa's coffin. The second nail came in May when Hoffa was called in front of a federal grand jury that had been impaneled to investigate "no show" jobs and mob influence at Local 299. On

countless other occasions in the past, he had snubbed his nose at similar government subpoenas, refusing to answer questions and pleading the Fifth Amendment.
But not on this occasion. Called to the stand on May 15, 1975, Hoffa testified in
detail about what he did and then was quoted by a local newspaper as saying that
he was "damn proud" of doing it.

In retaliation for Hoffa's continued public flirting with the feds, Frank
Fitzsimmons threatened to put a number of pro-Hoffa locals into trusteeship. In
late June, Hoffa ally Ralph Proctor, who would be murdered gangland-style eight
years later due to an unrelated conflict involving the union and the mob, was
jumped on the way to his car after a lunch meeting and beaten unconscious. Just
two weeks later on July 10th, Richard Fitzsimmons had his car blown up in the
parking lot of Nemo's Bar & Grill on Michigan Avenue, only a few short blocks
from Local 299. Many believed Hoffa ordered the bombing. Others believed it
was the work of people trying to make it look like Hoffa's doing, hoping that it
would lead to his demise. FBI documents reveal that around this same time, multiple informants stated that Hoffa had sought to take out murder contracts on
Frank and Richard Fitzsimmons as well as his hated rival, Tony Provenzano. Either
way, the incident served as the boiling point and paved the way for Hoffa's
undoing.

This series of events, occurring over a little less than two months, proved the
final straws in the saga and put into motion the most talked-about mob hit of all
time. While practically every FBI agent who ever worked on the investigation
claims to have a pretty good sense of what happened to Hoffa on the fateful afternoon of Wednesday, July 30, 1975, the case has never been officially solved. Using
over 500 pages of federal documents related to the investigation and the insight of
those members of law enforcement who worked the case, the following is the most
up-to-date and reliably likely account of what happened.

At some point in early 1974, a contract was issued on Hoffa's life in a decision
signed off on by Detroit Mafia don Joe Zerilli, Chicago mob boss Tony Accardo,
Pennsylvania Godfather Russell Buffalino, and Tony Salerno, the front boss for
the Genovese crime family. Because Hoffa "belonged" to the Detroit mob, Zerilli's
crime family was in charge of coordinating the details. With Zerilli getting up in
age, FBI records suggest that his heir apparent and nephew, Giacomo "Black Jack"
Tocco, and syndicate street boss Anthony "Tony Jack" Giacalone were the ones
who most likely oversaw the planning of the execution.

In the first weeks of July, FBI surveillance agents observed Salerno's proxy,
Tony Provenzano, flying into Detroit to meet with Roland McMasters and Tony
Giacalone, Hoffa's contact with the Detroit mob, at a hotel near Metro Airport in
Romulus. Tony Pro and Tony Jack were related through marriage—Giacalone was
married to the daughter of Giacomo "Big Jack" Provenzano, the Detroit Mafia's
longtime crew leader in Saginaw and an uncle of Tony Pro's. It is believed that the

meeting of the minds at the airport hotel was held to finalize the specifics of the high-profile kill. Since Hoffa knew he still needed Provenzano's support to get back into office with the Teamsters, it had been decided that a meeting with Provenzano—to secure his blessing—would be used as the lure. The mob knew full well that Hoffa's love of the union far surpassed his hatred for Tony Pro and that the prospect of getting things squared away with Provenzano and obtaining his pledge of delegates would be a sufficient setup strategy to get Hoffa out in the open. The assessment was spot-on.

The only problem was finding a place to meet where the mob could get Hoffa alone. For months, he was refusing to travel to New Jersey to see Provenzano. His only requirement was that Tony Pro come to Detroit to see him. Although he never intended to go to Michigan, Provenzano passed word to Hoffa through Tony Giacalone that he would be there on July 30th. William Buffalino, Hoffa attorney Russell Buffalino's first cousin and a longtime alleged Detroit mob associate, was marrying off his daughter on August 2nd in a lavish ceremony in Grosse Pointe, and many underworld luminaries were expected to descend on the city in the days leading up to the nuptials. This furnished the perfect excuse for his trip and Hoffa bought it hook, line, and sinker.

At a meeting over dinner at Hoffa's Lake Orion residence on July 26th, Tony Giacalone and his brother, fellow mob capo Vito "Billy Jack" Giacalone, informed Hoffa that the sit-down would take place at the Machus Red Fox, an upscale restaurant in Bloomfield Hills, one of the wealthiest bedroom communities in the country, at two in the afternoon. It was agreed that Tony Giacalone would be on hand to act as a mediator, although like Tony Pro, Giacalone had no intention of setting foot anywhere near Bloomfield Hills that day.

An elite assassination squad was assembled in the days leading up to the supposed meeting and was tasked with carrying out all the details of Hoffa's kidnapping, murder, and disposal. According to federal documents, the hit team most likely consisted of Provenzano lieutenants Salvatore "Sally Bugs" Briguglio and Tommy and Stevie Andretta; Russell Buffalino's right-hand man, Francis "Frank the Irishman" Sheeran; and Detroit mobsters Billy Giacalone and Raffealle "Jimmy Q" Quasarano. Briguglio, the Andrettas, and Sheeran, a close Hoffa confidant, flew into Detroit on the morning of July 30th and got ready to complete their assignment.

Sheeran claims in his 2004 book, *I Heard You Paint Houses: The Inside Story of the Mafia, the Teamsters and the Last Ride of Jimmy Hoffa*, that he met Briguglio and the Andrettas at a house on Beaverland Street off Seven Mile Road in Northeast Detroit in the hours prior to Hoffa's scheduled meeting with Giacalone and Provenzano, approximately 10 miles away. He then returned there at approximately at 3:30 and shot Hoffa in the back of the head as they entered the residence together for the sit-down. Whether or not you believe Frank Sheeran's account—much of which came from a deathbed confession given to his lawyer and co-author Charles Brandt—most of those with intimate knowledge of the investigation concede at the very least that he was closely involved with Hoffa's disappearance. FBI documents note Sheeran's presence at several top-echelon mob meetings, thought to be briefings regarding the events surrounding Hoffa's murder, as well as confirmation of his presence in the Detroit area on the day Hoffa went missing. As to his assertion that Hoffa was killed at the house on Beaverland, the FBI disregarded the theory because of the lack of DNA evidence in a forensic analysis of the home subsequent to Sheeran's 2004 confession and the inability to trace the residence to anyone with any relation to the underworld.

What is known for certain is the following: Hoffa left his waterfront property in Lake Orion at approximately 1:00 p.m. in his green Pontiac Granville and stopped by Airport Services Lines, a car courier business in Pontiac owned by one of his closest associates, Louis Linteau, known on the street as "Louie the Pope." Linteau, a former Teamster, and Hoffa used to be enemies but had mended their differences. By the time Hoffa left prison, Linteau had become his unofficial appointments secretary. It was well known in both underworld and labor union circles that Linteau acted as a buffer for Hoffa and that if anyone wanted a face-to-face meeting with him, they needed to contact Linteau first. The dinner meeting between Hoffa and the Giacalone brothers on July 26th, when they informed him of the July 30th sit-down, was arranged by Linteau. Hoffa stopped by his office on his way to the Machus Red Fox to check in before he went to see Tony Jack and Tony Pro. Linteau was out to lunch when Hoffa arrived, so Hoffa left a message for him before departing for his meeting at the Red Fox at approximately 1:45.

Arriving at the restaurant at approximately 2:00, Hoffa stood in the foyer waiting for Giacalone and Provenzano to show up. After making small talk with a half-dozen restaurant guests and employees, Hoffa left the premises at 2:45 and walked less than 100 yards to a hardware store payphone at a shopping mall. In his call, Hoffa told Linteau and his wife that he had been stood up and that he was going to leave immediately. Witness accounts from the parking lot have Hoffa being intercepted by three men in a Lincoln Mercury on his way from the payphone to his car, which was parked near the restaurant. After a brief conversation, Hoffa was observed getting into the Lincoln Mercury, which turned onto Maple Road. He was never seen alive again.

Those who saw the interaction between Hoffa and the men identified Sal Briguglio and Hoffa's surrogate son Chuckie O'Brien as two of the three occupants of the vehicle, which was believed to have most likely belonged to Joey Giacalone, Tony's youngest son. O'Brien, who was caught in the middle of the battle between Hoffa and the mob, was raised by Hoffa, but was also very close to Fitzsimmons and the Giacalone family. He is believed to have been used as a pawn in the plot to get his father figure out in the open so he could be killed. Not known as someone to be trusted with sensitive information, it is unlikely that O'Brien was let in on all the details of the plan. However, it's thought that he was used in the transporting of Hoffa from the restaurant to the execution site, because Hoffa, despite having had a recent falling out with O'Brien over issues related to Teamster politics, would feel safe getting into a car with Chuckie, not believing that the mob would involve him in a hit.

In his book, Frank Sheeran confirms O'Brien's role as the driver of the car that picked up Hoffa, but stated that he left before any violence took place. Admitting to driving Joey Giacalone's Lincoln that afternoon, O'Brien said in interviews with authorities that he used it to deliver a 40-pound prize salmon to Bobby Holmes, a longtime Teamster and close associate of Hoffa's. Known as a compulsive liar by friend and foe alike, O'Brien, the son of Hoffa's and Tony Jack's ex-lover Sylvia Pagano, proved to be telling the truth in that one specific instance, as reddish stains on the backseat of the vehicle tested positive for fish blood. However, there were so many other inconsistencies and holes in O'Brien's story about his activities during the afternoon of July 30th that the federal government is convinced of at least his peripheral involvement in the events leading to Hoffa's death.

Seized by the FBI in the days after Hoffa's disappearance, the Lincoln Mercury remains in a federal evidence storage locker, having been examined thoroughly over the years that followed. Police dogs recognized Hoffa's scent in both the car's backseat and trunk, and a single blood-coated hair, which was a DNA match to hairs from Hoffa's hairbrush, was found on the floor. Further testing uncovered additionally consistent DNA in the trunk and other parts of the car. Still there was not enough evidence to bring charges. All the principal suspects in the case either had ironclad alibis or ones that could neither be confirmed nor denied. Both Tony Giacalone and Tony Provenzano spent the entire afternoon of July 30th in public places surrounded by masses of people. Giacalone was at his unofficial headquarters, the Southfield Athletic Club, located on the first floor of the Travelers Towers office building. It was owned by Giacalone's and Hoffa's mutual acquaintance, Lenny Schultz, an old-time Jewish mob associate who often acted as a go-between for Tony Jack and the labor union brass. A man who made a habit of speaking to as few people as possible, Giacalone was unusually friendly that day at his club as he stopped to chat up several members and employees that he had never spoken to previously, in between taking phone calls and getting a massage and a haircut.

Around 2:30 that afternoon, O'Brien was observed meeting with Giacalone in a corridor of the club. Many in law enforcement believe this meeting was held to provide O'Brien with last-minute instructions, while O'Brien himself chalks it up to Giacalone just wanting to give him $200 as a graduation present for his son. Other FBI surveillance reports have Jack Tocco arriving at the Southfield Athletic Club at around 4:30, presumably to meet with Giacalone after the job was completed. Detroit Mafia lieutenants Peter "Bozzi" Vitale and Jimmy Quasarano, the syndicate's East Coast representatives, along with Sheeran, were seen going to visit Genovese family boss Tony Salerno at his headquarters, The Palma Boys Social Club in Harlem, in the early weeks of August 1975, for meetings that were viewed as "touch-base" sessions with the New York mob. Like Tony Jack, Tony Pro had an airtight alibi. Provenzano was at a New Jersey Teamsters hall playing cards the entire afternoon of July 30th. The only suspect in the case unaccounted for that afternoon was Billy Giacalone, who lost his surveillance team around 11:30 that morning and wasn't tracked down until dinnertime.

Because the Detroit Mafia owned a pair of crematoriums and several trash compactors within less than a half-hour's driving distance from where Hoffa was last seen, FBI reports suggest that his body may have been taken either to a funeral home or a sanitation facility in the area and disposed of there. Informants developed in the Detroit FBI office implicate Jimmy Quasarano, the Motor City crime family's soon-to-be consigliere, as the man in charge of making sure Hoffa's body was deconstructed as quickly as possible after he took his last breath, and Billy Giacalone as the Detroit representative responsible for overseeing the actual assassination.

Even though none of the principal characters in the murderous drama was ever charged with the crime itself, almost every single one of them either died or was imprisoned in the coming years on other racketeering-related charges. Detroit mob don Joe Zerilli passed away from natural causes in 1977. Tony Provenzano was convicted in 1978 of the murder of another Teamsters union official back in 1961 and died in prison in 1988. Tony Giacalone was sent to prison on charges of tax evasion and loansharking and completed a seven-year sentence before dying of cancer in 2001 while still under indictment in a massive racketeering case that was brought in 1996. Russell Buffalino spent time in prison during the late 1970s and most of the 1980s for extortion and attempted murder before dying of natural causes at a Pennsylvania nursing home in 1994. Sheeran, Salerno, and Zerilli's nephew and predecessor Jack Tocco were each convicted of racketeering charges and did time in prison, as was the case with Billy Giacalone, Jimmy Quasarano, and the Andretta brothers. Sal Briguglio was murdered on a street in Little Italy in 1978, after word leaked out that he might be cooperating with federal authorities against Provenzano and the Genoveses and could start divulging details about the Hoffa hit.

◇◇◇◇◇◇◇◇◇◇◇◇

In the years since Jimmy Hoffa disappeared, numerous theories have been proposed as to what happened to him and his body. Some of the more outlandish have been offered by prison inmates, often in the hope of trading the information for their freedom. A former close associate of Tony Provenzano, Donald "Tony the

Greek" Frankos, claimed that Hoffa's remains were buried beneath Giants Stadium in East Rutherford, New Jersey. A witness in an early-1980s Congressional hearing on the Hoffa case testified that Hoffa's body was taken to Florida and fed to alligators in a swamp. In the same hearing, another witness claimed that Hoffa's body was shipped to Georgia and buried underneath the Sheraton Savannah Resort Hotel, a construction project funded with Teamster money.

Theories like Frank Sheeran's have been given more weight by investigators. In 2006, the FBI in Detroit spent a week's time and a quarter of a million dollars of tax money to dig up a horse farm once owned by Roland McMasters, based on information they deemed credible from Donovan Wells, a onetime McMasters associate. Wells succeeded in exchanging the information, which later failed to prove accurate, for his release from prison on a drug-dealing conviction. Ralph "Little Ralphie" Piccardo, a credible informant from the Genovese crime family and a onetime driver for Tony Pro, told authorities that Hoffa's body was placed in an industrial steel drum and driven to a landfill outside of Detroit. Researcher Jeff Hanson believes he has tracked Hoffa's body to a Detroit Metro-area cemetery incinerator where there are record-keeping inconsistencies for cremations done on July 30, 1975. The incinerator is less than a mile from the house where Sheeran claims the murder took place. A number of FBI informants maintained that Hoffa's body was disposed of by one of the two area sanitation companies—Central Sanitation and Tri-County Sanitation—owned by members of the Detroit Mafia.

One of the less well known but more plausible theories stems from an idea developed by a group of retired FBI agents who worked the case in the 1980s, but don't wish to be identified. It is their belief that Hoffa was taken to the residence of Detroit mob soldier Carlo Licata, a mere two-mile drive from the Machus Red Fox on Telegraph Road, and killed there. Carlo Licata was a brother-in-law to Jack Tocco, who at the time of Hoffa's disappearance was Acting Boss of the Detroit Mafia.

A comment made to Frank Sheeran by Russell Buffalino seems to support the idea that Hoffa's body was disposed of at Bagnasco's Funeral Home in St. Clair Shores, owned and operated by Salvatore "Sammy B" Bagnasco, a brother-in-law to both Licata and Tocco. In his book, Sheeran recounts an incident in New York City where Buffalino informed him that Hoffa's body was "cremated at a funeral home in Detroit that was closely associated with the Detroit people," following a run-in with Pete Vitale on the street while he was leaving a restaurant meeting with Fat Tony Salerno in the weeks after the Hoffa hit.

Licata's house was known by authorities to be a frequent meeting spot for the Giacalone brothers and Hoffa, since it was centrally located between Hoffa's house in North Oakland County and Tony Jack's headquarters at the Southfield Athletic Club in South Oakland County. A transplant from California, Licata also had easy access to an incinerator at a local sanitation business he co-owned with Jimmy

Quasarano. To add more mystery and intrigue to the theory, Licata was found dead at the same residence, nestled on a secluded hill at 6380 Long Lake Road, on July 30, 1981, the six-year anniversary of Hoffa's disappearance. He had died of multiple gunshot wounds to the chest. Even though the death was officially ruled a suicide by the Oakland County Medical Examiner, many who worked the Hoffa case in its latter stages have their doubts. When some of these FBI agents began asking their informants on the street about the theory, they received resoundingly positive responses. According to these agents, it is a common belief on the street in Detroit that Hoffa's disappearance and Licata's death were at least loosely connected.

Carlo Licata was the son of Nick Licata, the former don of the Los Angeles Mafia in the late 1960s and early 1970s. Nick Licata had become a made member of the Mafia in Detroit in 1930, but he fled to the West Coast after a falling out with Joe Zerilli and Black Bill Tocco. Hooking up with the mob in Los Angeles, Nick ascended quickly up the ranks of the California Mafia and by the 1950s, he was in place to become an administrator. The only problem that arose with Licata's rise was his feud with Zerilli and Tocco in Michigan. Zerilli sat on the Mafia's national "commission," or unofficial board of directors, and if Licata wanted to become a don himself, he had to make peace.

In 1953, Nick Licata made an arrangement for his son, Carlo, who had recently made his bones in Los Angeles by killing the attorney of legendary California Jewish crime boss Meyer "Mickey C" Cohen, to marry Tocco's daughter and Zerilli's niece Josephine. The wedding was a huge ceremony in downtown Detroit that drew mob chieftains and dignitaries from across the country and officially served to bury the hatchet for the Tocco and Zerilli families. Federal documents related to the investigation of this theory indicate the informants told the FBI that at the time of his passing, Carlo Licata was in a dispute with his brother-in-law, Jack Tocco, over his treatment of Josephine. The informants allege that after a sit-down where Licata was told to stop drinking so much and to start treating his wife better, he became belligerent and threatened to use his knowledge of what happened to Hoffa as a bargaining chip. The FBI agents who favor the theory that Licata's house was the location of the hit believe it's possible that Licata himself was killed in the same spot on the anniversary of the Hoffa murder as a message that no one is safe from harm, not even family members, if they even think about turning on the crime syndicate.

The Days Otto and Ralph Didn't Come Home

A little over two years after Jimmy Hoffa was wiped off the map by the Mafia, one of his former top allies, Otto Wendell, kicked off a trend of onetime close associates of the slain labor boss getting slain themselves—a trend that continued for another seven years. Wendell was a longtime powerbroker in the Detroit-area labor union scene, known to be a whiz with numbers and, like Hoffa, a man often observed in the company of organized crime figures. On December 12, 1977, Wendell was found shot twice in the abdomen in his car on a rural road three miles from his home in Livingston County. He was alive, but barely hanging on. A .38 caliber revolver belonging to Wendell was found next to him and was later determined to be the gun that fired the shots. Rushed to the hospital, he fell into a deep coma for close to two weeks before finally succumbing to his injuries on Christmas Eve.

Otto Wendell's death at the age of 63 was initially ruled a suicide, but was soon relabeled a homicide following the impaneling of a grand jury. Several factors led to this change. First and foremost, it was quickly discovered that Wendell, who at the time of his death was the treasurer of Hoffa's old Local 299, out by Tigers Stadium, was scheduled to testify at the extortion trial of reputed Detroit Mafia captain Vincent "Little Vince" Meli, set to start in the early months of 1978. He was also rumored to have testified in front of a number of grand juries regarding his knowledge of organized crime influence within the Teamsters union. The word around town was that Otto Wendell had loose lips. This perception, whether true or false, was what most likely got him killed.

◇◇◇◇◇◇◇◇◇◇◇◇

Much like Jack Tocco and Tony Zerilli, Little Vince Meli was a Mafia prince and heir apparent to a leadership post in the local crime family from the time he was an infant. Meli was the son of mob soldier Frank "The Music Man" Meli and the favorite nephew of longtime Detroit Mafia underboss Angelo "The Chairman" Meli, one of the founders of the city's La Cosa Nostra syndicate. Little Vince, whose nickname differentiated him from his first cousin, Vincent "Big Vince" Meli, his uncle Angelo's son, was born in San Cataldo, Sicily, on January 2, 1921. Coming to Detroit in the early 1930s, he grew up being bred to join the family business. After graduating from Notre Dame in 1942 with a degree in economics, he enlisted in the Army and went overseas to fight in World War II. His natural smarts and savvy, as well as his ability to speak multiple foreign languages, got him assigned to the Army's Intelligence Division. Eventually, Meli was named captain of an elite special forces unit that was akin to today's Delta Force or Navy Seals. He was a natural hero. In his two years serving in Europe, Meli earned two Purple Hearts and the Presidential Medal of Honor and was in one of the first groups of U.S. military personnel to enter and liberate the Nazi concentration camps in 1945.

Following the war, Meli returned home to Detroit and joined the family business. Almost immediately, he was recruited to help his uncle Angelo infiltrate the local labor unions and stage a takeover of the city's vending machine industry. Teaming with his father and three other mobsters and with the financial backing of his uncle, he started a trio of jukebox machine distributorships—Meltone Music, Jay-Cee Music, and White Music—and became highly influential in the city's burgeoning record industry. Meli's name surfaced in FBI reports in the late 1950s, relating to the persistent rumors that Berry Gordy used a mob loan to start Motown, allegations the music mogul has always steadfastly denied. Early in the next decade, in U.S. Senate hearings on organized crime, Meli was identified as an up-and-comer in the Detroit Mafia and a recent made member. Federal Narcotics Bureau documents from that era allege that syndicate drug proceeds were continuously being funneled through Meli's jukebox businesses, with Little Vince and his partners retaining a sizeable percentage of the transactions.

With such an astonishing résumé, some people question Meli's choice of career direction: "This guy was a superstar and could have done anything he wanted in life after his time in the military," said a retired FBI agent who declined to be identified. "He probably could have become a Mike Illitch or a Bill Davidson, a self-made multimillionaire by legitimate means if he had chosen to go down a different path. But instead he chose the easy way out and joined up with his father and uncle. Now that's not saying he didn't have extreme business acumen, because he did. He had some very successful legitimate business endeavors in his life. However, he also was heavily involved in organized crime in the area and in a lot of ways just decided to be a thug instead of an upstanding member of society."

Sticking with Motor City mob tradition, Little Vince's life on the domestic front crossed paths with his life on the business front. After coming back from overseas, he married Grace Di Mercurio, the daughter of Detroit Mafia soldier Frank "Frankie D" Di Mercurio, settled in Grosse Pointe Woods, and had six children. Little Vince's sister was married to William Buffalino, and his first cousin, "Big Vince," was married to the daughter of Mafia captain "Cockeyed Sam" Perone, while Big Vince's two sisters were both married to powerful mafiosi, Jack Tocco and Frank "Cheech" Livorsi from New York.

Starting in the 1960s, FBI documents allege that Meli rose to the level of capo in the crime family and spearheaded an infiltration of the Detroit-area steel-hauling industry on their behalf. For over a decade, he helped operate J&J Cartage, a massively successful steel-hauling firm that was owned by Joseph "House Jack" Cusmano and James "Smiling Jack" Russo, both reputed organized crime associates. Desiring to expand his reach in the industry in 1975, Meli and Russo, described in law enforcement files from the time as Meli's personal bodyguard and driver, opened another steel-hauling firm called Alco Express. Before they could get Alco off the ground and properly running at full capacity, Meli and Russo, along with Cusmano, were hit with a federal extortion rap stemming from work at J&J Cartage. In the indictment, the three were said to be extorting portions of drivers' pension funds by using Meli's reputation in the mob as leverage in closed-door meetings with employees. Despite having been charged over the past two decades with an assortment of state and federal crimes ranging from gambling, counterfeiting, and extortion to labor racketeering and income tax evasion, Little Vince had never been convicted of a single one.

While awaiting trial, Meli and Russo worked hard and built up Alco Express to such a point of profitability that if they had to shut down J&J Cartage due to their pending legal problems, they would be able to make a seamless transition. This effort was made significantly easier for one big reason. Due to a series of complicated circumstances, Alco was never unionized and operated free of normal labor restrictions. Detroit's newly formed Local 124 was supposed to bring Alco under its control, but that never happened and the company operated without its workers being properly represented. As a result, money that should have been going toward health, welfare, and pension benefits was going straight into Alco's pockets. Keeping close tabs on Meli and Russo while they were both out on bond awaiting trial, the FBI took a great interest in activities at Alco. The government intended to enter what was happening there into evidence at the J&J Cartage trial.

Otto Wendell, acting as treasurer of Local 299, Michigan's Teamster nerve center, handled paperwork and payments due related to Alco's non-unionized operation, and because of that, he was on the prosecution's witness list. Because Wendell had a great deal of pertinent knowledge, the feds wanted him on the stand, answering questions under oath. Also being badgered by the press and from within the union itself was Ralph Proctor, a Teamsters bigwig and longtime associate of Wendell's. Like Wendell, he was a former confidant of slain Teamsters boss Jimmy Hoffa. Proctor stated publicly that he was investigating complaints about Alco's methods of operation, yet no apparent headway was being made. Those who worked on the investigation believed this lack of progress was intentional since Proctor was a known social companion of both Meli and Russo and received a great deal of his own power in the union because of his relationship to them. Wendell held the key to a lot of pieces in this puzzle, but by the time the trial began in mid-1978, he wasn't alive to testify. Authorities believe he was killed by the mob to stop him from divulging what he knew.

◇◇◇◇◇◇◇◇◇◇◇◇

While Otto Wendell lay clinging to life in a hospital bed after being shot several times in December 1977, the FBI rushed to his side, looking for answers that could help identify the perpetrators. Although unable to speak, before he lapsed into a final deep coma, Wendell indicated he wanted to write something. He scribbled three hard-to-read words on a pad of paper. One translation of the words penned by Wendell came out as "Mealy Mouthed Roxy." Agents believed this was a reference to George Roxburgh, a business agent and trustee of Local 299 as well as a known associate of organized crime figures. Roxburgh was no stranger to violence as a reputed longtime member of Roland McMaster's inner circle. Five years earlier, in June 1972, Roxburgh was shot three times while sitting in his car in Royal Oak. He lost an eye, but survived the shotgun attack and continued as an alleged enforcer for the Teamsters. His name surfaced peripherally in the disappearance of Jimmy Hoffa as well.

It soon came out through the investigation that Wendell had been planning to run for the presidency of Local 299, but he had dropped out of the race a few weeks before his shooting. According to those close to him, Wendell had stated several times that he felt his life was in danger. He was close to Jimmy Hoffa and was well aware of the consequences of crossing the various organized crime figures who pulled strings behind the curtain in the Teamsters union. The FBI believes Wendell suffered the same fate as Hoffa. Seven years later, Ralph Proctor was felled in similar circumstances—dead as a result of a union-related dispute with the Mafia.

◇◇◇◇◇◇◇◇◇◇◇◇

At approximately 1:00 a.m. on August 10, 1984, 61-year-old Ralph Proctor, the former president of Teamsters Local 124, was found shot to death in the front seat of his 1981 Cadillac Seville in the parking lot of a Livonia shopping mall located at Six Mile and Newburgh, about a half-mile from his home. The car's engine was still running and the headlights were on. He had last been seen earlier in the evening by his wife as he left home to meet a business associate. A woman who lived in a house adjacent to the shopping mall told police she heard a series of "popping" noises about 10:15. It was determined by the county medical examiner that Proctor had been shot in the cheek with a large-caliber weapon by someone in the passenger seat, and eight times in the back of the head with a .22 caliber gun by someone sitting behind him. There were no signs of a struggle or of a robbery, and it was described as an execution-style murder. Due to the professional nature of the murder and Proctor's relationship with the Teamsters, investigators looked for a connection to union politics and organized crime. They quickly found one.

Proctor, a World War II veteran, had been a truck driver and member of Local 299, the home base of Jimmy Hoffa during his reign of power. The man they called "The Silver Fox" for his perfectly coifed gray hair and immaculate appearance was a staunch Hoffa loyalist and even shed blood for the beleaguered labor boss. When tensions between Hoffa and the mob were at their peak near the end of his life in the summer of 1975, Proctor was jumped and physically assaulted while leaving a bar in Melvindale. He was left with a fractured jaw and a pair of broken ribs for siding with Hoffa instead of the Mafia-backed union.

Following Hoffa's disappearance a month later, Proctor continued his involvement with the Teamsters and made a quick ascent up the ranks of union leadership. In 1979, he was elected president of the newly created Local 124, formed specifically to handle the needs of the large number of steel haulers in the Detroit area. This was where, much like Wendell, he bumped heads with the mob and specifically with Vince Meli, a man described in U.S. Congressional hearings from 1984 as the Detroit Mafia's representative in the steel-hauling industry.

Slated to retire at the end of 1985, Proctor abruptly stepped down as president of Local 124 in early 1984, almost two years early. Investigators believe that he was forced out of the presidency because he had become too much of a thorn in the side of the nefarious influences that were pulling strings behind him in the union. FBI documents point to personal disputes Proctor had with Meli and Local 299 president Pete Karagozian as likely contributing factors in his premature departure from office. Things got so heated between him and Karagozian that Karagozian fired Proctor's son, Dennis, from his job as a business agent for Local 299. Immediately after stepping down as head of the local, Proctor opened up a trailer repair company in Dearborn. Within months there were more rumors of problems with Local 124 and with other Teamster officials in the area. People were complaining that Proctor had started his company while still president of Local 124 and had used his influence to get contracts for his new business ventures. According to interviews conducted by police following Proctor's murder, his successor as president, William Klann, had to start informing vendors that Proctor was no longer representing the union in any way.

On August 9, 1984, the last night of his life and a mere four months after stepping down from the union presidency, Proctor left his Livonia residence for what he told his wife would be a short business meeting up the street at Wing Yee's Chinese restaurant. He would never return. Many of those intimately familiar with the federal investigation into Proctor's murder believe the person he was going to meet that late-summer evening over 25 years ago was Anthony "Chicago Tony" La Piana, Vince Meli's son-in-law and a man authorities suspected to have been a high-ranking member of the Detroit Mafia.

◇◇◇◇◇◇◇◇◇◇◇◇

Anthony La Piana Jr. was born in Chicago on December 20, 1943. His father was a longtime Teamsters union powerbroker, and he was exposed to the ins and outs of labor politics at a very young age. After serving in the Marine Corps right out of high school, La Piana returned to the Windy City and took a job with a freight-hauling business. When he was 24, he was arrested by the FBI and charged with hijacking a truck in Illinois. Eventually acquitted at trial in 1967, the following year he came to live in Detroit part-time as a result of a job he took with another, bigger trucking company that had hubs all across the Midwest. Recently divorced from his high school sweetheart, he soon met and fell in love with Phyllis Meli, daughter of Little Vince.

La Piana, whose nickname is a reference to his hometown, married Phyllis in 1974 and settled with his new bride in Grosse Pointe Woods. According to FBI documents, Chicago Tony had organized crime affiliations dating back to his days as a teenager in Illinois. At a future unrelated deposition, he would admit to being childhood best friends with Anthony "Little Tony" Borselino, a hit man for the Chicago mob who was slain gangland-style in 1979. Federal investigators also believe that from the moment he married into Vince Meli's family, La Piana became a prized pupil and ace protégé of his new father-in-law. Buoyed by his father's already well-established ties in the Teamsters and his father-in-law's muscle, Chicago Tony is alleged to have become an extremely juiced-in player in national labor politics, despite not holding a union office. That didn't mean he couldn't do business with the county's organized labor elite, because he did plenty. As the owner of a pair of insurance companies, Tony gained lucrative contracts with various mega-sized labor unions for blanket employee healthcare coverage, making him a very wealthy man.

By the early 1980s, La Piana's name began to get a lot of attention in federal law enforcement circles. Street informants for the Detroit FBI began identifying him as an up-and-comer in the local Mafia as early as the late 1970s. International Brotherhood of Teamsters president Jackie Presser, who after his death from a heart attack in 1988 was identified as a highly confidential government snitch, had keyed the feds in to La Piana immediately. FBI documents reveal that Presser informed his handlers that almost as soon as he was elected president in 1983, he was approached by La Piana, who promptly identified himself as a representative for organized crime families in both Detroit and Chicago and instructed him that any problems with either syndicate were to be sent his way. Presser also told the FBI that La Piana pressured him to help settle a pension fund debt for his personal business and to name Chicago Mafia member Dominic "The Big Banana" Senese as an organizer for an Illinois Teamsters outpost. Federal officials identified La Piana as an "inducted member" of the Detroit Mafia family as early as 1990, and in 2000, Nove Tocco, a mobster turned government informant, told the FBI that Chicago Tony had been elevated to the level of capo and was "running his own crew." During testimony at a racketeering trial of members of the city's mob hierarchy in 1998, it was revealed that Detroit don Jack Tocco had informed a witness that for any problems he was having with the labor unions, he should "go see Tony La Piana."

Although the co-owner of one of his insurance companies was convicted on federal charges of falsifying documents in the mid-1980s, Chicago Tony escaped the investigation unscathed. The same thing happened when his name surfaced in several parts of a federal indictment that brought down Florida Teamsters boss Walter "Buster" Brown on charges of corruption in 2001, but failed to include La Piana. To this day, he has never been convicted of a single felony or any count of criminal conduct. Whatever his status in the underworld, one thing was for sure: Tony La Piana and Ralph Proctor had been friends for over a decade when Proctor died in August 1984. This even La Piana admits as true. According to police files relating to Proctor's murder, the pair met through Vince Meli in the early 1970s when Proctor was part of Jimmy Hoffa's inner circle. Whether La Piana was with Proctor at the time of his death or was supposed to be with him is a different story. La Piana claims he was nowhere near Livonia on August 10th, nor was he ever supposed to meet up with Proctor that night. Law enforcement believes otherwise.

In interviews with authorities following her husband's death, Doris Proctor said that in the last months of his life, it had been routine for her husband to meet with Tony La Piana on Thursday nights. The meetings would usually last an hour and would take place after dinner, before the Proctors' last cup of coffee prior to retiring for the evening. On most occasions, La Piana would call the house and talk to Doris right before her husband left, telling her to pass along the rendezvous information. The night of Ralph Proctor's murder, the second Thursday of August 1984, Doris never spoke to La Piana on the phone. Ralph took the call and left the house after dinner, telling her he was going to meet "Tony." He told her that he would be back in time for them to watch the nightly news together at eleven. Doris told police she knew "Tony" to be Tony La Piana, who she believed was in the process of trying to help her husband sell some property he owned.

Investigators unearthed other possible reasons for Proctor's series of meetings with La Piana. One was that Proctor was haggling with Local 124 and Local 299 over money he loaned the union several years before to help get Local 124 off the ground. In the final six months of his life, Proctor made it more than evident to anybody who would listen that the Teamsters owed him $100,000 and they weren't paying him back. The ill will felt toward him by Vince Meli wasn't helping matters. Meli reportedly blamed Proctor in part for his extortion conviction years before, which had resulted in a prison sentence starting the previous January, and he repeatedly badmouthed him in public. Even though Little Vince was in prison, he still carried quite a bit of weight with the unions from behind bars, and Proctor allegedly needed him to sign off with the Teamsters before they would release the funds. More than one informant told federal authorities that the money Proctor felt he was owed by the Teamsters was the actual reason for the series of meetings between Proctor and La Piana, who was said to be acting as a conduit to his father-in-law.

On more than one occasion, Proctor is alleged to have hurled threats in the direction of certain figures with deep organized crime connections about what he would do if his money was not repaid. One of these men was reputed to be Roland McMasters, the longtime mob-backed union enforcer known to be the Teamsters' unofficial sergeant-at-arms and a social companion of his. Everyone, most importantly the mob, knew full well that Proctor had quite a bit of knowledge about the shenanigans involved with union politics and that if he began to speak, whether to the media or the police, many important underworld interests could be put in severe jeopardy. Gary Proctor, Ralph's son, told police of a conversation he had with McMasters in the days leading up to his father's murder in which McMasters remarked, "Tell your father to stop making so many waves."

When authorities visited McMasters, he claimed he hadn't seen or spoken to Ralph Proctor in months. When they visited Tony La Piana, he refused to speak to them. Issuing a statement through his attorney, La Piana said he was with his family that evening at the Meli residence in Grosse Pointe Woods, but declined to expand any further or undergo any in-person questioning. In the press, La Piana's attorney explained that when Proctor told his wife that he was going to meet La Piana, that was merely an excuse for him to go meet someone else. This statement may have alluded to Proctor's reputation as a ladies man, according to several of his former co-workers and associates. No charges were ever filed in this case, but those involved in the investigation believe they have an idea of what happened. Although none of them has ever been indicted for playing any role in Proctor's killing, the Detroit FBI office still considers La Piana, Meli, and McMasters its top suspects. Another name that came up in the investigation was Louie La Hood, a onetime driver and bodyguard of Meli's, who like McMasters was often described as a heavily influential union strong arm, but who by 1984 was running a bar and banquet hall on the East Side called "The Barristers Lounge." McMasters died in 2006 at the ripe old age of 97. Meli lived to be 87.

Neither Ralph Proctor's nor Otto Wendel's murder has ever been solved. Vincent Meli died of bone cancer in 2008. As for Tony La Piana, he is believed by the FBI to remain an important member of the Detroit Mafia. Neither case has been closed. The stories of both homicides involve many of the same individuals, and even though they took place seven years apart, each highlights a violent connection between Teamsters and Detroit mobsters that has been present for decades.

THE DETROIT
DRUG PIPELINE

Smacktown U.S.A.

By Dr. James Buccellato and Scott M. Burnstein

Detroit, February 21, 1962.

It was two in the morning and Gerlando was locking up his bar for the night. Walking out the back door of his establishment, the bar owner was horrified to find a dead pig blocking his exit. Seeing its front and hind legs bound by rope, he inspected the animal and concluded the swine had died from asphyxiation. Gerlando knew that the pathetic animal was placed there as a warning. By the next day, patrons of the bar were already gossiping about the dead pig. Gerlando owned Frankie G's, a popular hangout for wiseguys in Detroit. Well acquainted with underworld symbolism, customers recognized the pig carcass as a message: *squealers die.*

Earlier in the week police had visited the bar, asking patrons about Roy Calabrese, a local pimp, numbers runner, and regular at Frankie G's. Although not a fully inducted mob soldier, Roy was nevertheless a very connected figure in the Detroit underworld. Specifically, he was tied into the Partinico faction of the local Italian crime syndicate. A few nights earlier—Valentine's Day to be exact—police found Calabrese's body garroted in the trunk of his own car. They located the vehicle in a Kroger's parking lot in St. Clair Shores, a suburb of Detroit. There was no doubt what the dead pig meant and that it was directed toward Gerlando: *keep your mouth shut about Roy Calabrese.*

Though unable to solve the murder, police were able to connect the victim to a shadowy faction of the Detroit syndicate known in the underworld as the "lower Sicilians." To be precise, the group traced its heritage to the Sicilian town of Partinico. Like other elements of the Detroit mob, the group was involved in traditional rackets such as illegal gambling and labor corruption. But it was the heroin trade that distinguished the Partinico faction from other criminal groups. It made them superpowers.

Detroit and the Global Heroin Trade

Researchers tend to underplay Detroit when examining the global history of heroin trafficking. Social scientist Eric C. Schneider's impressive study of the opium trade, for example, places New York at the center of heroin distribution in North America. According to Schneider, between the 1940s and 1980s, New York dominated the smack trade. Dealers in other urban cities had to go through the Big Apple for supplies.

Few would challenge the notion. There is no question that syndicates in New York facilitated a staggering amount of illicit narcotics traffic. But often lost in the discussion of the North American and international drug market is the importance of the Motor City. Even Schneider himself singles out Detroit as the exception to the rule, having special access to the suppliers in New York. The facts are clear. When it came to heroin, an overwhelming amount of evidence suggests that it was the Detroit Mafia that was supplying the New York underworld for close to three decades following World War II, not the other way around. To be more precise, it was a group within the larger Detroit crime family that was doling out "H" at a breakneck pace. This Sicilian faction of Detroit's Mafia was known as the Partinico group, and was led by some of the city's most deadly hoodlums. The Partinicos supplied almost the entire country at that time. Besides New York, almost every big city across the nation was supplied with heroin that was brought into the United States by members of the Detroit Partinicos.

Three important factors placed Detroit at the nexus of the North American heroin trade. First, unlike many other Italian American syndicates, Detroit maintained close relationships with Sicilian crime families overseas. Their Mafia brothers across the Atlantic had direct access to opium growers in the Middle East. Traffickers processed the opium into heroin in Europe and shipped the product to distributors in Detroit. Second, the Detroit–Windsor border has always been a major hub of international trade. Sicilian suppliers often used cargo ships bound for Montreal to move their product. The heroin made its way down to Windsor and onward across the border. Lastly, Detroit's mob was heavily involved in labor racketeering and related industries such as trucking and steel. As a result, drug traffickers in the Motor City used these connections to develop a sophisticated distribution network.

Detroit's involvement in the drug trade began with its deep Sicilian connections. As with other big cities, Sicilian immigrants poured into Detroit during late 1800s and early 1900s, looking for economic opportunities. Many of them went on to become successful entrepreneurs, doctors, engineers, and civil servants. Unfortunately, a criminal element emerged in Detroit's Sicilian community as well. Local newspapers began documenting Italian organized criminal activities as early as 1908. During the early years of syndicate history, Sicilian gangsters tended to group together with compatriots from their hometowns. Mobsters arriving in Detroit from Partinico, for example, would link up with Partinicesi mafiosi already operating in the city. Out of this milieu, certain groups operated international criminal enterprises with the aid of comrades back in the old country. Heroin trafficking was one of the most profitable examples of such joint illegal operations.

The Detroit Mafia produced three subgroups known for remaining exceptionally close to their Sicilian counterparts overseas: the Partinico faction (also known as the lower Sicilian group), the Windsor faction (a Canadian crew linked to the French Connection heroin ring out of Marseilles), and the Cinisi faction (affiliated with the Badalamenti crime family of Palermo).

John Priziola and the Partinico Faction

Led by Giovanni "Papa John" Priziola, the Partinico faction was the oldest and most powerful of the groups operating in the Motor City. Standing just over five feet three inches tall, the diminutive gangster climbed the ranks of the Detroit underworld by combining violence with exceptional leadership skills and heavily entrenched connections. Starting off his criminal career in the area as a rum-runner during Prohibition, Papa John rose to the rank of consigliere in the 1930s, third in command and top advisor to longtime Godfather Joe Zerilli until his death in 1979.

Arriving in Detroit in 1909 at the age of 16, Priziola soon earned a reputation on the street as a dependable earner and an unscrupulous killer. Between 1917 and 1931, Papa John piled up a number of arrests for larceny, bootlegging, concealed weapons, narcotics, and murder. Similar to other mafiosi from his era, Priziola made his first fortune during Prohibition in the bootlegging industry. During the 1920s, he co-owned a sugar house and liquor-cutting factory with Detroit mobster Nicolo "Nick the Executioner" Ditta. Together they supplied booze to blind-pig establishments throughout the city. Papa John generated a second fortune during World War II by orchestrating a gas rationing coupon scam that is alleged to have netted him millions.

In addition to establishing himself as one of the local mob's top moneymakers, Priziola had another advantage that enhanced his position on the streets: his heritage. Whereas other local wiseguys at the time chose to lead lives of crime, Papa John Priziola was born into the Mafia. FBI informants told authorities that Priziola had a reputation as a killer before arriving in Detroit, dating all the way back to his days as a youngster in Sicily. It is speculated that Papa John "made his bones" during a blood feud involving his father. Priziola's father, Giuseppe, was a high-ranking mobster back in Partinico. The elder Priziola had fallen victim to the murderous intrigue of his own son-in-law. After Giuseppe's killing, the assassin fled Sicily for the United States. Partisans of the Priziola clan managed to lure the killer back to Italy a short time later. The Priziola family had their revenge. Italian authorities soon discovered the son-in-law cut into over 800 pieces.

Back in Detroit, Papa John solidified his position as an underworld powerbroker by linking up with other Partinicesi gangsters such as Frank "Frankie Three Fingers" Coppola and Raffaele "Jimmy Q" Quasarano. Initially, Coppola operated as the official leader, or capo, of the Partinico faction. Though younger than Papa John, Coppola ranked higher as a mafioso in Sicily, and he carried his status with him from the old country to America. Together, Coppola, Priziola, and Quasarano operated a number of lucrative gambling joints including the infamous Lucky Star Policy House. The police raided the gambling den in 1947 and determined the group was taking in around $40,000 a day through the Lucky Star.

Like other venture capitalists, Frankie Three Fingers, Papa John, and Jimmy Q—sometimes also referred to as "Jimmy the Goon"—wanted to parlay their earnings. With lots of capital to invest and solid connections back in Sicily, the Partinico group decided to jump head first into the heroin market. Sweetening the deal and making things substantially easier in moving their product, Coppola and Quasarano had recently aided the Detroit mob in a successful infiltration of the International Brotherhood of Teamsters. Because of the union's relationship to the trucking industry, the Partinico faction had access to a national distribution system. With direct access to heroin suppliers in Sicily and control of a delivery network in the United States, the Partinico group established an ideal drug-dealing infrastructure.

Frankie Coppola's connection to the Teamsters is one of the more discomforting moments in the history of that proud labor movement. Coppola was particularly close to Teamsters' president Jimmy Hoffa. The relationship dated all the way back to the days of Coppola's first months in America. Shortly after Frankie Three Fingers arrived in Detroit, he started up a romantic relationship with Sylvia Pagano. Coincidentally, Pagano, an aspiring actress who dated several of the city's most powerful mobsters, was a former lover of Jimmy Hoffa. Sylvia introduced Coppola to her old paramour and a lucrative partnership emerged.

Hoffa's fledging labor movement had been fighting off union-busting goons for years. After meeting Frankie Three Fingers, Hoffa decided to team with Coppola and his cohorts in the mob and counter their antagonists with the Teamsters' own squad of thugs. Coppola, along with other Detroit mobsters including Pete Licavoli and Santo "Cockeyed Sam" Perrone, assisted the Teamsters in their street wars with rival unions like the Congress of Industrial Organizations. Of course there were tradeoffs. Coppola provided the muscle, and in exchange

Hoffa granted the Partinico group access to Teamster-controlled trucking networks. Later, Hoffa used the Teamsters to provide political cover for the Partinico
faction by appointing Priziola and Quasarano as union officials in Local 985.

As for the heroin trade, FBI documents suggest that Frank Coppola established a drug smuggling route out of Florida as early as the 1920s, only months
after entering the country. Frankie Three Fingers was on the run from Italian prosecutors for a 1919 homicide in Palermo when he entered the United States in
1925. In addition to running drugs, Coppola spent time as a bootlegger in Los
Angeles before arriving in Detroit in 1931. By the 1940s, the Partinico group had
amassed such a fortune from labor racketeering and illegal gambling that its foray
into the international narcotics trade was a natural progression. The authorities did
eventually catch up with Coppola in 1947, and deported him to Italy. He tried to
reenter the U.S. in 1948 and 1949, but was intercepted by American officials both
times and returned to Sicily.

Ironically, Coppola's deportation led to an escalation of heroin smuggling to
Detroit. Back in Sicily, he was in a position to take direct control of the supply side
of the network. Initially, Sicilian mafiosi acquired heroin from government sanc-
tioned morphine producers in Italy. After identifying corruptible officials at the
pharmaceutical companies, Sicilian gangsters would arrange for the firms to inflate
production over regulated limits and buy the surplus heroin. Investigators with the
Federal Bureau of Narcotics estimated that the arrangement produced approximately 800 kilos of heroin for Sicilian crime organizations.

The partnership worked well until American authorities pressured the Italian
government to crack down on corruption in the pharmaceutical industry.
Eventually, Italian authorities issued a total ban on the production of heroin. With
pharmaceutical companies out of commission, Italian American gangsters had to
look to other suppliers. The Corsican mob from Marseilles was more than happy
to satisfy the market.

"Cockeyed Joe" and the Windsor Connection

Before continuing to describe the Partinico faction's involvement in narcotics, it is
important to note the Windsor group's role in the heroin trade as well. Going by
underworld mapping systems, Windsor, Ontario was considered part of Detroit's
territory; that is to say, the Motor City crime family–controlled rackets on the
Canadian side of the Detroit River, a mere five-minute drive from downtown.

From the 1930s through the 1950s, Giuseppe "Cockeyed Joe" Catalanotte was
capo of the Windsor crew. Like Papa John Priziola, Catalanotte came from Mafia
royalty. His brother, Salvatore "Singing Sam" Catalanotte, was one of the original
mob bosses of Detroit and is considered by some experts the city's first modern-
day don. Not one to ride his brother's coattails, Cockeyed Joe built a reputation as

a vicious gangster in his own right. By the time he took over syndicate operations in Canada, Cockeyed Joe had an extensive arrest record going back to the early 1920s. Catalanotte's record included charges for murder, assault, extortion, and narcotics violations.

When Detroit police raided Cockeyed Joe's apartment in 1930, they were astounded to find an arsenal of over 60 firearms. Detroit police officer Marvin Lane broke his hand wrestling a loaded gun away from Catalanotte, who reached for the pistol as police searched the premises. Interestingly, investigators linked one of the confiscated guns to the assassination of popular radio host Gerald Buckley, though Catalanotte was never charged with the crime. After serving a short stint behind bars, Cockeyed Joe was back on the streets and looking for fresh rackets.

The 1940s were a shaky period for the country's narcotics industry. World War II had severely disrupted the narcotics trade between Europe and North America. When the war ended in 1945, Cockeyed Joe recognized the lucrative potential of reintroducing the drug pipeline into the Detroit area. Catalanotte, along with his top lieutenants Onofrio "Nono" Minaudo, Paul "The Sicilian" Cimino, and Nicholas "Canadian Nick" Cicchini, transformed the Windsor–Detroit border into the primary hub of international narcotics trafficking.

By being in charge of looking after the Detroit mob's rackets in Windsor, Catalanotte became acquainted with other powerful gangsters in the Canadian underworld. Jimmy Renda, for example, a mobster out of Riverside, Ontario, was part of Cockeyed Joe's criminal orbit. Renda put Catalanotte in contact with heroin traffickers from Montreal. Combining linguistic and criminal similarities, French Canadian mobsters in Quebec worked well with Corsican gangsters from Marseilles.

The global nuances were fascinating. Corsican mobsters had contacts with French-speaking Lebanese gangsters with access to opium growers in Turkey. Turkish opium producers would cook the opium into a morphine base and sell it to Lebanese middlemen. Eventually, the product would make its way to French smugglers. The Corsicans had established an elaborate network of clandestine conversion labs in Marseilles to process the morphine base into heroin. Finally, Corsicans would smuggle the heroin onto cargo ships headed for Canada. American and French investigators estimated that by the early 1950s, the so-called French Connection was supplying North America with over 100 kilograms of heroin per month. Controlling the Windsor–Detroit border, Catalanotte was in a perfect position to capitalize on the illicit traffic. Central in importance to this network was Catalanotte's association with Dominic Albertini. As the official head chemist of the French Connection heroin ring, Albertini was recognized as one of the most powerful gangsters in Marseilles. Jimmy Renda introduced Catalanotte to Albertini and as a result an extremely profitable transnational heroin partnership emerged.

In 1952, Cockeyed Joe even tried to smuggle Albertini into Detroit to establish additional distribution outlets in the United States. Federal authorities at the time believed that Catalanotte hoped to introduce Albertini to the Partinico faction in the city and build new business relationships between the two megawatt mob groups. Before any agreements could be established, however, American authorities intercepted Albertini at the Windsor border. Interestingly, Albertini was caught at the border by means of surveillance set up for another Detroit mobster. Federal agents were monitoring Peter Di Lorenzo, a suspected racketeer, counterfeiter, and human trafficker when they observed Dominic Albertini leaving Di Lorenzo's business. Agents arrested the French chemist as he tried to enter Detroit. Albertini offered the agents a $100,000 bribe but was rebuked. He was convicted of illegal entry and sentenced to two years of which he served a year and a day.

Investigators were closing in on Catalanotte as well. Cockeyed Joe's drug network started to unravel when a confidential informant began trading information to federal agents in 1950. The informant worked with a Midwest drug trafficker named Robert "Texas Bob" Kimbell, who was transporting marijuana into Detroit in 125-pound bushels. One of Kimbell's primary customers was a dealer named Michael Lockett. The feds found out through their informant that Lockett had introduced Kimbell to Italian heroin traffickers in Detroit.

Intrigued by the allegations, agents with the Federal Bureau of Narcotics set up a fake heroin buy to nail Texas Bob. Kimbell fell for the trap and agreed to cooperate with the government in return for a lighter sentence. As a result, Texas Bob started introducing undercover agents to lower-level Italian heroin suppliers operating out of the mob-controlled Detroit–Windsor hub. The undercover agents developed relationships with a number of "connected" dealers such as Andy Bottancino, Nick Prano, and Jimmy Galici, a known made member of the Detroit Mafia.

During the investigation it was discovered that the primary supplier for this group of drug lieutenants was a mysterious mafioso known only as "The Old Man." It quickly became clear that The Old Man was Cockeyed Joe Catalanotte. Proving it, on the other hand, wasn't so easy. By the end of 1950, agents had arrested Lockett, Bottancino, Prano, and Galici on narcotics charges, but were unable to find someone willing to testify against their ringleader, Catalanotte. They all went to trial and were convicted, though Kimball never made it to the witness stand as he had been killed in a drug deal gone wrong in San Antonio.

Staying hot on Catalanotte's trail, investigators infiltrated Cockeyed Joe's crew once again only a year later. In 1951, undercover agents started making buys from figures in Detroit's Chinese underworld. Within months, they busted James Paing and Jay Lum for trafficking, and the two began cooperating with the federal investigators. Paing and Lum passed on the names of their Italian suppliers—Louis Oddo, Robert Tassiano, and Sam Caruso—and agreed to participate in a sting operation. Paing placed his drug order with Caruso, who like Jimmy Galici was a known made member of the Detroit Mafia, and then passed the request on to Oddo. Caruso and Oddo arranged for the heroin to be delivered to a gas station owned by Tassiano.

Informants explained to authorities that per standard protocol, Caruso would wait several days before passing the drug proceeds on to his boss. Agents waited, keeping Caruso under surveillance. Finally, on February 21, 1952, law enforcement followed him to a meeting with the ever-elusive Old Man. Agents witnessed Caruso passing drug money to none other than Cockeyed Joe Catalanotte. Police arrested Cockeyed Joe and within the year a federal court convicted him on narcotics charges. Catalanotte's incarceration, however, didn't even come close to stopping the flow of heroin into Detroit.

Drug Lords

The Partinico group took advantage of Catalanotte's legal troubles and with Cockeyed Joe locked up, established itself as the prominent heroin organization in Detroit. Back in Sicily, Frank Coppola and other recently exiled American Mafia dons like Charles "Lucky" Luciano forged their own partnerships with Corsican traffickers. With such connections in place, Coppola supplied his partners in Detroit with copious amounts of heroin.

Meanwhile, law enforcement began to catch on to the fact that a new, more sophisticated drug network was firmly in place after monitoring an increased amount of travel to Sicily by Detroit-area gangsters. Following Coppola's deportation, authorities observed two Partinico group members in particular traveling cross-continent quite often. The feds observed Jimmy Quasarano and another Priziola disciple and top Michigan-based mob lieutenant, Salvatore "Little Sammy" Finazzo, making frequent trips overseas to meet with Partinicese mob leaders in Sicily.

Agents suspected Quasarano and Finazzo were in Sicily to negotiate and finance heroin deliveries to the United States. Finazzo was born in Partinico, but moved to the U.S. as a child, settling first in St. Louis and then relocating to Detroit. His status within the local underworld was cemented in 1922 when his sister married future mob boss Joe Zerilli. In contrast, Jimmy Q was born in Pennsylvania, but raised in Sicily. His mother moved the family back to their ancestral home of Partinico after Quasarano's father died in a coal-mining accident. Back in Detroit, Jimmy Q and Little Sammy Finazzo co-owned the Motor City Boxing Gym and were tasked with overseeing a number of Papa John Priziola's gambling and loansharking operations.

If Coppola was the founder of the Partinico group and Priziola was its leader, then Jimmy Q was the crew's enforcer. After spending his early youth in Partinico,

Quasarano moved back to the United States as a teenager. Committed to the gangster life, at the age of 21, he made his way to Detroit to work for Partinicese Godfather Frank Coppola. Authorities arrested Quasarano a dozen times between 1931 and 1945. Jimmy Q was arrested on narcotics charges in 1941, but he agreed to enlist in the Army in exchange for dropped charges. The military granted Quasarano a medical discharge shortly thereafter, and by the late 1940s, Jimmy Q was back in action and traveling to Italy to negotiate narcotics shipments. He had solid drug connections that extended beyond Frankie Three Fingers. Quasarano's father-in-law, for example, was Vittorio "Don Vito" Vitale, a powerful Mafia don from Castellammare del Golfo in Sicily. Not only did Don Vito have excellent heroin sources to bestow upon his new son-in-law, but Jimmy Q could use the pretense of "family visits" to Vitale as a perfect alibi for traveling to Italy so often.

Through his father-in-law, Quasarano also became connected to Salvatore "Toto" Vitale, the *sotocapo*, or second-in-command, of the Mafia family in Partinico. Like Coppola, Toto Vitale spent time in the United States before being deported back to Italy in 1937. In addition to supplying Detroit with heroin, Toto was the key supplier for another Sicilian group operating out of Missouri. Sal's cousin, John "Johnny V" Vitale, captained a crew of Partinicesi gangsters in St. Louis. Members of the St. Louis faction included Anthony "Tony Pip" Lopiparo, Anthony "Tony G" Giordano, and Ralph "Shorty" Caleca. As with Quasarano and Finazzo from Detroit, federal investigators observed Lopiparo and Giordano, whose brother Salvatore "Sammy G" Giordano was a made member of the Mafia in Michigan, traveling to Sicily to meet with Salvatore Vitale, presumably to negotiate heroin shipments, on numerous occasions.

Whereas the Catalanotte group had been smuggling heroin down from Montreal across the Windsor–Detroit border, the Partinico Mafia shipped their product to Detroit directly. Traffickers used any number of ingenious ways to smuggle the product, including hiding heroin in boxes of canned sardines, canned tomatoes and oranges, and in olive oil drums. Often the syndicate used passengers flying to America as unwitting drug mules, paying baggage handlers at the airport to slip narcotics into random people's luggage.

Once in the U.S., the product made its way to Detroit mafioso Peter Gaudino and his Gaudino Imported and Domestic Groceries Company on Mack Avenue, located on the East Side of Detroit. Gaudino was a veteran trafficker who freelanced between the Partinico faction and the Catalanotte group. The Partinico organization would also ship heroin to Peter "West Coast Pete" Tocco's fish market on Joseph Campau Street, in that Tocco was Priziola's son-in-law.

It is noteworthy that federal investigators went in front of Congress and identified the Detroit-Partinico drug operation as the primary supply line of heroin to the Midwest and East Coast Mafia families. Within Detroit, most of the product made its way to African American dealers. Priziola had forged strong partnerships with Detroit's black gangsters. FBI files note that Papa John even hosted a multi-cultural underworld summit of sorts. In 1962, Priziola invited the top African American gambling czars to a joint meeting with the Italians, and together they reorganized illegal gambling in Detroit, constructing what was known on the streets as the "New Frontier." Priziola's group used these intergang alliances to distribute heroin as well.

Surprisingly, Priziola's biggest customers were not local dealers. Primarily, the Partinico group supplied the Lucchese crime family of New York. As with other crime syndicates, after World War II, New York families began searching for new heroin sources. At this time, the Detroit Mafia had the strongest ties to heroin traffickers in Sicily. Even the Bonanno crime family, known for being the most Sicilian of the Italian American syndicates, did not fully develop its drug network until after 1957. Up until the late 1950s, even the most powerful New York crime families had to look to Detroit for their heroin supply.

Giovanni "Big John" Ormento, a captain in the Lucchese family in New York, was the Partinico group's primary customer. Standing five feet 10 and weighing over 250 pounds, Big John's arrest record included charges for narcotics, firearms, and bookmaking. During one prison stay, Ormento's psychiatric evaluators described him as both "paranoid" and possessing "superior intelligence." The mental health staff predicted that Ormento "would return to crime" upon release. They were right.

In the New York underworld, Big John ran the infamous "107th Street Mob" in Harlem. The group operated one of the city's largest narcotics distribution networks. Ormento was also a labor racketeer with ties to Midwestern trucking organizations. It was through these networks that he became affiliated with corrupt Teamsters officials and influential East Coast Mafia powers like John "Johnny Dio" Dioguardi and Frank "Cheech" Livorsi. Ormento eventually married Livorsi's daughter. Livorsi's other daughter married the son of Detroit Mafia underboss Angelo "The Chairman" Meli.

Big John met his Detroit suppliers through a labyrinth of familial connections. Angelo Meli was hosting a banquet in Ormento's honor at the Bowery Night Club in Hamtramck when he introduced Big John to Papa John Priziola and Jimmy Q Quasarano. In addition to having solid Teamsters connections, Ormento owned OSS Trucking Inc. and was a labor representative for the Garment Center Truck Owners Association. Strategically, he was in the perfect position to facilitate a large-scale drug distribution network. After meeting Papa John and Jimmy Q, Ormento found a heroin supply line to finalize the operation.

Unfortunately for the Partinico faction, the tumultuous realm of underworld politics threatened to undo Detroit's grip on the lucrative heroin pipeline. Tensions between Frank Coppola and Salvatore Vitale began festering after the 1949 assassination of Santo Fleres, the boss of the Partinico Mafia. Up until that point,

Coppola was operating out of Mexico and working with the Matranga crime family from San Diego.

The Mexican government actually granted Frank Coppola permission to live in Tijuana, ostensibly for the purposes of studying agriculture. Instead of farming, Coppola set up gambling dens and casinos. Working with the Matrangas across the border, he also established new routes for human trafficking and drug smuggling. As long as Salvatore Vitale was in Sicily and Coppola was in Tijuana, the two hot-tempered crime lords avoided conflict. That changed when the Mexican government arrested and deported Coppola in 1950.

Back in Sicily, Coppola handpicked Gaspare Centineo to replace the murdered Santo Fleres as the new boss of the mob in Partinico. Considering traditional Mafia protocol, this was an unconventional selection. Partinico underboss Toto Vitale was theoretically next in line for the top spot. Coppola's unique political connections with the Italian government, however, gave Frankie Three Fingers some added leeway in making his final decision, a significant advantage when navigating the machinations of the underworld.

Frankie Three Fingers was a political kingmaker in Sicily with connections to powerful Italian senators such as Girolamo Messeri. Furthermore, Coppola's brother was a priest and powerbroker in the local Catholic church. As a result, few politicians in Partinico could survive without the support of the Coppola brothers. Unafraid to namedrop, Frank Coppola would often brag that "it was Vittorio Emanuele Orlando who advised me to go to the United States." Orlando, the former prime minister of Italy, was originally a parliamentary deputy from Partinico. Officially, Gaspare Centineo may have been the new crime boss of Partinico, but veteran gangsters like Sal Vitale knew that the real power behind the family was Coppola.

Toto Vitale was a heavy hitter in his own right, and was not somebody to be taken lightly. As underboss he established connections with Marseilles and was on the frontlines of developing the heroin pipeline to Detroit. Vitale also had the infamous Charles "Lucky" Luciano in his corner. Luciano was the point man for introducing gangsters like Vitale to Corsican traffickers. Coppola hoped to remove Luciano and Vitale and reposition himself as the link between Detroit and Marseilles.

This was not the first time Coppola had agitated the Luciano organization. Prior to his deportation from the United States, Coppola invested in both legal and illegal gambling operations in New Orleans. For these ventures he partnered with Louisiana crime boss Salvatore "Silver Dollar Sam" Carollo and Luciano's American representative Frank Costello. Although it is unclear what triggered the dispute, FBI documents indicate that the relationship between Costello and Coppola soured shortly after the partnership began. Informants alleged that Costello went to the Mafia's ruling council in New York, known as the Commission, seeking permission to assassinate Coppola. Luckily for Coppola, Commission leaders turned down Costello's request and the United States Government deported him before the feud could escalate.

Complicating things further, Salvatore Vitale alienated his customers in Detroit by supplying adulterated heroin. Still in control of the heroin pipeline for the time being, Vitale sent 14 kilos of product to Jimmy Quasarano in Detroit and in return accepted a $75,000 down payment. Jimmy Q was outraged when he discovered that the heroin shipment was mostly sugar, and he wanted to take immediate revenge. Papa John Priziola, who was financing the Detroit side of the deal, accused Vitale of a double cross. Vitale proclaimed his innocence and responded that he must have been deceived by his contacts in Marseilles. To try and make amends with his Detroit receivers, Vitale arranged for $100,000 worth of heroin to be delivered with no down payment tendered.

The two sides agreed that Joe Matranga from the San Diego mob was a neutral party and could be trusted to pick up the heroin in New York. Matranga was related to both Priziola and Vitale through marriage. He was married to Priziola's daughter and his sister was married to Sal Vitale. Matranga made the pickup, but he was subsequently robbed. Three masked men broke into his hotel room and took the stash at gunpoint. Although they were unable to prove it, Matranga and Vitale suspected that Priziola and Quasarano arranged the robbery. Vitale demanded a meeting to settle these disputes. Senior mafiosi from Detroit presided over the meeting, known on the street as a sit-down, between Vitale's American representatives and Priziola's group. The mob arbitrators did not rule on the New York hijacking, but they did find in Vitale's favor concerning the earlier shipment of "garbage heroin." Priziola and Quasarano were told to settle their debts with Vitale peacefully.

Relations between the two groups remained cold after the sit-down. In the months following the dispute, Quasarano traveled to Italy to meet with Vitale. The Partinicesi underboss was expecting Jimmy Q to arrive with cash and negotiate further drug shipments. Vitale wanted to reenter the United States and hoped Quasarano and the Detroit group would help smuggle him back into the country. Instead, Jimmy Q explained that "things were too hot" to either smuggle Vitale into the United States or arrange further heroin deliveries. Furthermore, Quasarano did not arrive with any cash payments to square away earlier drug debts. Federal agents monitoring the situation suspected that Jimmy Q was insincere. Investigators believed Quasarano was buying heroin from Partinico the whole time, but from another source: Frank Coppola. The government interpreted the provocations by Priziola and Quasarano as signs that they were backing their former boss Coppola in his power play against Vitale.

Meanwhile, investigators were closing in on the Partinico group in Sicily. American law enforcement busted Sicilian gangster Frank Callaci with three kilos of heroin in May 1951. It was suspected that Toto Vitale was Callaci's supplier and Italian police arrested him as well. Astonishingly, federal agents found letters on Vitale written by John Priziola, complete with Priziola's own personalized letter-head and Grosse Pointe Woods address. The notes instructed Vitale to keep a low profile until further notice. Authorities suspected that coded language in the letter referred to drug trafficking and the smuggling of illegal aliens. Vitale was eventually released from custody, and he made a run for the United States. The run was unsuccessful, and he was arrested again by American customs officials in December 1952.

Back in Italy, federal narcotics agents continued to chip away at the Partinico drug operation. Agents in Rome had been shadowing a drug courier from the St. Louis faction of the Partinico group. Surveillance led investigators to Frank Coppola's estate in Anzio. Informants supplied information suggesting the courier was there to pick up six kilos of heroin for delivery to Detroit. Apparently, something spooked the courier and he left the estate without making the pickup. The agents decided to remain at their surveillance post and it paid off. Serafino Mancuso was soon observed visiting the location and picking up a green trunk. Mancuso was one of Coppola's drug lieutenants from Partinico's neighboring town of Alcamo. Trailing Mancuso in the vehicle, agents arrested him at the Alcamo train station.

Law enforcement found the suspected six kilos of heroin concealed in the four walls of the specially constructed trunk. Evidence after the bust suggested that the $42,000 worth of heroin was heading for Detroit. Subsequently, the Italian government issued arrest warrants for Frank Coppola, John Priziola, and Jimmy Quasarano. Unfortunately for investigators, someone tipped off Coppola and he went into hiding. The Italian courts tried Priziola and Quasarano in absentia but dropped the charges, believing that conviction would be pointless without physical defendants. With Coppola on the run and Salvatore Vitale in prison, the heroin pipeline to Detroit experienced a temporary interruption.

By 1955, the Partinico drug network was back in operation. Italian authorities eventually caught up with Coppola and arrested him on unrelated charges that included murder and kidnapping. He beat the rap and returned to the streets. Vitale's incarceration was also temporary. After being picked up by U.S. Customs agents, he was sentenced to serve three years from an earlier conviction but was released from prison two years early on a technicality. At that point, American authorities hoped to deport him for the second time, but the proceedings were caught up in red tape and Vitale got a reprieve. While his deportation was under appeal, he set up operations with the Matranga family in Southern California. With Vitale out of prison, Priziola and Quasarano could no longer avoid paying off their earlier drug debts. The Detroit group started off by paying $20,000 of the money it owed Vitale, and soon the heroin deliveries were back on schedule. It did not take long, however, for old tensions to resurface. When Vitale sent $36,000 worth of heroin to Detroit and Papa John and Jimmy Q refused to pay, the flames of discontent were stoked once again. Incensed by the Detroiters' attitude, Toto Vitale threatened to have one of Quasarano's relatives in Partinico murdered if payment did not arrive.

In the meantime, veteran members of the Partinico factions such as the LoMedico brothers tried to mediate a peaceful settlement. Vito LoMedico worked with the Sicilian branch while Frank LoMedico assisted the Detroit group. The San Diego crime family tried to intervene, too. Joe Matranga, who was at the same time Priziola's son-in-law and Vitale's brother-in-law, urged his father-in-law to pay the drug bill. Detroit Godfather Joe Zerilli and New York drug trafficker John Ormento also visited Vitale in San Diego, each gangster luminary hoping to negotiate an agreement. Instead, Vitale grew more impatient and raised his demands to $60,000. He also told Joe Matranga that he would have Priziola and Quasarano killed if they failed to pay.

Underworld figures on both sides of the issue arranged an emergency sit-down between the two parties in 1956. Vitale confided in his wife that he would travel to Detroit for the meeting, collect his money, then fly off to Marseilles and Italy to collect other outstanding drug debts. FBI surveillance teams observed Vitale in Windsor, meeting with Peter Di Lorenzo and an "unidentified" son of Detroit mob czar Black Bill Tocco (his sons Jack and Tony were both active in the crime family at the time). That was the last recorded sighting of Salvatore Vitale.

Interviewed by the FBI, Vitale's son-in-law speculated that his father-in-law was lured to Detroit for a supposed meeting, and then executed. The son-in-law asked Matranga what happened but was told "to mind his own business." Soon federal investigators presumed Vitale had been murdered as well. With their rival out of the way, Coppola and Priziola not only resumed the drug pipeline to Detroit, they set about reorganizing the global heroin trade altogether. It was an incredibly ambitious proposition, but one the pair had the power and ingenuity to pull off.

The Grand Hotel des Palmes in Palermo is noted for its elegance and style. Featuring fine Italian tapestries, grand facades, antique chandeliers, and parquet floors, the hotel is considered an ideal location for hosting high-level conferences and meetings. As a guest, Richard Wagner composed part of his opera, *Parsifal*. In October 1957, the hotel attracted a different crowd of guests. Local police found it peculiar that a large number of reputed mobsters were converging on the site. Investigators monitored the hotel for days, noting an impressive list of Italian American and Sicilian gangsters passing through the doors. Police identified a number of underworld notables including Lucky Luciano, Frank Coppola, and Vito Vitale. Surveillance teams began to suspect that Italian American crime boss Joseph "Joe Bananas" Bonanno, in town to visit Luciano, was chairing some type of underworld summit. Other than Joe Bonanno and his New York entourage, only one other American mafioso was identified at the infamous conference: Detroit's own Papa John Priziola.

Already dealing in heroin, the criminal organizations on both sides of the Atlantic decided to meet and discuss streamlining the delivery process to increase supplies to America. Through his connections in the Caribbean, Coppola arranged an increase in heroin shipments concealed in food packages through Cuba. The heroin would make its way to Teamsters-affiliated crime bosses in the South such as Santo Trafficante in Florida and Carlos Marcello in New Orleans. Using his political connections with Vatican banker Michele Sindona, Coppola arranged intricate money-laundering schemes for the voluminous drug profits that were pouring in. The transatlantic agreement between the crime families solidified the Italian American Mafia's monopoly on the importation of heroin. But as the Partinicesi strengthened their position, the Catalanotte crew out of Windsor continued to struggle.

Canadian Collapse

The U.S. judicial system convicted Cockeyed Joe Catalanotte on narcotics charges in 1953. Yet after issuing a seven-year sentence, the court reversed its decision and released him in 1957 on the condition that he be deported to Italy. The Canadian capo's stay in Italy was not long and soon he was back in North America, landing in Cuba where he linked up with his former Windsor crew lieutenant Onofrio "Nono" Minaudo.

Married to Catalanotte's sister, Nono was a trusted member of the Catalanotte inner circle. From their Caribbean base, the veteran gangsters initiated a new heroin route. The Canadian mobsters in exile still had solid drug supply connections in Sicily, including Cockeyed Joe's older brother Vincenzo Catalanotte, who everybody called "Jimmy." Originally operating out of Detroit, Jimmy was deported to his home country after finishing a narcotics sentence in 1934. Back in Sicily, Jimmy specialized in bootlegging cigarettes. With smuggling routes and tactics already in place, it was only logical to add heroin to the illicit traffic.

Not long after getting things in their new narcotics operation up and running in Havana, Cuban authorities intervened and arrested Joe Catalanotte and Onofrio Minaudo as undesirable aliens in 1958, booting them out of the country. Exiled from Cuba, Catalanotte tried to enter New York, but was arrested and deported to Mexico. Undeterred, both Cockeyed Joe and his brother-in-law Nono set about returning to Canada. Catalanotte gained a temporary visa to enter the country in 1958, while Minaudo entered Windsor illegally.

American investigators suspected that Catalanotte was sneaking into Detroit to visit relatives at the time. Meanwhile, Nono Minaudo had his own complicated immigration history with North American authorities. Minaudo was dodging murder, attempted murder, assault, theft, and larceny charges in Italy when he entered the United States illegally in 1924. He migrated to Detroit and invested in a bowling alley and olive oil import company. Detroit police, however, suspected that Nono was also involved in armed robbery, prostitution, and labor racketeering. Marrying into the Catalanotte family, Minaudo joined the Windsor group and helped smuggle heroin across the Detroit River until the United States deported him to Cuba in 1954.

Minaudo used his political connections at the Canadian embassy in Havana to secure a short-term visa and re-entered Canada a few years later, staying for close to a decade. This seven-year stint on Canadian soil was highly scandalous, considering his prior convictions and deportations. The hullaballoo increased when Minister of External Affairs Paul Martin admitted that as a private lawyer he represented the infamous mobster. The scandal intensified and Canadian authorities had little option but to deport Minaudo. Informants told the FBI that Nono dreaded the possibility of being deported to his home country, and he had good reason. Within weeks of setting foot back in Sicily, he was gunned down by assassins in 1965.

Initially, the FBI suspected the assassination had a Detroit connection. After further investigation, however, agents shifted blame to local Sicilian mafiosi. The murder was never solved, but investigators focused on two theories in particular. One theory positioned Minaudo as the victim of a vendetta extending back to his early years in Sicily, while the other linked his murder to Sicilian loan sharks. Most experts tend to subscribe to the vendetta theory. Meanwhile, Catalanotte's visa expired and the Canadians deported him back to Mexico. It did not take long before agents from the U.S. Federal Bureau of Narcotics busted Cockeyed Joe while trying to set up another drug smuggling operation in Tijuana. Isolated and facing serious jail time, Joe felt he had no other option but to offer his services as an informant to the government. Federal narcotics agent Bill Durkin was intrigued by the desperate gangster's offer. Still, Durkin recognized that Catalanotte's limited knowledge of the Mexican underworld was of little use to police investigations south of the border.

To maximize Catalanotte as a source of information, federal agents had to feed the veteran narcotics trafficker back into his traditional smuggling network. For years, Cockeyed Joe facilitated the transnational flow of heroin between Europe and North America. Marseilles was the point of departure for the drug network and that's where the government placed Catalanotte, a ploy to make sure their prize snitch was at the nerve center of the Corsican heroin empire.

Federal narcotics agent Robert De Fauw was in the midst of investigating the infamous French Connection heroin ring when Catalanotte turned up in Marseilles as an informant. According to De Fauw, the Corsicans knew Catalanotte from past dealings and continued to believe Cockeyed Joe represented Detroit's Mafia family. With stellar drug-dealing credentials, Catalanotte was able to infiltrate the top Corsican syndicates. Initially, Cockeyed Joe linked up with the Guerini crime family. Fighting as part of the French resistance during World War II, the Guerini brothers made a number of valuable contacts with labor leaders, socialists, and members of the French intelligence community. Such connections helped facilitate the brothers' takeover of the Marseilles waterfront. Trusting that everything with Catalanotte was on the up-and-up, the brothers arranged a number of heroin deliveries through Montreal, believing they were supplying Cockeyed Joe's Detroit connections. Meanwhile, each shipment provided the government with details about the Guerini organization's delivery methods.

Now integrated into the Corsican underworld, Catalanotte also started dealing with French mobster Joseph Orsini. In addition to being a Nazi collaborator during World War II, Orsini was an experienced counterfeiter and drug smuggler. He acted as the Ansaldi crime family's representative in North America before being deported by the United States in 1958. Orsini was also the Guerini organization's chief competitor in the drug racket. Recognizing that tension existed between the two drug gangs, the government decided to play one group off against the other. De Fauw used Catalanotte to begin the intrigue. As part of the rouse, Cockeyed Joe went to Orsini, alleging that the Guerini brothers were supplying police with information about his drug shipments and conversion labs. In response, Orsini ordered the assassination of Antoine Guerini.

The gutsy mob hit ignited a serious of retaliations that rocked the French underworld. Meme Guerini, for example, apprehended an Orsini associate and tortured him prior to throwing the victim off a cliff. De Fauw recalls that the chosen method of assassination during the war was the motorcycle drive-by shooting. Gunmen would drive past at high speeds and unload rounds at their targets, speeding off before retaliation shots could be fired.

For three years, the Federal Bureau of Narcotics used Catalanotte's services to build a case against the Corsican traffickers. Now that the rival drug organizations were dismantling each other, it became the ideal time to utilize Joe's information and begin arresting members of the drug network. The investigation even snared high-ranking members of the Royal Canadian Mounted Police, including a corrupted staff sergeant on the Corsican payroll. Joe's primary condition for informing on the French, however, was that he would never give up any information on his Detroit *amici*, or Mafia brethren. The feds respected his decision.

"He was a real mafioso," Robert De Fauw recalled.

Quite often the gangster and the federal agent shared dinner in Marseilles. According to De Fauw, old one-eyed Joe was a pretty good cook. While in Spain on business, De Fauw purchased two pendants from the Shrine of the Black Madonna for his informant. The agent instructed Catalanotte to send the medals to the gangster's wife and child back in Detroit. Caught in a rare moment of sensitivity, Cockeyed Joe, the old-school mob tough guy, "broke down and cried like a baby" in gratefulness. Though the agent developed a fondness for Joe, he knew Catalanotte was a killer and was always careful to have "his sidearm" close by when dealing with the gangster.

Nevertheless, De Fauw recognized Catalanotte's invaluable contributions to the case and promised him that the government would check with immigration authorities about permitting the informant to visit Detroit. Unfortunately for Cockeyed Joe, French investigators were not as sympathetic. Making things worse, American agents suspected that the Corsicans had moles inside the French intelligence community. As a result, De Fauw never completely trusted his Marseilles colleagues. He even checked his automobile for car bombs each morning before setting off to work. Once local investigators became aware of Catalanotte's cooperation, French narcotics agents went after him. Under the circumstances, feds knew that protecting a known drug trafficker would have created diplomatic tension between the Cold War allies. American agents had to let their informer fend for himself. De Fauw instructed Joe to "lay low" for a while. Catalanotte ignored the advice and fled to Italy where he was arrested shortly after. De Fauw soon lost track of his ace informant.

With Minaudo dead and Catalanotte on the run, Nicholas Cicchini stepped in to take over Detroit's Canadian operations. Cicchini was a baker in the legitimate world. On the streets, however, the gangster specialized in bookmaking, counterfeiting, and smuggling illegal aliens. Soon Cicchini took over the lucrative drug-trafficking racket vacated by Catalanotte. Combining his two vocations, Cicchini smuggled heroin into Detroit by hiding the product in loaves of bread.

Cicchini's drug network started to unravel when Canadian authorities arrested Moises Costillo in 1956. Costillo was attempting to smuggle heroin across the Windsor–Detroit tunnel. The Costillo bust led to the arrest of Pete Devlin. Undercover agents with the Royal Canadian Mounted Police arrested Devlin attempting to sell 20 ounces of pure heroin. Devlin gave up information on his sources, and soon the RCMP concluded that Enrique Peralta was the ringleader of the medium-sized drug operation. But investigators ultimately wanted to know who was supplying the supplier.

The name John Simon turned up as the local supplier with connections to the "Italians." By 1961, patient undercover investigators finally started dealing with Simon directly. Agents earned his trust and eventually Simon introduced them to the boss of the entire network: Nick Cicchini. During their first meeting, Cicchini offered to sell the agents $100,000 worth of counterfeit U.S. $50 bills. Intrigued by the offer, the agents were nevertheless investigating drug trafficking and continued to pressure their new contact for heroin rather than counterfeit bills. Cicchini took the bait and offered to sell 100 percent pure heroin for $11,000 a kilo.

The undercover agents agreed to the price and arranged for a followup meeting at a local bar in Windsor. Cicchini arrived at the tavern with half a kilo as a sample. Agents paid for the product with marked bills, then took the heroin to the lab for testing. Cicchini's dope tested at 99.2 percent purity. Agents and Cicchini met for a third time, but the gangster informed his new customers that his heroin supply was dry at that time. Instead, he offered to sell the agents counterfeit bills once again, this time a million dollars worth.

Meanwhile, investigators suspected that Cicchini was buying his heroin from the Agueci brothers of Toronto. Alberto and Vito Agueci were members of the Magaddino crime family based in Buffalo, New York. The brothers had excellent heroin contacts in Sicily, and if one followed the pipeline to its source, they would find the Corsicans, specifically Dominic Albertini's half brother Joseph Cesari. Unfortunately for investigators, Cicchini assured his new clients that they would "never meet" his partners. Sensing he was not bluffing, agents decided to end the investigation and arrest both John Simon and Nicholas Cicchini. At 67 years old, the Canadian capo was sentenced to 12 years in prison for drug trafficking.

The New Order

Once the Canadian drug network collapsed, federal investigators identified the Partinico faction as the last "independent source of heroin" in Detroit in Congressional hearings from 1963. Well into the decade, the Partinicesi not only dominated the heroin trade, but continued to earn their violent reputation. After eliminating Salvatore Vitale, Leo Di Fatta was the next body to fall. Di Fatta's father was a longtime family friend of the Priziolas and was even best man at Papa John's first wedding. Priziola attempted to mentor his friend's son, but Leo insisted on leading the life of a petty stickup man. Disappointed that Leo wouldn't come under his wing, but unable to cut ties with the renegade hood altogether because of the fondness he held for Leo's dad, Papa John even posted the $5,000 bond for Leo after he was arrested during a botched robbery.

Leo Di Fatta's career path became more dangerous when he started holding up mob-connected businesses in the Detroit area. Though Di Fatta received a severe beating as a result, he knew that as long as his father was alive, he would be under Priziola's protection and spared the ultimate punishment. Unfortunately for Leo, the robberies lasted longer than his father. Not long after the old man died, police found Leo Di Fatta's "trussed and weighted body" in Lake Erie. Confidential informants reported that Priziola dispatched local enforcer and emerging syndicate street boss Anthony "Tony Jack" Giacalone to fix the Di Fatta problem permanently.

Vitale and Di Fatta weren't the last bodies to drop. With the bloodthirsty mobsters still not content with the state of their rank and file, the gangland slayings continued. Roy Calabrese started off as a runner in one of John Priziola's betting parlors. Eventually, the young wiseguy graduated to the position of bookie in the numbers racket. On the side, Calabrese hustled as a small-time pimp. The would-be gangster obviously underestimated his employers' reputations when he hatched a scheme to rip off his own gambling house. On the streets, the scam was known as "going with the tickets." After learning the winning numbers for the day's illegal lottery, Calabrese would leak the digits to a co-conspirator on the street. His accomplice would then prepare a mock betting slip to match the winning digits.

Soon Roy's associates at Frankie G's bar noticed sizeable increases in the young bookie's disposable income. Papa John Priziola also took notice and suspected his employee of ripping him off. Calabrese endured a beating accompanied by a warning to clean up his act. Recklessly, he continued the scam, refusing to heed the advice of the Detroit Mafia and choosing to test and cross them instead. That was until Valentine's Day, 1962, when time ran out on his scam and his life at the same time. After finishing dinner, Calabrese told his mother that he was leaving to meet with friends. Hours later, the St. Clair Shores Police Department found Calabrese's garroted body in the trunk of his car.

According to FBI informants, the next murder committed by the group caused a rift in the organization's hierarchy between Papa John and veteran heroin trafficker Peter Gaudino, known to freelance in the drug trade and alternate his deals between the Partinicesi group and the Windsor crew. He was also godfather to a son of Detroit gangster Paul "The Sicilian" Cimino. Gaudino's beef with Priziola related to the disappearance of Cimino. Congressional investigators had identified Cimino as Joe Catalanotte's "right-hand man" in the drug trade. In 1962, as Cimino faced a deportation hearing with the Immigration and Naturalization Service, Priziola feared his fellow mobster would start ratting on his drug partners in Detroit. No longer under Cockeyed Joe's protection, Cimino was an easy target. He disappeared before he could meet with immigration officials. The consensus on the street was that Cimino was murdered. One informant told the FBI with confidence, "You'll never see him again."

A few years later, Peter "Tino" Lombardo, a member of Priziola's California operation as well as an identified Mafia soldier, was also killed. FBI documents indicate two possible motives for Lombardo's homicide. First, informants were indicating to the FBI that the Partinicesi suspected Lombardo was a rat. Another more likely motive for the Lombardo hit was his role in an intra-family squabble that pitted new street boss Tony Giacalone against old-school Detroit mob capos Santo Perrone and Pete Licavoli. FBI documents from the era reveal Lombardo was suspected of helping plant a bomb underneath Giacalone's car that was detected by a Giacalone lieutenant before it could detonate. Authorities believed that Lombardo was ordered by Perrone to blow up Giacalone in retaliation for Perrone's loss of his leg from a car bomb set by the Giacalone crew in 1963. The tension all stemmed from the changing of the guard in the syndicate from the new regime led by Giacalone and a group of crusty old-schoolers, represented most

fervently by Perrone, sometimes called "Sammy the Shark," and Licavoli, sometimes referred to as "Horseface Pete," who resented taking orders from their
younger counterpart.

Meanwhile, federal narcotics agents in Detroit were only able to make one
modest case against the Partinico group in the entire time it was operating at full
tilt. In 1959, agents nailed Andrew Bottancino, the same low-level trafficker who
worked with the Windsor network years earlier, and Vincent "Crazy Jimmy"
Finazzo, a recognized made member of the Detroit mob and the son of Sam
Finazzo, grandson of Don Joe Zerilli, for heroin trafficking in 1961. Well versed on
the proper mob etiquette in such situations, when he was convicted and sentenced
to five years in prison, Crazy Jimmy kept quiet and served his time while the bosses
remained free.

Federal law enforcement received another breakthrough in its war on international drug trafficking in 1965. The FBI received notice from a confidential source
in Italy that the Italian government was issuing 17 arrest warrants for suspects
linked to the Sicilian drug trade. The list of indicted suspects included John
Priziola, Raffaele Quasarano, and John Ormento. Sicilian police launched the
operation by raiding the villa of former Bonanno crime family underboss Giovanni
Bonventre in Castellammare del Golfo.

Italian prosecutor Giuseppe Mattina submitted "22 volumes of testimony and
evidence" to Judge Aldo Vigneir, linking the indicted to an international drug
cartel. Vigneir even traveled to the United States to interview the infamous mob
turncoat, Joseph Valachi. Unfortunately for law enforcement, the United States
and Italy had yet to formalize an extradition treaty. As a result, the Italians once
again dropped the charges against Priziola and Quasarano. Italian police also
arrested Frank Coppola a few months after the raid on Bonventre's home in a
related narcotics investigation. But like Papa John and Jimmy Q, Frankie Three
Fingers Coppola beat the rap.

Despite the intensified police scrutiny, Priziola apparently maintained a sense
of humor. Robert De Fauw recalls how the diminutive boss joshed agents during
one surveillance operation. De Fauw's agents were tailing Priziola when the gangster stopped by a local Catholic church. Leaving Mass, Quasarano opened the car
door for his boss when, as if reenacting a scene from a movie, Papa John walked
past his driver and headed straight for the "undercover" vehicle. Priziola knocked
on the agents' windshield and said, "If you guys want to know where I'm going,
why don't you just ask?"

By the late 1960s, the Partinicesi groups in Sicily and Detroit experienced different trajectories in global drug trafficking. In Partinico, Frank Coppola intensified his Mafia family's involvement in heroin smuggling by forming alliances with
powerful Sicilian dons like Salvatore Greco and Luciano Leggio. Frankie Three

Fingers also mentored the next generation of Partinicesi mafiosi, including his nephews Augustino and Giacamo Coppola and his son-in-law Giuseppe Corso.

Unlike their Sicilian counterparts, however, the Detroit faction scaled back their drug operations by the 1970s. Two factors contributed to the Priziola group's declining participation in the drug trade; most importantly, the 1957 Palermo narcotics conference established direct heroin links between the New York and Sicilian Mafia families. Up until that point, Detroit's Partinico group had privileged contacts with the Sicilian heroin exporters. As a result, Detroit supplied New York's crime organizations. After 1957, the Bonanno and Gambino crime families, in particular, established their own independent sources of heroin supply. Secondly, content with supplying New York, Priziola's crew became less interested in supplying the local heroin market in Detroit and, by the 1950s, began allowing competitors to come in and set up shop pushing heroin in exchange for a street tax.

Robert De Fauw maintains that as a result of these two factors, Priziola's crew began focusing less on narcotics and instead expanded their interests further into labor racketeering, extortion, and bookmaking. Just as the highly competitive narcotics market convinced Priziola's group to move away from dope, another faction of the Detroit mob emerged and embraced the new global heroin trade.

Last Run

The Badalamenti group represents the third faction of the Detroit Mafia that is heavily involved in the narcotics trade. Cinisi is a Sicilian coastal town outside of Palermo, and also the ancestral home of the Badalamenti clan. There the family existed as one of Cinisi's ruling Mafia factions. In their early years of racketeering, the clan specialized in trafficking black market cigarettes. The family also held a virtual monopoly in Palermo's fruit and produce market. Younger members of the Badalamenti clan, along with other extended family, immigrated to southern Michigan in the 1940s. Brothers Emanuele and Gaetano Badalamenti, for example, settled in Monroe and operated a local market. The siblings were also members of the Cinisi Mafia and were connected to the Tocco mob in Detroit. The local Mafia leadership soon placed Emanuele, also known as "Rough Manny," in charge of all Mafia-related racketeering south of Detroit all the way to the Ohio border.

Other prominent mafiosi from the Cinisi area arrived in Michigan around the same time, including Salvatore Bartolotta, Filippo Manzella, Antonio Palazzolo, and Salvatore Palazzolo. In 1928, the Palermo judicial system tried Bartolotta, the Palazzolos, and Salvatore Badalamenti for being part of a Mafia criminal conspiracy. By the time immigration authorities deported Gaetano Badalamenti in 1950, the Cinisi group had already established itself as an important faction of the greater Detroit underworld.

Back in Sicily, the Badalamenti family transitioned from trafficking black market cigarettes to supplying heroin. Evidence of this transition emerged in 1958 when Italian authorities arrested Gaetano's brother Vito and their cousin Cesare Badalamenti during an undercover narcotics investigation. The cousins served modest sentences and by the mid-1960s, Cesare joined his Badalamenti relatives in Michigan.

In addition to owning a real estate and a construction company in the Detroit area, Cesare began trafficking heroin again. Settling in the suburb of Mt. Clemens, Cesare Badalamenti tapped into a pre-existing heroin network that already had Cinisi group fingerprints. The Badalamenti family was linked to the Coppolas in Partinico; an example is the relationship Gaetano Badalamenti and Frank Coppola developed in Detroit before their respective deportations. Later, U.S. Customs officials linked Badalamenti's nephew Dominico Coppola to an 81-kilo shipment of heroin uncovered in an Italian ocean liner bound for New York.

Joe Indelicato represented another link in the pre-existing Detroit–Sicily heroin pipeline. Indelicato operated out of Canada and was a business and social acquaintance of Joe Catalanotte and Nick Cicchini. In 1956, authorities busted Indelicato in New York with half a million dollars of heroin, yet remarkably, he only served a five-year sentence. Out of prison, Indelicato acted as the drug courier between the Badalamentis in Sicily and their Detroit cousin Cesare, who by that time was put in charge of all of the city's "Zips," or imported Sicilian foot soldiers. As with the Catalanotte–Cicchini network, Indelicato and Badalamenti transported heroin across the Detroit–Windsor border with relative ease.

By the early 1980s, a number of the original Cinisi mafiosi in Michigan had passed away. A younger generation soon emerged to fill the void. From his Sicilian base of operations, Gaetano Badalamenti continued to supply his American nephews and cousins with cocaine and heroin. Scattered throughout rural locations in the Midwest, Badalamenti's relatives used pizzerias as fronts for receiving and distributing narcotics.

Law enforcement uncovered a Michigan connection while surveilling Pietro "Sicilian Pete" Alfano, a suspected heroin trafficker living in Illinois. Agents noted that Alfano made frequent calls to Sam Evola Jr. in Temperance, Michigan. On the surface, Evola was a law-abiding drywall contractor living near the Ohio border. Closer inspection revealed that Evola was the son of Detroit mafioso Salvatore "Sammy Blue Eyes" Evola. The elder Evola was an old-school mobster with ties to Joe Catalanotte, Sam Finazzo, and Jimmy Quasarano. More importantly, investigators realized that the younger Sam Evola was married to Cristina Badalamenti, Gaetano Badalamenti's niece. Agents also discovered that Alfano was Badalamenti's nephew. According to investigators, the blood ties were no coincidence, and agents suspected that the ringleader of this rural American drug operation was none other than the infamous crime lord Gaetano Badalamenti, known around the world as simply "Don Tano."

Hoping to uncover a deeper Sicilian connection, the DEA and FBI increased surveillance on Alfano, Evola, and their cousin, Emanuele Palazzolo (yet another Badalamenti nephew). Agents monitored several phone conversations between the trio and a mysterious international caller. The surveillance teams suspected that often-heard phrases like "salted sardines" and "playing cards" were codes for narcotics shipments and purchases.

Yet another breakthrough in the case occurred as agents observed Alfano, Evola, and Palazzolo traveling to New York at different times to meet with suspected East Coast traffickers. Once in New York, Cinisi group members would meet with drug dealers connected to the Sicilian faction of the Bonanno crime family. Intriguingly, agents discovered another common link between the Cinisi group and their Bonanno associates: like Alfano and Palazzolo, the New York gangsters owned a number of pizzerias, but these were spread throughout the East Coast rather than the Midwest. With so many Sicilian drug suppliers operating pizza chains across America, federal agents dubbed their investigation the "Pizza Connection."

Putting the pieces together, field agents hypothesized that Gaetano Badalamenti was supplying the American Mafia with narcotics while using Sicilian traffickers to facilitate the operation. According to investigators, the mysterious international caller dealing with Alfano must have been Badalamenti. Yet for investigators this was only a hypothesis; directors at the DEA and FBI were unconvinced. Why would a major Sicilian crime boss like Badalamenti communicate directly with lower-level operatives in rural, Midwestern America? To answer that question, agents had to examine recent power struggles taking place within the Sicilian Mafia.

For decades, the major crime families of Palermo, including Badalamenti, Bontate, and Inzerillo, ran the heroin trade as a consortium. The Palermo cartel brought in other crime organizations from surrounding areas like Partinico and Castellammare del Golfo, yet one Mafia family felt marginalized by the arrangement. As boss of the Corleone family, Luciano Leggio resented the hegemonic positions of Badalamenti and his Palermitan allies in the narcotics trade. Quietly and patiently, the Corleonesi plotted against the consortium. To the great embarrassment of the Cinisi boss, Leggio's henchmen carried out a number of kidnappings on Badalamenti-controlled territories.

By humiliating the Cinisi boss, Leggio demonstrated to other crime families in the area that Badalamenti was vulnerable. The Corleone boss soon started scheming with middle-echelon mafiosi in the Palermo families. "Why should the bosses in Palermo hoard all the drug profits while foot soldiers in the organizations go hungry?" asked Leggio. Infuriated by such provocations, Badalamenti and his allies plotted the murder of Leggio's right-hand man, Salvatore "Toto" Riina. Yet by cultivating relationships with the disgruntled mafiosi of rival families, Leggio had spies in place that informed him about the Riina murder plot. Now was the time for the Corleonesi to organize an outright insurrection.

Beginning in 1981, Corleonesi hit squads picked off the old dons one by one. Among others, Leggio's hit teams gunned down Salvatore Inzerillo, Stefano Bontate, and Gaetano's cousin, Antonino Badalamenti. The Great Mafia War was actually a slaughter as the Corleonesi killed hundreds of rival gangsters associated with the Palermo drug consortium. Gaetano Badalamenti lost a number of relatives during the war, including a nephew who was tortured and chopped into pieces. Two of Badalamenti's nephews in the United States, Salvatore and Matteo Sollena (close to the Gambino family in New York), were shot to death as well. Once in command of the Sicilian Mafia commission, the Corleonesi expelled Badalamenti from the Cinisi family. Gaetano knew that his expulsion was a death sentence, and fled to Brazil.

Hiding out in Latin America, the former Cinisi boss reorganized the remnants of his drug empire. Remarkably, even though the Corleonesi had a contract out on his life, they nevertheless permitted Badalamenti's reentry into the drug trade. Now that Leggio and Riina were in control of the Sicilian Mafia, Badalamenti's remaining people had to kick up a percentage of any drug profits to the new bosses. The Corleonesi still planned on killing Gaetano, but in their bizarre logic, they figured they should still make some money off of him before pulling the trigger.

Don Tano faced logistical problems as well. Most of his trusted lieutenants were wiped out during the Great Mafia War. To insulate themselves from prosecution, mob bosses typically avoid dealing in narcotics directly and instead delegate those responsibilities to lower-level operatives. In the case of the Cinisi crime family, however, the top and middle layers of the organization were killed during the war. If the former don wanted to sell drugs to nephews in the American Midwest, for example, he would now have to communicate with them directly.

Back in Michigan, federal agents monitored Sam Evola Jr. as he frantically tried to collect drug money from his buyers. Bugged phone conversations revealed that the mysterious international supplier was furious that his American contacts were tardy with their drug payments. Apparently, Evola sold $400,000 worth of cocaine and heroin on consignment to a local dealer who, even after several weeks, was unable to pay for the product. Over the phone, Alfano and Evola debated whether or not they should kill the delinquent drug client. Both knew that if they did not come up with the money, they would end up dead themselves.

The wiretaps on Pietro Alfano produced more crucial information when agents heard an operator announce, "I have a call from Brazil," followed by the voice of the mysterious international caller. The feds knew Gaetano Badalamenti had to be in Brazil. Not long after, investigators overheard Badalamenti order Alfano to meet him in Madrid. American law enforcement agents followed Alfano to Spain, tailed him in Madrid, and observed as he led police straight to the prized target. Spanish police officially arrested Badalamenti and his nephew and handed them over to the FBI on April 8th.

Investigators now had enough evidence to justify a series of warrants, and on April 9, 1984, they launched simultaneous raids on the homes of Alfano, Evola, and Palazzolo. Before leaving for Spain, Alfano had procured an impressive arsenal as agents discovered bullet-proof vests, hollow-point ammunition, silencers, an AR-15 assault rifle, and a number of handguns in his house. Agents also found a modest amount of cocaine during the raid on Sam Evola's place.

More importantly, they found Evola's passport and realized that he had been traveling to Brazil in the recent past. They also discovered a notebook with what appeared to be coded language scribbled throughout the pages. The codes matched a number of cryptic messages the FBI had intercepted from the Alfano wiretaps. Badalamenti was passing on the codes to his nephews so that they could communicate without revealing their true agendas. Meanwhile, Evola's cocaine tested at 95 percent purity, signaling that it came directly from Latin America, presumably Brazil.

The feds rounded up dozens of other suspects in the "Pizza Connection" investigation, and in 1985 the case went to trial. Gaetano Badalamenti was convicted of being the ringleader and sentenced to 45 years in prison. Pietro Alfano survived an assassination attempt during a recess in the trial. He was left paralyzed, however, and was later sentenced to 15 years. Sam Evola pled guilty to the cocaine charges, but refused to testify against his co-conspirators. He received a 15-year sentence. Agents suspected that Evola's brother took over the narcotics operation after Sam's arrest and conviction.

Over the years, Italian organized crime in Detroit became less involved in the heroin trade. By the 1980s, cocaine replaced heroin as the major drug commodity in the Motor City as well. During that decade, undercover drug enforcement agents busted Robert "Bobby the Animal" La Puma, a soldier in the Giacalone crew, on cocaine charges. And in 1988, British undercover police thwarted a plan by the Detroit mob to ship millions of dollars worth of cocaine to dealers in the United Kingdom. Detroit mafiosi were caught hiding the kilos in industrial equipment heading across the Atlantic. Despite these notable examples of Italian involvement in narcotics trafficking, African American syndicates and outlaw motorcycle gangs largely replaced the traditional Italian mob as the city's major drug suppliers.

Still, the Partinico, Windsor, and Cinisi groups of Detroit's Mafia were pioneers in the global drug trade. While Detroit's local crime family may no longer be major players in the narcotics trade, other Italian American crime organizations continue to expand their involvement in heroin and cocaine trafficking. Secondly, the Partinico and Windsor crews initiated the type of transnational templates for global drug trafficking utilized today. Currently, local African American drug organizations purchase cocaine from Colombian cartels who contract with Mexican gangs for delivery to Detroit. This is precisely the type of globalized supply and distribution originated by the likes of Priziola, Catalanotte, and Badalamenti.

End of the Line

John Priziola went into semi-retirement during the 1970s. He became an active mobster again following the death of Detroit godfather Joseph Zerilli in 1976. Papa John's leadership stabilized the Detroit underworld as the local Mafia transitioned to the era of Giacomo "Black Jack" Tocco, Black Bill's oldest son and Joe Zerilli's nephew. Priziola died of a heart attack in 1979, having never served any significant time for drug trafficking or anything else for that matter. Jimmy Q served as Jack Tocco's first consigliere, but had to step down due to a conviction in an extortion case. Once out of prison, Quasarano remained a valuable member of the Detroit Mafia until his death in 2001.

UNDERWATERWORLD

The Four Bears Water Park Murders

By Kyle Duda and Scott M. Burnstein

Contracting pink eye is a risk you take when you go to a water park. Death and prison are the risks you take when you get involved with organized crime. But what happens when organized crime mixes with the over-chlorinated water of a public water park? I guess you'll just have to ask Butch. He's the only one still standing.

Public water parks aren't the cleanest of locations, but ultimately they serve a purpose. Organized crime isn't the most ethical way to make a living, but it's something that nonetheless exists and ultimately plays a role in society, whether out in the open or deep beneath the surface. Although entrenched in the shadows of public perception across Metro Detroit, the Mafia is an undeniable force—existing, often with a shiny veneer of respectability, in many different avenues of life. Using a public water park as an analogy for organized crime isn't all that difficult, especially since in the Motor City, at least according to federal documents, they were long linked in tandem.

Whether you choose to dabble in organized crime, or just like to frequent public water parks, there are inherent risks that everyone involved knows and accepts. So, for the sake of your family—or for the sake of The Family, you cast your reservations aside and "jump in," accepting the less-than-sanitary conditions. Once you're there, "in the water," so to speak, you're there. Like it or not, it can't be undone. While water parks throughout the land emit a certain grimy charm (not to mention serving as a microbiologist's wet dream with all the different forms of germs swarming around such establishments), the filth uncovered in the bottom of your run-of-the-mill public pool pales in comparison to the real dirt that was alleged to have gone down at Four Bears Water Park in Shelby Township, Michigan, in the 1980s.

From 1983 to 2004, the suburban park created summer memories for countless families. Ask almost any resident of Metro Detroit about Four Bears and chances are he or she will rattle on about the park's grand water slides, wave pool, or bumper boats—a far cry from a would-be coke overdose, a self-inflicted gunshot wound to the chest, and a slew of allegations and whispers that kept local and federal law enforcement officials relatively busy for much of the final two decades of the 20th century.

The park, located in the heart of suburbia, a little more than 20 miles north of Detroit, lasted 21 years before it was demolished in favor of luxury homes and condominiums. But its legacy lives on. It was truly a Metro Detroit staple. The man who made it all possible—the same man who was once at the center of numerous allegations linking him to organized crime and other nefarious activities—was the water park's notorious owner, Louis Stramaglia, a man his friends affectionately referred to as "Butch." Stramaglia, a wealthy businessman, alleged mob associate, and owner of a slew of companies around the country, was known to carry himself with a larger-than-life bravado and intimidating flair.

"Butch is hard-core, not someone to be messed around with," said a former federal agent who asked not to be identified. "He was someone we always had our eyes on."

Whispers of shenanigans and more-than-questionable business practices related to his asset portfolio were rampant.

"There were rumors that drug money and profits from some other illegal operations were being run through Four Bears," said an unnamed federal agent. "Whether Butch was aware of this, we could never prove."

And the feds almost had him. They were the thinnest thread away from nailing Stramaglia to the wall for good, putting him behind bars for the better part of the rest of his life. But Butch averted the grasp of law enforcement and remained virtually unscathed. For nearly a decade, Stramaglia and his construction company, Vito Trucking and Excavating, found themselves in the newspaper headlines for all the wrong reasons: shoddy work, kickbacks, sweetheart deals, intimidation tactics, and other racketeering-related activities. This reputed behavior helped trigger a 32-month criminal investigation that ended with Butch facing more than 80 years in prison. The water park and construction impresario was charged with embezzling $1.7 million from a highly lucrative, publicly financed deal he struck with Dade County in Florida to build the Sawgrass Expressway, a 23-mile stretch of highway that would cost $200 million to complete. With his veil of legitimacy shattered, Stramaglia was found guilty on all 38 felony counts and was sentenced to 50 years in prison. But always the scamster, Butch found a way to get out. After just two years in the can, Stramaglia was a free man. A federal judge overturned all 38 felony counts on a technicality, and in 1993, Butch returned to Detroit. As luck would have it, the only two other men who might be able to put him back in prison were dead, laid to rest six feet under years earlier, their deaths shrouded in mystery. Butch's name would pop up in both investigations, but he would never be charged in either case.

◇◇◇◇◇◇◇◇◇◇◇◇◇

According to members of law enforcement familiar with his persona, Stramaglia came off as a thug.

"Now, I'm not trying to accentuate stereotypes, but this guy was straight out of central casting for one of *The Godfather* movies," Oakland County Sheriff's Office detective Terry Cashman commented. "He drove a big black Cadillac, wore real expensive suits, always had a cigar in his mouth; basically, trying to portray a real hard ass."

With Butch, though, it was definitely not a put-on. He himself would tell you that.

"I'm a good-timer, I like to party, I ain't no Ivy Leaguer. I'm a little rough around the edges," he once said to a newspaper reporter.

Butch didn't need the aid of an ivory tower institution to make his own powerful connections. He knew how the game worked—whether in the street or when dealing with greedy politicians—and made sure to surround himself with the right people who could sway things in his favor. When Butch was banned from bidding in Lee County, Florida, due to complaints about his subpar work on an East Lee County sewer project, federal records show he brought in some high-class call girls to entertain the right people aboard his yacht, *The Prodigal Son*, to make sure his name was removed from the prohibition list.

"Let's be grown up about this; if what I'm doing is wrong, they ought to lock up every fucking lobbyist in Washington," Butch told the reporter. "I do business like any businessman, no more, no less."

Perhaps none of Stramaglia's connections was more powerful than the infamous Giacomo "Black Jack" Tocco, Detroit's convicted Mafia don, reputed to be the head of the Motor City mob family since in the 1970s. Despite his rap sheet— a racketeering bust in the mid-1990s and subsequent incarceration—the bespectacled and business-savvy Tocco had infiltrated mainstream high society in suburban Detroit with relative ease. Over the past 60 years, he claimed ownership of a wide variety of successful legitimate businesses, such as Melrose Linen, Hazel Park Racetrack, Hillcrest Country Club in Clinton Township, and the Warren Tennis Club. Butch didn't try to hide his relationship with Tocco. And why would he? In certain power circles, a friendship with Tocco was something to flaunt. Access to Tocco and the honor of being seen in his company provided instant credibility. More importantly, said one former fed, "it bred an environment of fear for those who may have contemplated crossing Butch."

"I've known Jack Tocco—what difference does it make?...I'd rather have Jack Tocco for a friend than 20 FBI agents," Butch told *The Miami Herald* in 1983.

A friendship with Jack Tocco or any member of the Mafia also required responsibilities beyond playing tennis and appearing at one of their offspring's weddings. And if these responsibilities weren't met or if something or someone got in the mob's way, there were sure to be dire consequences. While the Detroit mob in particular is not known for its overt violence when compared to its blood-lusting contemporaries in New York, Chicago, and Philadelphia, lives frequently tend to get lost amid the chaos of the Motor City underworld. These types of men and their associates are quite capable of killing to preserve the bottom line or to prevent a lengthy prison stint. Butch was surely well aware of the game and how it worked, specifically its potentially homicidal ramifications. When his baby brother Frank, the vice president of both Four Bears Water Park and Butch's construction company, turned up dead in January 1989, things hit home harder than ever. Or did they?

◇◇◇◇◇◇◇◇◇◇◇◇

Frank was no angel. He knew what he was getting into, and was alleged to have been just as shady a businessman as his brother was. However, while Butch was perceived on the streets as a standup guy, steady as a rock, Frank was considered the opposite.

"He wasn't as hardcore as his older brother," said one former federal agent familiar with the pair. "Frankie was known as more of a wild card, not trusted as much as Butch, but we still had him on our radar."

Throughout the 1980s, Frank Stramaglia made a name for himself around the city for his partying ways. He got caught up in the fast-paced, easy-come, easy-go lifestyle. Of course, in the '80s, no party was complete without the biggest cliché of the decade—cocaine. The trendy white powder was one of Frank's biggest vices. It was well known that he was a heavy user of the drug and had battled addiction since his late-teen years. So it wasn't particularly surprising when the 33-year-old was found dead in 1989 from what was thought to be a cocaine overdose after a night of revelry. His death scene was the embodiment of an individual with a penchant for life's many excesses: Frank was slumped and naked in a running hot tub with a condom, a porno mag, and a coke straw all floating just an arm's reach away. All that was missing to hammer home the hedonistic theme was a Rolling Stones song blaring in the background.

On January 1, 1989, Frank and a person believed by authorities to have been Helen Collins, a longtime social companion, checked into Room 333 at the Comfort Inn off Hall Road in Utica. He never made it down to the lobby for checkout. The hotel's general manager, Michael Walker, went to check on the room when nobody answered the phone. He discovered Frank's body slouched over the right side of the running whirlpool. Frank was almost completely submerged in the soapy tub save for the left side of his face. There was some foamy, semi-coagulated blood near his head and an unknown black scum floating in the water. The police incident report notes that the large, well-appointed room was remarkably clean. After removing Frank's body and draining the tub, a plastic bottle of aspirin was found at the bottom.

With very few clues and an immaculate crime scene, police had little to go on. Helen Collins, the water park's former comptroller, denied being with Stramaglia at the Comfort Inn, despite the fact that hotel personnel saw her with him when he checked in. Authorities soon discovered that Frank got his cocaine from his best friend, Mark Giancotti, a suspected mob-backed drug dealer who lived in Troy. Giancotti had replaced Collins as the comptroller at Four Bears in December 1987. Following the initial examinations, Utica police ruled Frank's death to be accidental. It should have been an open-and-shut case. Frank liked to party. He also liked cocaine and had overindulged in the past. But things got complicated when Giancotti turned up dead just a little more than one month later under suspicious circumstances. Giancotti, like Frank, was a partier. He not only sold cocaine, he used it as well. On February 7, 1989, Giancotti's body was discovered in his car in the parking lot of a Meijer supermarket in Rochester Hills. His death was a tad messier than Frank's perceived overdose. Mark Giancotti left this world with the aid of a bullet to the chest. A .357 Magnum revolver was found lying next to him.

"We got a call to come out to Meijer's at around 2:30 in the morning," recalled Lieutenant Terry Cashman in a 2010 interview. "I remember it was very cold outside and when we got there, we were directed to a car in the parking lot surrounded by several uniformed officers. Approaching the vehicle, I could see a white male, around 30 to 35 years old, slumped over the seat with a pistol on the floor at his feet. He was shot twice in the chest."

It would be one thing if two employees at the same company died in the same month. Chalk it up to coincidence or a freak occurrence. But when you're dealing with two deaths just a few weeks apart, involving two men from the same business who both had alleged ties to organized crime, questions begin to arise. Why would a perfectly healthy, 30-year-old man with a zest for nightlife, a burgeoning cocaine operation, and all the perks that came with success shoot himself in the chest, let alone in the parking lot of a discount supermarket? It just didn't make sense.

"The more we started to dig, the more we started to believe this death was not a suicide, but rather most likely, if not certainly, a murder," Cashman stated. "It's very rare for men to commit suicide by shooting themselves in the chest, and the gunpowder residue test came back negative, which would be virtually impossible if you were shooting yourself."

It soon became obvious that there was much more than met the eye in the untimely passing of Giancotti and Stramaglia.

"Immediately, our informants started to tell us that Giancotti's death was connected to the death of Frank Stramaglia," Cashman continued. "These two were said to run in fast circles and to be cocaine users. Stramaglia was Giancotti's boss, but they were viewed as equals by most people. We eventually got word from the FBI that the Stramaglias and Giancotti were said to be associated with the local organized crime family. The more we looked into things, the more obvious it became that the two deaths dovetailed."

There was no question that Mark Giancotti's death was the result of foul play. Test results determined that the gun left behind was indeed the weapon used to kill Giancotti. But the ballistics report showed that Mark didn't fire the gun. Police released a composite sketch of a man who had been seen talking to Giancotti in a 1976 Cadillac El Dorado with another man in the back seat, 90 minutes before Mark was found in his own car parked nearby. Unfortunately for the investigation, the two men in the car were never identified. Informants would tell federal authorities in the coming months that the men in the El Dorado were both members of the local crime syndicate. All that was certain was that two men with ties to Four Bears Water Park were dead in a matter of two months. But why? Apparently, the Detroit mob works in mysterious ways.

"The Detroit Mafia is very adept at shrouding their hits in mystery, carrying things out in a way that leaves more questions than answers," said a former federal prosecutor.

Following Giancotti's death, Werner Spitz, a consulting medical examiner from neighboring Macomb County, stepped in and performed an autopsy on Frank Stramaglia. The examination bore some intriguing results. Most glaring was the fact that Stramaglia's body was found to have 19 times the lethal dose of cocaine in his system. And even more bizarre, the drug had been cut with cadmium, a toxic compound found in battery acid, gardening fertilizer, and house paint. Cadmium is not what normal drug pushers use to cut cocaine, but it could easily be mixed with cocaine because it also is a white powder, Spitz noted in his report. He added that cadmium is expensive and generally unavailable to the public.

"If I told you to go out and find me some cadmium, most people wouldn't know where to turn," he commented.

The connection between the two deaths was clear, despite the fact that Stramaglia's death was never officially ruled a murder. Carl Marlinga, the Macomb County prosecutor at the time of the two deaths, has a strong opinion on the matter. "The two murders were made to look like a suicide, but obviously they were not suicides," Marlinga said in a 2010 interview. "Somebody was sending a message."

Law enforcement officials then turned their focus to someone quite familiar to them: Butch Stramaglia. As Terry Cashman recalled, Butch was more than willing to give out his fair share of overt cryptic messages.

"So, we eventually make it over to Butch's house to talk to him about the case," Cashman continued. "When we got to his house, we were taken to see Butch in his office. We told him why we were there and he said, with a bit of a smirk on his face, 'I thought that guy killed himself.' As soon as we told him we thought it might not have been a suicide, he said, 'I had nothing to do with that.' He paused for a second and then said, 'I could have if I had wanted to, but I didn't.' And then with a half-laugh he said, 'I could have you two guys whacked if I wanted to.' Leaving Butch's house, I've got to say we came away with a stronger belief that he had something to do with it than we did when we first got there."

In Mario Puzo's *The Godfather*, the don of Detroit goes on a tirade about how he doesn't want drugs sold to children. Butch thought in a similar manner. He didn't want drugs near his kid brother. Police began exploring a revenge angle for the homicide, theorizing that Butch might have had the motive to kill Mark Giancotti if he believed that Giancotti provided Frank with the drugs that wound up overdosing him.

"Both Frank Stramaglia and Mark Giancotti were seen out together quite a bit at the local night spots in the months leading up to their deaths, and it was said they were always treated like VIPs and always surrounded by a lot of girls and hangers-on," Cashman reported. "It was told to us that Stramaglia got his drugs from Giancotti and that his brother Butch didn't like Giancotti as a result. Butch had put out a lot of time and effort to get his brother clean, and obviously it never stuck. Plus, Frank and Butch were both in recent trouble with some racketeering charges down in Florida, so the waters around them at that time were kind of choppy, to say the least. The deeper we got into the investigation, the more we believed Butch possibly had something to do with the Giancotti's homicide."

Following the meeting with Butch, Cashman and his partner Bill Harvey hit a dead end in their investigation and turned things over to the FBI. One agent familiar with the case reaffirmed some of Cashman's notions.

"We were called into the case pretty early, within a couple weeks of Mark Giancotti showing up dead," said a former federal agent who asked not to be identified. "The Frank Stramaglia death a few weeks before was real suspicious, and when his buddy Giancotti wound up going under similar circumstances, it was a no-brainer to get involved. We were aware of Giancotti as an associate of organized crime in the Detroit area, and Stramaglia and his brother had been in our sights for a while in terms of their association with the Mafia around here. The DEA was telling us that Giancotti was a mid-level cocaine dealer. Stramaglia and his brother Butch were under federal indictment down in Florida. After collecting the facts, there was no doubt in our minds that these two deaths were related, and at least one or both of them were carried out on the orders of the top brass of the mob."

Trying to connect the dots became an arduous process. Things weren't lining up right, and soon speculation began to overmatch reason. Rumors swirled, but nothing concrete could be made when trying to link the deaths of Mark Giancotti and Frank Stramaglia to the mob. Organized crime and the construction industry have been synonymous with each other for decades. It might seem stereotypical, but in the case of the Stramaglias, it appeared true. In addition to running Four Bears, Butch and Frank were major players in the construction world. They served as president and vice president of Vito's Trucking and Excavating. The company handled many construction projects in Florida, none bigger than the multi-million-dollar Sawgrass Expressway in Broward County.

It didn't take long before the Stramaglia brothers and Vito Trucking and Excavating were coming under intense scrutiny in the Sunshine State. Earlier in the decade, the Stramaglias and some of their executives were charged with grand theft and racketeering for a sewer project in Orange County, Florida. Butch also pled guilty to income tax evasion involving a sewer project in Lee County and was ordered to pay damages to the county for deficient work. But the biggest allegation lent itself to the Stramaglias' involvement in the construction of Sawgrass Expressway in Broward County, where the Stramaglias were under indictment and investigation for racketeering, theft, and bribery. Close to two million dollars was missing, and it was believed—although never proven—to have been allocated to other Stramaglia-owned companies. One of those companies was alleged to have been the Four Bears Water Park. The FBI was starting to look at how the Stramaglias might be helping certain Detroit-area wiseguys, one of them being Jack Tocco, launder their own individual illegal proceeds.

A trial loomed over the heads of the Stramaglia brothers as 1988 came to a close. According to federal documents, Frank was rumored to have approached investigators and inquired about the possibility of cooperating in the weeks before his death. If Four Bears was being used to launder money, certainly Giancotti would have been privy to this information, making him another loose end to eliminate.

"Surveillance records showed that both Giancotti and Stramaglia were seen in the presence of members of organized crime in the days, even hours, leading up to their deaths. We had it on pretty good authority that Giancotti was with Stramaglia at the hotel where he wound up dead," said one federal official. "In my opinion, either Giancotti or the mob got wind of Frank's talks in Florida and got spooked that the reverberations would be felt up here. Either way, someone intentionally OD'd Frank and Giancotti got it back in return for being involved. Now, we know Giancotti and Frank were said to be close friends, but in that world something like that really didn't mean much. Most likely, Giancotti either took it upon himself to do something and got taken out as punishment or was told to do something and got taken out to cover other people's tracks."

As mentioned above, there are no certainties. Nobody has ever been charged in either case. Over two decades removed from the pair of deaths, law enforcement has wittled the case down to three possible theories:

1. Frank Stramaglia accidentally overdosed on cocaine that was given to him by Mark Giancotti. Giancotti was then killed by a friend of Stramaglia—perhaps Butch—for this fatal error. Stramaglia's gun was used to send a message, letting people know why Giancotti was killed.
2. Stramaglia was intentionally given a lethal amount of cocaine by Giancotti to stop Stramaglia from linking him to the money laundering going on at Four Bears. Giancotti was subsequently killed by friends of Stramaglia—perhaps Butch—with Stramaglia's gun to send a message, letting people know why Giancotti was killed.
3. Stramaglia and Giancotti were killed to prevent them from talking about the Sawgrass Expressway case in Florida. Their deaths guaranteed that nobody else would be implicated in the illicit activities going down in Florida. Stramaglia's gun was used to make sure that a particular point was made about why they were killed.

It's tough to find the truth, especially when dealing with individuals who pride themselves on their secrecy. Only two things are certain: Frank and Mark are dead. If you want more answers, you're going to have to ask Butch. But he'll probably tell you to go jump in a public pool.

A HAUNTING ON ST. AUBIN STREET

The Detroit Occult Murders

A personal essay by Alan Bradley

The year was 1929 and Detroit was bursting at the seams, immigrants from the edges of the world burrowing their way into the city's flesh. In 1910, the city had 285,000 souls; by 1929, a million and a half pairs of feet scurried back and forth to their factory posts, their wooden tenements. Has any city ever grown so fast as the little river fort founded by Antoine de la Mothe Cadillac? Such a question is unanswerable, given our palsied grasp on the facts of history, but suffice it to say that in those days Detroit was a cauldron of many ingredients, fired to a boil by assembly lines running night and day, with rooming houses renting beds out by the eight-hour shift. A giant work camp is really all it was, its Babel-tongued citizens united only by sweat and toil. The land of opportunity, yes—but a land of different opportunities for different people.

Our story concerns three men: two foreigners and a man of native birth from some unknown corner of the southern croplands. These men each came to Detroit with their own strange dreams and made use of the opportunities they found. Let us meet our first subject, an expert opportunist in this land of milk-fed suckers and honey-drenched rubes: Benedetto Evangelista, a.k.a. Bennie Evangelist, a self-proclaimed "Divine Prophet." Benny plied his trade of spiritual flimflam on Detroit's East Side, near Eastern Market, where the farmers brought their lettuce and potatoes every morning to sell to the Italian shopkeepers and vegetable cart men that plied their honest trade in little Italy, while Bennie plied his tricks out of the home he shared with his wife and four small children on St. Aubin Street. Born in Naples, Italy in 1896 as Benedetto Evangelista, Bennie's first beachhead in the New World was in Philadelphia, where he joined an older brother named Antonio.

Antonio, by his own account, disowned Benedetto when he began having mystical visions of a non-Catholic nature and sent him to York, Pennsylvania and a job on a railroad construction crew. Bennie's best friend in York (a fellow Neapolitan) was one Aurelius Angelino, and the two of them began to dabble in the occult. Apparently, Aurelius was unable to take the Ouija boards and tarot cards with the proper grain of salt, because in 1919, he started hacking his family to death with an axe, being stopped only after two of his children were dead. Needless to say, Aurelius was sent to a prison for the criminally insane, while Bennie himself moved on to Detroit to start anew for the third time (three being an auspicious number).

What sort of a place did young Benedetto, seer of visions, find when he arrived in his new home? Streets paved with gold! Hudson's downtown department store was the tallest in the world. Henry Ford's introduction of the five-dollar-a-day wage and the auto industry's general overflowing abundance were transforming peasants into a proto-bourgeoisie. But Detroit was a stern mother to her children: she would love them, yes—but only if they came to work! Only if they came to sacrifice their bodies in the foundries like virgins tossed into the hungry volcano of industry. And so they came, and the days of their lives were melted away like pig iron in the forge, and the gold in the street could only be pried loose by the picks and axes of the industrialist strongmen, white and Protestant by law, as it was they themselves who made the law.

The anger they must have had, some of them. Those foreign aliens, those Appalachian trash, those black sphinxes. No wonder they sought solace in their concocted religions; Benedetto even reconstructed the universe right in his base-ment. In fact, if you stood at street level on the corner of St. Aubin and Mack Avenue and cocked your head at just the proper angle, you could see inside the basement window of the Evangelista home, and there was his personal cosmology for all to see, a hand-painted sign announcing to the public:

"Great Celestial Planet Exhibition."

From papier-mâché and wires and wood he had built, all by himself, nine planets and a sun with an electric eye that sat in the center. Benedetto had learned the trade of carpentry somewhere, and in a boomtown like Detroit this had afforded him the prosperity to escape the assembly line chain gang and to dabble in real estate, as well as build the universe he saw in his mind right there in his own basement. The planets, according to the newspaper accounts, were orbiting demons, circles of monstrosity and they hung low to the ground, so that Evangelista's dis-ciples, or customers, could touch them.

The mystic, the prophet, the faith-healer, the snake-oil salesman, the charmer, the cheater, the psychotic—they all found fertile soil in which to plant themselves when they arrived in Detroit, and Evangelista was one of these men. In addition to his carpentry and real estate, he sold potions and did psychic healings upon those who paid his fees, which went as high as $10.00 (two full days on the assembly line). He was doing quite well for himself, having taken on a wife, and along with their four children they had settled into a house at 3457 St. Aubin. Benedetto Evangelista now called himself Bennie Evangelist, without the foreigner's vowel at the end. Their home appeared to be (the only evidence a faded microfiche) a large and comfortable one, with a wide porch and fresh green paint adorning its wooden planks; an oasis where the luxuries of self-discovery could be indulged as the streetcars passed by, carrying laborers to work.

"Divine Prophet, Wife, 4 Children Hacked to Death"
"Wholesale tragedy laid to fanatics, humble St. Aubin home is scene of murders"

The Detroit Free Press broke the news to the stunned city on Independence Day, 1929. A man named Vincent Elias had come to the Evangelist home on the day before at 10:30 a.m. to discuss a real estate deal with Bennie, and had found Bennie sitting behind his desk, his hands across his chest. His headless body was slumped forward and his severed head lay on the floor beside his chair. The three older children, all girls, were found in a room on the second floor, their heads crushed with an axe. His wife, Santina, was found in the marital bed with the young boy, Mario, at her side. They, too, had been hacked in the skull.

The victims: Bennie Evangelist, age 43; Santina, his wife, age 40; children Angeline (eight years old); Margaret (later said to be a boy named Matthew), age six; Jean (four); and Mario, the other/only boy, age 18 months. (An interesting sidelight: To show just how things we take now for granted, such as Italians being named Mario, had not yet become incorporated into Americana, the newspapers reported the infant boy's name as "Marrow.")

Nearly the entire homicide division was dispatched to the crime scene, though one should not confuse the application of all this police manpower with any sort of competence. When the police arrived, alongside Evangelist's severed head, they found three large, framed photographs of a child in a coffin. The photos were later determined to be of a son that the couple once had, but who had died before his first birthday some years earlier. What could this have meant?

And now the strangeness begins to build upon itself. Numerous copies of a book Evangelist had written and self-published littered the room. It was titled, *The Oldest History of the World Discovered by Occult Science*. Its opening lines were:

"My story is from my own views and signs that I see from 12 to 3 A.M. I began on February 2, 1906 in Philadelphia, Penn., and it was completed on February 2, 1926, in the city of Detroit, County of Wayne, State of Michigan. On this new earth the last one was created by God the Father Celestial and the great prophet Miel. We call it today the great Union Federation of America. I am with the power of God and I respect this Nation. In this book I shall express all my views of past twenty years. In this great continent are all the generations. By the willingness of God, my respect to this nation, I shall do my best to tell you of the old world. I shall tell about the world before God was created up until this last generation, and I shall explain to you your descendants."

The Detroit police, a semi-pro team at best, failed to keep newspaper reporters and the dozens of gawkers from contaminating the crime scene, destroying any potential clues save one, a bloody fingerprint on the doorknob of the home. To make matters even more difficult, most of Evangelist's neighbors and clients were recent Italian immigrants and were less than willing to provide information to law enforcement. Detectives were unable to compel even one of Evangelist's people into making an official statement that could have provided at least some starting point from which to launch their investigation. Evangelist's own records and the collection of personal items (including articles of women's clothing, often used for casting love spells) found in the home proved that hundreds of people had come to him for services, but scarcely a handful even admitted they had known him:

"Several pieces of women's undergarments, each tagged with the name of its owner, police point out, reveal that the so-called mystic indulged in practices of 'voodooism,' or devil worship. Such garments, 'voodooism' has it, can lead to the finding of a missing person, when they are properly handled by one versed in the mystic arts of that belief." (*Detroit Free Press*, July 5, 1929)

The police used the limited evidence at hand to pursue three very different theories. The first one revolved around several notes found in the Evangelist home that pointed to Bennie being extorted by *La Mano Nera*, or the "Black Hand." The Black Hand was a loose confederation of Italian criminals that used intimidation and murder to extort money from Italian immigrants. The great opera tenor Enrico Caruso fell victim to them. In one 90-day stretch, 15 people were murdered by the so-called Shotgun Man on a single block in Chicago's Little Italy. One of the letters dated six months before the murders told Evangelist: "This is your last chance."

The problem with the Black Hand extortion theory was that by 1929, the group had long since "evolved" into the traditional Mafia structure of Italian organized crime, and crude extortion schemes were a thing of the past. Caruso's run in with *La Mano Nera* dated back to 1910 and "Shotgun Man" had disappeared from Chicago before 1920. Whoever was trying to extort Bennie was almost certainly an amateur just looking for an easy mark, not part of a syndicate capable of the grisly murders that took place on St. Aubin Street.

The second theory was significantly more plausible. A 42-year-old man from the area named Umberto Tecchio visited the Evangelist home the night before the bodies were found. He was making final payment on a house Evangelist had sold him. Tecchio, along with Angelo Depoli, a friend who'd accompanied him to St. Aubin Street the night before the murder, were brought in for questioning the next day when an axe, a "keen-edged" banana knife, and a pair of suspiciously clean work boots were found in the barn behind their boarding house. Tecchio and Depoli not only didn't confess to the murders, but stated that nothing out of the ordinary had happened, and they'd gone out drinking after dropping the last payment on Tecchio's home off to Bennie Evangelist. Newspaper accounts state that Tecchio, just three months prior to the massacre, had knifed his brother-in-law to death in an argument. How he escaped prosecution is unclear, but it certainly gave investigators reason to consider him a prime suspect. However, with no physical evidence and no confession, Tecchio was released, and he died a few years later in 1934. After Umberto Tecchio's death, the continuing investigation into Detroit's largest mass murder uncovered a newspaper delivery boy who told police he had seen Tecchio on Evangelist's front porch on the morning of the murders. But what is that recollection worth in the face of no motive, no evidence, and no confession? Who can say?

Now for the last hypothesis. In 1923, Benedetto's old friend Aurelius Angelino (the axe murderer of his own two children) escaped from the Pennsylvania prison for the criminally insane—and was never seen again. Had Angelino somehow made his way to Detroit, where his old friend had set up his eerie basement shrine? It's certainly possible, but what proof is there? The Detroit police seemed to have put more credence and invested more of their time on Umberto Tecchio, but looking back after more than 80 years, the very nature of the crime seems the most damning evidence against Aurelius Angelino.

The "M.O.," or *modus operandi,* closely matches Aurelius' own crime back in York, and it is not hard to imagine that he slowly made his way west to Detroit and finally tracked down his old partner in "voodooism." And when Aurelius arrived at the door of the now-prosperous Benedetto, and when he thought back over the prison horrors of the almost 10 years that stood between that moment and their last meeting, what rage must have boiled inside him—and to see Benedetto, there in his personal fiefdom and with his own personal universe built by his own hands, hanging from the basement ceiling! Since Bennie was found dead in his wizard's garb, sitting calmly at his desk, and since Bennie himself wrote that he received his visions from 12:00 to 3:00 a.m., is it difficult to imagine Aurelius Angelino, escaped madman and convicted axe murderer, slithering in an open window while Bennie sat in his trance in the early hours of July 3, 1929? Once inside the Evangelist home, what difficulty would Aurelius have had in decapitating the man who had left him behind in York to rot in an insane asylum while he not only indulged his occult dreams, but grew rich from selling spells and potions? And yet, after Angelino's escape from Pennsylvania's lax custody in 1923, no record of his existence, whether in Detroit or anywhere else, can be found. How can a family of six be slaughtered by the sharp edge of an axe and the blunt force of its handle and the killer disappear without a trace? For the purposes of closing the murder case of Bennie Evangelist (as no arrest was ever made), let us just say that an evil spirit exacted retribution of some kind upon Bennie and his unwitting family and disappeared into the dark night of Detroit.

"Evangelist, no doubt, was insane," said the parish priest who supervised the family's burial at Mount Olivet Cemetery, "but I do not believe Evangelist was sincere in practicing the creed he had established. Rather, I believe he founded the mysterious cult with all of its weird props and practices with the sole idea of making money."

◇◇◇◇◇◇◇◇◇◇◇◇

"Around the time of the first World War, the Negroes in the southern states became attracted to the northern industrial cities, such as Detroit, Pittsburgh, and Chicago. They believed implicitly that the North, unlike the South, presented rare opportunities to improve the economic and cultural standards of the Negro. As a result of the prevalent illiteracy among these people and the large numbers of them who immigrated to the North, possibilities for employment diminished. The Depression period completely dispelled the rest of their hopes and reduced greatly their living standards. During these years, many militant and cultist groups arose which reflected the Negroes' intense desire for racial improvement and recognition and which based the position of the Negro in American society on the treatment afforded him by the white people" (FBI case files concerning the Nation of Islam).

Now it was 1932, and to paraphrase the anonymous author of the FBI commentary above, the Depression completely dispelled the hopes and reduced the standard of living for African Americans. So let us meet Robert Harris, a black man from Tennessee, who arrived in town just a few short months after the great crash of October '29 and the unsolved massacre of the Evangelista family on St. Aubin Street. It was a different Detroit than the one Bennie Evangelist had lived in—not so much gold in the streets, especially for someone like Robert Harris.

Robert soon fell in with a nascent religious movement, led by one W.D. Fard, known as "The Order of Islam." The Order eventually came to be known as "The Nation of Islam," and in that long-ago day, just as it was in the time of Malcolm X and Louis Farrakhan, the group was a beacon of hope for the descendants of African slaves that came to its secret meeting places, halls, and temples. W.D. Fard (a figure we will discuss in detail after a brief excursion into the deeds of his follower, Robert Harris) had coined an apt, almost Biblical term for the world in which the black man lived in 1932: "The Wilderness of North America."

A long tract could be produced on the difficulties of a 44-year-old black man (the grandson of slaves) in the 30-percent-unemployed Detroit of the Great Depression, an elaborate psychological analysis of why he did the thing he did. But instead I will quote a brief part of Robert Harris' statement to the Detroit police with regard to the murder he committed:

> "The ninth hour of the 20th day had come Sunday. It was predestined 1,500 years ago that at that hour I must make a human sacrifice to my gods. It must not be a member of the Order of Islam, but some stranger—the first person I met after leaving my home."

Harris went on to confess what he did with James Smith. Smith, who lived with him and his family in a rooming house at 1429 Dubois Street in the heart of Detroit's overpopulated "Black Bottom" neighborhood, was brought into the cold and (safe to assume) poorly furnished front room that morning in November 1932, where Harris' wife and children sat waiting as they had been commanded by their hardfisted husband and father. An important moment was at hand for the family. Harris told homicide detectives that Smith was a willing sacrifice. He "mounted an altar, stretched his arms, and looked up." At the stroke of noon, Harris went on to say, he plunged a knife into James Smith's heart, then crushed his skull with an automobile axle "just to quiet him." When police arrived, they found an eight-inch knife stuck into Smith's heart so deeply that only the handle protruded from his corpse.

Once taken into custody, Harris, who also used the alias "Robert Kerrian," supplied to him by the Order of Islam as a replacement for his "slave" name, struggled in desperation with police when they tried to take a fingerprint of his left hand, which was gloved. The glove was eventually removed by force. "My right hand belongs to everyone," Harris had told the detectives, "but my left hand belongs to the King." Once he was nominally subdued and in the close custody of the homicide division at police headquarters, Robert Harris/Kerrian continued his maniacal confession to the stunned investigators. The murder victim, James Smith, was supposedly a member of the same cult and was living with Harris and his family at 1429 Dubois Street (coincidentally, Dubois is exactly one block east of St. Aubin Street, where the Evangelista family had been slaughtered):

> "I told him that I had been commanded to kill somebody by the Gods of Islam. At first he didn't want to be killed, but when I showed him that he

would be the savior of the world and go to heaven right away, he said all right. The day had come, Sunday. He had to be killed just at noon, so I set a clock in front of the altar where everybody could see it. Smith was sitting in a chair in front of the altar. My wife was timekeeper. As the hour drew near, I said, 'Smith, do you still want to be killed?' because the command ordered me not to kill anybody who didn't want to be killed. Smith nodded his head. When it was just 12 o'clock, I said, 'Smith, get up and stand on the altar.' I grabbed my dirk [knife] and stabbed him like this."

A piece of paper, possibly found in some magazine or book, was discovered at the crime scene. Some said it was a passage from the original manual of the Order of Islam, which the Nation of Islam denies. It said: "The unbeliever must be stabbed through the heart." *The Detroit Free Press* printed the following on November 22, 1932:

"Harris admitted that he slew Smith as part of the rites of his weird religion, while his wife, 'Queen' Bertha Harris, and their children and 'disciples' looked on. Detective Oscar Berry of the Homicide Squad checked his assertion, announced that all the evidence indicated its truth, and speculated upon the hold which the jungle cult may have upon certain ignorant elements of Detroit's Negro population."

Harris' wife, "Queen" Bertha, told police that she and her children had been forced to prepare for and watch the murder under the threat of death themselves. Bertha made statements that she had been pulled from the marital bed and thrashed when she had first caught wind of Harris' macabre plan, but that she and the children were all considered "disciples" by Harris and had no choice but to attend the ritual. Police declined to bring charges against Bertha Harris.

Embarrassed and desperate after their bungled investigation of the Evangelista murders on St. Aubin Street, the Detroit police initially hoped Harris would be identified as the killer in the still-unsolved Evangelista slayings, but when Harris' fingerprints were compared with the bloody fingerprint they found on the doorknob at the Evangelista home, the prints didn't match. Harris himself denied knowing anything about the Bennie Evangelist family massacre.

Now our final, and perhaps most interesting, subject enters the stage. He is Wallie Dodd Ford, a.k.a. W.D. Fard Mohammed, a.k.a. Professor Fard, a.k.a. Fard Mohammed. W.D. Fard, as he is most frequently known, was soon identified as the leader of the religious order or cult (depending on one's point of view) that included both Robert Harris and James Smith. Fard was quickly rousted out of the organization's headquarters at 3408 Hastings Street for questioning. According to the newspapers, a crowd of nearly 500, claiming to be members of the Order of

Islam and being led by men wearing a red fez atop their heads, invaded Detroit police headquarters after the raid on the Hastings Street temple to protest the detention of W. D. Fard and his secretary, "Ugan Ali." After realizing that their demands to release Fard and Ali wouldn't be met, the 500 men and women quietly left and the questioning of the suspects began. When Fard was asked by the police just exactly who he was, he told them: "I am the supreme being on Earth." When asked about Robert Harris and the sacrificial murder he had committed, Fard said that Harris "apparently misunderstood my teachings."

Robert Harris, W.D. Fard, and Fard's secretary Ugan Ali were sent to the psychopathic ward of Detroit Receiving Hospital for observation by psychiatrist Dr. David Clark. The police department's initial theory was that Fard and his secretary had deluded cult member Harris into homicidal tendencies. But Ugan Ali made this official statement to the police department: "Our fundamental purpose is to uplift our own people; members are taught not to eat certain foods, to employ their time usefully, and that by their efforts the world can be rid of evil by 1934. Harris had no standing in the order and was not regarded as a leader. Many people avoided him because of the wild things he sometimes said."

Robert Harris' brother Edward made statements to the police that his sibling had seemed demented: "Worries over money caused my brother to lose his mind. He has been acting queerly in the last few weeks, preaching a lot and stopping people on the streets. Nobody paid much attention to him." Ugan Ali and W.D. Fard told detectives that there was nothing in the teachings of the Order of Islam that promoted use of "sacrificial rites," and that the order did not bear any responsibility for Robert Harris' actions. Fard went on to say that he did not know Harris, and couldn't remember him from the many meetings he must have attended. Nobody paid much attention to him.

When the fingerprints of "W.D. Fard" were compared to those of "Wallie Dodd Ford," a former California prison inmate, they were a perfect match. Years later, during their investigations into the activities of the Nation of Islam in the late 1950s, the FBI obtained a World War I draft card in the name of Wallie Dodd Ford on which he described himself as living in California, owning a restaurant, and having been born in the Shinka province of Afghanistan. He listed his date of birth as 1893. On a 1920 U.S. Census form, he listed his place of birth as New Zealand, with parents of English and Polynesian lineage. Portland, Oregon also came up in the FBI investigation as a possible place of birth.

After serving a three-year stretch in San Quentin (1926–1929) for violation of the California state narcotic laws, Wallie Dodd Ford disappeared from the public record—that is, until the Detroit police homicide detectives ran the fingerprints of "Master Fard" as they investigated the horrific cult sacrifice of James Smith by Robert Harris on Sunday, November 20, 1932.

W.D. Fard probably arrived in Detroit from Chicago after the Great Crash of 1929. (Just like Robert Harris, he had arrived in the industrial promised land just a few months too late.) A fog surrounded his true identity and motives then, as it did throughout his life; the records of his movements and methods are as murky as his place of birth. Chicago police claim that Fard became involved in an internal power struggle within a group known as the Moorish Science Temple. When the temple's founder, "Noble Drew Ali" (Timothy Drew), was found dead in his home while awaiting trial for the murder of rival "Sheikh" Claude Green, Wallie Ford/ Fard asserted that he was the reincarnation of Noble Drew Ali and attempted to seize power of the fast-growing and increasingly powerful temple. Just as his claim of being Noble Drew Ali's reincarnated heir to power was being rebuffed within the Moorish Science Temple, the stock market crash occurred. W.D. Fard declared it a sign and a punishment upon the world for failing to accept his messianic assertions, and he fled to Detroit.

Fard arrived to find the city a very different place than the one Bennie Evangelist saw as a source of easy prosperity during the prior decade. No longer the land of opportunity and auto magnets begging for more workers, but a place where men begged for work and were desperate for a solution to capitalism run amok. Once in Detroit, this lithe and handsome man with skin the color of the lightest melanin began to peddle silk and other trinkets in the mostly black Elmwood district of the city's lower East Side, also known as Black Bottom. But the most important thing he peddled was himself. Fard sold his image to those dreamless, hopeless people who had traded the sharecropper's shack for even worse shacks—so cold in Detroit's winter nights, so many living without indoor plumbing right in the heart of the world's industrial center.

Wallie Ford's people watched the jobs they'd dreamed of when they came north go to someone else, always someone else—a Serb or a Syrian or a Pole or one of those same "white trash" they thought they'd left behind. So the most valuable thing he sold to them, even more exotic than the faux silks and baubles, was hope. Hope that they would learn the secret, hope they would be given the key to their own redemption and power without the white man's help. Ford began to create a persona for himself, first as Professor Fard, then as Master Fard. He told them that he had come from Mecca in the Arabian Peninsula, and that the descendants of slaves in America were not African, but "Asiatic." He told them that they should cast off their slave names, just as Robert Harris would later cast off his, and take a new, Asiatic name, just as Robert Harris took the name "Kerrian" on the eve of his crime. He taught his new pupils hidden knowledge and disseminated pamphlets with titles such as *The Lost Found Nation of Islam: A thorough knowledge of our miserable state of condition in a mathematical way, when we were found by our savior W.D. Fard.*

Here are some excerpts from Fard's manifestos:

- The original man is the Asiatic Black man, creator God and owner of the universe and father of civilization.
- It took John the Baptist 600 years to make a white man out of a colored man.
- There ain't no other devil on the planet earth under the earth but the white man.
- The uncle of Mr. W.D. Fard lived in the wilderness of North America and he lived other than his own self; therefore his pulse beat 78 times per minute, and this killed him at 45 years of age. How many times did his pulse beat in 45 years?

The Detroit Free Press had this to say on November 22, 1932:

"Police court records in Middle Western industrial centers have revealed the amazing growth in recent years of Negro cults with strange Islamic symbols and titles. Complaints against them have been so petty, however, that they have not been investigated for Voodoo, and it is generally believed that their Mohammedanism exists only in a meaningless but impressive mixture of Allahs, Mohamets and other Mohammedan incantations. High priestesses and priests of Allah, clad in pseudo-Oriental costumes, are frequent defendants in Police Court swindling cases. Praying on the superstitions and susceptibility of Negroes, they have robbed families of their savings. Their victims, however, have been gulled mostly through a belief in the high priest's ability to foretell the future, and the cases have not borne the marks of the race's fear of Voodoo."

When police conducted a raid on the room of Wallace Fard in a hotel at 1 West Jefferson Avenue, thousands of letters written to "Master Fard" were found piled on the floor. *The Detroit Free Press* reported: "in every instance, the letters were written painstakingly on cheap note paper. All were written in almost unintelligible scrawls in lead pencil. The import of each was the same. The signer of each wanted his 'slave name' changed to a Mohammedan one, and was willing to pay Fard for the service of crossing out the sender's legal name and substituting in its place one such as Mohammed, or Bey, or Ali. Numerous gaudy identification cards were also found in the place."

The following extract is from the transcript of Robert Harris' guilty plea in front of Judge Boyne at Detroit Recorder's Court, Friday, November 25, 1932:

Judge Boyne: "Take off your cap." Harris does not comply.

Harris: "I am king here."

Judge Boyne: "Oh, no, you are not, I'm the king here."

Harris: "No, sir, I'm the king here and everywhere." Discussion interrupted as a bailiff of the court removes Harris' cap.

Judge Boyne: "Did you kill James J. Smith?"

Harris: "Yes, I did." Harris replaces the cap on his head; it is again removed by the bailiff.

Harris: "I did kill this man at 1429 Dubois Street."

Judge Boyne: "Why did you kill him?"

Harris: "It was crucifixion time, that's why I killed him."

Judge Boyne: "What did you kill him with?"

Harris: "With the crucifixion; I said, 'aliker alump' and he fell dead. He died because it's a dumb civilization." But Harris starts to walk toward the door.

Judge Boyne: "You'd better wait a minute." Harris then grabs a box of rubber bands from the clerk's desk and begins stuffing them into his pocket.

Judge Boyne: "Put those back."

Harris: "No, I'm king here." Harris continues to stuff the rubber bands into his pocket. He also puts his cap back on his head. The court bailiff recovers the rubber bands while another takes the cap from Harris' head (his final dethronement) and leads him out of Judge Boyne's court and into a prison cell. From there he exits the stage of history.

Prison records from that era are hard to find, and the final fate of Robert Harris is long lost, but it could be easily imagined that he may have been released from the Ionia Prison for the Criminally Insane many years later, as his maniacal energy weakened along with the strength of his body, and Robert Harris/Kerrian "the King" walked the streets of Detroit once more as an old man in the tumultuous decade of the 1960s. The house where Harris killed his willing victim and the temple where he once worshipped at the feet of Master Fard would have been long gone by then. He would have had no real bearings on the world, no landmarks to moor his tenuous grasp on reality. Perhaps Robert Harris muttered on the street to people passing by as he begged for change, his old voice a harbinger for the coming riot and the deaths that would fill the city of Detroit as it hurtled toward the century's terminus. By then it had become known as "The Murder City" and took its place upon the altar of history to be sacrificed, unwanted and unneeded, like the man named James Smith, into whom Robert Harris had plunged his knife inside that little tenement room so many years before.

By 1934, W.D. Fard, pressured by the Detroit police to leave town, had also disappeared from history. There were rumors that he resurfaced in California and Pakistan years later, but they were never confirmed. Competing stories said that he had been murdered at the hand of his successor Elijah Poole, a.k.a. Elijah Muhammad, the mentor of Malcolm X, but no real proof exists of that. The FBI, for its part, maintained an open case file on him until 1960, and a former lover claimed that he had returned to his native New Zealand after fleeing Detroit. Whatever happened to Wallie Dodd Ford, one thing is certain: the spirit that transformed his body into W.D. Fard ceased to exist. The self-proclaimed "Supreme Being on Earth" was never heard from again, and no evidence of Master Fard has been uncovered since June 1934.

Three men—two foreigners and a stranger in his own land—came to Detroit many years ago with a dream. It was the same dream everyone who came here had: to build a new and better life, to place their bodies onto the assembly line of the modern age and emerge perfectly formed at the end of the line. Note the single commonality among them: they all created an alternate personality when they arrived in the greatest boomtown America has ever known. Benedetto Evangelista, Wallie Dodd Ford, and Robert Harris were so committed to changing their place in the world that they created new identities for themselves, and their Doppelgängers unleashed a trio of Mr. Hydes upon Detroit.

YEAR OF DEATH

A Homicidal Housecleaning

The mid-1980s were a tumultuous and violent time for traditional Italian organized crime in America, highlighted by major convictions of mob leaders around the country, bosses being murdered by their own underlings, and ongoing wars among regional mob factions. Often overlooked during this time period, but right there in the thick of things, was the local Detroit Mafia. Normally cited as a paragon of stability and nonviolence, the organization went through its own period of unrest in 1985, when at least nine people were executed by the mob in a span of less than six months.

Experts attribute most of the killings to the Mafia's effort to control lucrative gambling and drug operations, specifically the wholesale suburban cocaine market, and getting all their ducks in line in anticipation of future casino legalization within the city limits. Others were credited to the settling of old grudges and the "opening of the books" for membership in the crime family, creating opportunities for proposed members to "make their bones" by committing murder. For a crime family notorious for utilizing violence as only a last-resort measure, 1985 was the deadliest year in Detroit organized crime circles since the bloody Prohibition era. Despite the syndicate's reputation for nonviolence, there are many who believe that might not be the most accurate categorization.

"In reality, they can be a very violent group; they just mask it extremely well," said retired FBI agent Bill Randall. "They're well-versed at putting a lot of layers between themselves and the street, distancing themselves just far enough away from guys like us, but not too far away so they can still assert their authority. Guys get their heads broken open or people show up missing and you might know for sure who ordered it, but there's no way you're ever going to prove it or bring charges because the guy you're fingering is five people removed from the guy who pulled the job."

Former U.S. Prosecutor Keith Corbett concurs: "These guys are experts committing murder and then veiling the circumstances around the crime in so much mystery and confusion that it prevents the ability to build any real cases against them. Homicide investigations surrounding the mob in Detroit go cold quickly. There's just too much insulation between the top guys and the street guys. You're dealing with true professionals in their craft, which in this case happens to be murder."

◇◇◇◇◇◇◇◇◇◇◇◇

The Mafia murder spree began in early April in the East Side suburb of Sterling Heights. Located in Macomb County, Sterling Heights is not known for criminality. There's a good reason. Starting in the late 1960s, many high-powered Motor City mafiosi relocated from Detroit proper into the peaceful upper-middle-class suburb, a bedroom community roughly 25 miles outside the city limits. As a result, there was a hands-off edict for most underworld activity in the area for fear it would bring unwanted heat from law enforcement on the newly enshrined gangster suburbanites. That edict was broken in 1985.

On Tuesday, April 4th, police found the bodies of Eugene Mancen, 32; Frederick Sanderson, 33; and Laverio Teramine, 52, in a business suite in the Time-Reality Office Complex on Fourteen Mile Road. All three had been knocked unconscious and shot in the head with a .22 caliber gun. Police theorized that Mancen and Sanderson were operating a dual sports-betting and drug-dealing operation out of the building, while Teramine, a nephew of local mobster Anthony "Terrible Tony" Teramine, just happened to be in the wrong place at the wrong time. He was only present in Mancen and Sanderson's office at the time of the homicides to pick up gambling winnings from the previous evening's NCAA men's basketball championship game between Georgetown and Villanova.

Macomb County officials subsequently released information that Mancen had been threatened the week prior to his murder by Detroit mob associate Paul Leggio, who physically assaulted him and demanded $200,000 in back street taxes to the Mafia in exchange for the right to operate. Leggio was a nefarious character who had grown up around organized crime, immersed in its culture for his entire life. He was a bookie, drug dealer, and alleged underworld partner of Robert "Bobby the Animal" La Puma, a well-known top enforcer for Anthony "Tony Jack" Giacalone, the Detroit Mafia's street boss, and his younger brother Vito "Billy Jack" Giacalone, a fellow captain and mob administrator.

The hulking La Puma was a best friend and running buddy of Tony Giacalone's ace protégé, Ronald "Hollywood Ronnie" Morelli. Throughout the late 1960s and 1970s, the pair made an intimidating duo, parading around town flanked by an entourage of goons, including Leggio and local mob princes Danny "The Trigger" Triglia and Augustino "Little Augie" Giordano, sons of powerful Mafia lieutenants Joseph "Joe the Whip" Triglia and Salvatore "Sammy G" Giordano. Led by Morelli and La Puma, and backed by the Giacalone brothers, the crew of young hoods made their presence felt throughout the area's racket landscape and in all of the most popular local nightlife hotspots, strong-arming past anybody who dared to get in their way. Ronald Morelli, a notorious ladies man, worked his way up the ladder from Tony Jack's driver to acting capo of his crew. Tony Jack took a liking to Morelli, who bore a striking resemblance to NFL star quarterback Joe Namath because like himself, Hollywood Ronnie didn't spring from traditional Motor City mob royalty. By the 1970s, Morelli was put in charge of all loan-sharking operations in the Metro Detroit area on behalf of the Giacalone brothers.

In 1971, Morelli and La Puma were both nailed on charges of extortion and illegal gambling in a pair of separate indictments that came down within four months of each other. Indicted alongside them on both charges was Sol "Good Looking Solly" Shindel, a well-known Jewish mob associate and gambler. Shindel, the point man on all of the Giacalone brothers' sports betting operations, was a frequent social companion of both Morelli and La Puma and ran his gambling empire from the Anchor Bar downtown.

According to federal documents in the case, the mob feared that Shindel, whose behavior had become increasingly erratic in the previous months, would become a government witness. Backing himself even further into a corner, in early December 1971, he allegedly stole money from the Giacalones and went on a gambling binge in Las Vegas, accompanied by Morelli and La Puma. Two days after returning from his trip to Sin City, Sol Shindel was found murdered in his house in Southfield, shot in the face. As the investigation into Shindel's homicide got under way, Morelli and La Puma quickly became top suspects. The pair of enforcers would have their names arise in other federal murder investigations in the years to come as well. In 1972, their names surfaced in the George "Little Pete" Katranis murder investigation. Katranis, the son of longtime Greektown gangster and mob associate Petros "Pete the Greek" Katranis, was alleged to have started freelancing in the loan-sharking and extortion business. Morelli and La Puma were close friends with Katranis and his brother Mike and were suspected to have used their personal relationship to lure "Little Pete" to his death.

When mob collector Tommy LaBerrie turned up dead in 1976, informants were again telling the authorities that Morelli and La Puma had something to do with it. They were never charged with any of the crimes, but they had their reputations on the street enhanced by the innuendo and speculation. Going on to die of a heart attack in prison in September 1985, serving the final months of a conviction for extortion, Ronald Morelli has a legacy that is still much talked about to this day. Robert La Puma wound up taking a drug arrest in 1987, alongside Paul Leggio, and serving time in federal prison before living briefly in Florida and then returning to Metro Detroit in the mid-2000s.

Police believe that Leggio contracted out the April 1985 triple homicide in Sterling Heights to James "Red" Freeman, a close associate, who is alleged to have been instructed to bring in a hit team of Italian mobsters from St. Louis to carry out the executions. Freeman himself had had an interesting criminal past. He had been acquitted in a previous triple murder in which two men and a woman were beheaded at a Detroit social club in 1979. Indicted with him in the beheadings was reputed drug kingpin Francis "Big Frank Nitti" Usher, a onetime lieutenant under the Giacalones while coming up through the ranks of the local underworld.

While no one was ever arrested in the Sterling Heights murders of 1985, Paul Leggio was convicted in 1987 of witness tampering, obstruction of justice, and firearms charges in unrelated cases. He eventually died in prison. Former Macomb County Prosecutor Carl Marlinga has long insisted that the contracted murder of Mancen and Sanderson was part of an effort by organized crime to control lucrative illegal betting operations before the possible legalization of casino gambling in Detroit, and that it was also the motive for the murders of three other Detroit area bookies that same year.

"Those murders were rooted in the fact that the mob wanted to consolidate their interests as fast as possible for the fear that casinos were going to come into the city and scoop up big chunks of their gambling profits," Marlinga maintained. "They already controlled a majority of the action anyway, but they wanted to grab up as much as they could of what was left out there before the state came in and cut into the market. It was a power grab and it would prove a sign of things to come."

In 1993, Sterling Heights police arrested four individuals—John Finazzo, Freddie Andelmo, Michelle Urban, and Carolyn Hojnacki—for running a gambling operation out of the same Time-Reality building that was the site of the 1985 murders. Hojancki was also arrested in the Wolverine Golf Club gambling case in 1992 that centered on the activities of reputed mob capo Jack "Fat Jackie" Lucido and several members of his family, alleged to have been using the Macomb Township golf club as a headquarters for a city-wide gambling empire. Fat Jackie Lucido, the son of longtime crime family lieutenant Salvatore "Sammy Lou" Lucido, who died on April 9, 1985, and all of his co-defendants were eventually acquitted of the charges.

One of the murders that Carl Marlinga and his office linked to the Sterling Heights homicide case was the killing of Harold "Harry Mack" Maciarz on May 9, 1985. Maciarz, 56, was found dead in the trunk of his Mercury Grand Marquis on the East Side of Detroit. Police described the murder as a "professional hit"; Maciarz had been shot several times in the back of the head. Authorities believed that both the Harry Mack hit and the Mancen, Sanderson, and Teramine murders were committed by the Detroit Mafia as a means of consolidating all illegal gambling going on in the area in the midst of casino gambling legislation being bandied about in the state senate. Mancen and Sanderson were bookies. Harry Mack was a policy boss, an integral cog in the mob's numbers business.

Back in 1982, Maciarz was busted as part of an $80-million-a-year illegal lottery ring. The lucrative policy operation was being conducted under the auspices of Dominick "Fats" Corrado, the Detroit mob's capo in charge of policy. At the time of his death, Maciarz was known to be involved in illegal gambling, and the investigation into Maciarz's death showed that his gambling operation and that of Mancen and Sanderson dealt with common associates. Another murder that appeared to have connections to the Detroit mob was that of Colleen Smith of Clinton Township. Smith, 21, was last seen on May 18, 1985 at a popular Macomb County nightspot. The following day, she was found shot to death in an alley in Highland Park.

While pushing for a grand jury to investigate unsolved crimes in Macomb County, Carl Marlinga and the Sterling Heights police issued statements that suggested local organized crime involvement in various entertainment hotspots around the county, including the one where Smith was last seen. Police also stated their belief that Smith's murder was tied to narcotics and organized crime. Throughout the investigation into her death, informants told authorities that Smith had been involved in some sort of romantic relationship with Detroit mob enforcer Bernard "Bernie the Hammer" Marchesani, 61, a seasoned mob vet who was on the run from the law at the time of the crime.

Nine months later, in early 1986, federal marshals apprehended Marchesani as he stepped out of a Van Buren Township apartment. He had been a fugitive since failing to appear in court for his 1981 indictment on extortion charges alongside Detroit Mafia underboss Anthony "Tony Z" Zerilli. During his arrest, Marchesani, at one time the man in charge of all loan-sharking in the area, was found in possession of $28,000 in cash, four handguns, a shotgun, and a bag of illegal narcotics. Although he was never charged with the crime, authorities questioned Bernie the Hammer regarding the Colleen Smith murder. Some investigators believe that Marchesani killed Smith after she threatened to reveal his whereabouts to the police.

Bernie had a long history of connections to mob violence. A witness at Tony Zerilli's extortion trial told jurors that he was terrified of owing money to Marchesani, reputed to be Zerilli's primary muscle on the streets, because "he didn't want to end up like Pete Vassalo." Vassalo was a collector for Giacalone-backed loan-sharking operations in the 1960s. He was killed in 1972, his body found floating in the Detroit River, in retribution for the accidental murder of an indebted client that the mob deemed responsible for the subsequent arrests of Marchesani and the Giacalone brothers on loan-sharking charges.

The most high-profile mob hit of the 1980s was the July 1985 murder of long-time Detroit Mafia lieutenant Peter "Fast Pete" Cavataio. As far back as 1963,

Cavataio had been publicly identified as a member of the Detroit organized crime family and had a criminal history dating back to the early 1950s. Fast Pete, nick-named for his chosen lifestyle, was found dead, bound and shot several times in an abandoned garage on Harvey Street near the Ambassador Bridge on July 6, 1985. There was evidence that he had been tortured first.

Cavataio, who also went by the street handle "Pete the Baker" because he owned and operated a number of bakeries around the city and in Canada, had been a thorn in the mob's side for quite a long time, but it had not always been like that. At one point in his younger days, Pete was tabbed as an up-and-comer in local underworld circles. He had all the right credentials to be a future leader. First, he was the son of Dominic Cavataio and the nephew of Julian Cavataio, two well-respected made members of the Detroit mob who had been heavy money earners for the syndicate since its earliest days. Secondly, Fast Pete married within the crime family, wedding the daughter of powerful capo Pietro "Machine Gun Pete" Corrado. His bride was also the granddaughter of Boss Joe Zerilli. Through his marriage, Cavataio became best friends with his brother-in-law, Fats Corrado, who was named capo of his father's crew when Machine Gun Pete died of a heart attack in 1957. Finally, Fast Pete came under the mentorship of powerful local mobsters Salvatore "Little Sammy" Finazzo and Raffeale "Jimmy Q" Quasarano, significantly increasing his status as a future staple of the syndicate.

Immediately after being pegged as a rising star in the Detroit Mafia, the expectations began going to Pete's head. Cavataio was impulsive, reckless, and defiant. He also developed a dangerous habit of having affairs with other mobsters' wives and girlfriends. Becoming the target of a federal drug probe didn't help mat-ters, and neither did going into debt to more than one mob-sponsored bookmaker and refusing to pay what he owed. By the early 1980s, Fast Pete Cavataio had gone from being viewed as a future captain to a clear liability. For a while, Cavataio was able to use his close friendship with Fats Corrado as a free pass for his transgres-sions. But that would only last as long as Corrado was alive. When Fats died of a heart attack on June 26, 1985, Cavataio's time was up. As soon as Corrado stopped breathing, a murder contract was issued on Fast Pete's life. Less than two weeks later, he was dead. Cavataio was the last made member of the Detroit Mafia to be executed.

Several years later, former Giacalone enforcer John Pree admitted his involve-ment, along with other members of the Giacalone crew, in the murder of Cavataio. This included stabbing him with a red-hot knife in order to get him to reveal the whereabouts of what the mob believed to be stolen funds. Pree, who was arrested for staging a series of home invasions in 1991 and 1992, later recanted his claim, but many law enforcement officials believe that Pree's initial claims were valid and that his recantation was only a result of Mafia intimidation and interference.

Fast Pete's murder would have ripple effects. On September 16, 1985, the bodies of James Stabile, 58; his wife Camille, 56; and I.T. Hill, 55, were found in the Stabiles' East Side market. James Stabile was a well-known bookmaker who worked under the direction of Pete Cavataio, and he had been questioned after Cavataio's murder. Besides his bookmaking activities, Stabile was suspected of running a drug operation out of his market. Hill was an employee who, like Laverio Teramine a few months earlier, just happened to be in the wrong place at the wrong time. The Stabiles had both been shot and Hill had been repeatedly stabbed. The triple murder, the second in the area since the spring, caught the eye of organized crime investigators because of Stabile's connection to Cavataio. It was suspected that the killings resulted from the mob's desire to make a move on Cavataio's business interests after his death and to eliminate any remaining loyalists.

Things got even murkier when Gary Hobbs, a 35-year old local gambler, was arrested and convicted for the crime. Hobbs admitted to the killings but claimed that they were the result of a gambling debt. This would fit with the authorities' belief that it was not a professional job. Hobbs was issued a life prison sentence, but his motive and truthfulness were still questioned by many involved in the case, including Carl Marlinga and the Macomb County Prosecutor's Office. In 1987, Marlinga told reporters that he believed that the triple murder in Sterling Heights in 1985 was linked to the killings of several bookies in Detroit that same year as part of an effort by organized crime to take control of certain gambling and drug operations.

"There was a great deal of bloodshed in a very short amount of time," Marlinga noted as he reflected on the string of homicides in 2010. "We attributed the violence to the mob's desire to get everybody in line and re-establish their dominance in traditional black market rackets. As much as I pushed and as hard as we investigated, we could only uncover so much information and it wasn't enough to bring down indictments. The people in charge of organized crime around here are very sharp leaders and their ability to pull off such a string of murders and not have any trails leading back to them demonstrates that higher level of criminality."